SPIRITUAL WELL-BEING AND SOCIAL SUPPORT

A Pathway to Mental Health of Adolescents

Dr. Johnson Ponthempilly SDB

Chennai • Bangalore

CLEVER FOX PUBLISHING
Chennai, India

Published by CLEVER FOX PUBLISHING 2023
Copyright © Dr. Johnson Ponthempilly SDB 2023

All Rights Reserved.
ISBN: 978-93-56481-25-1

This book has been published with all reasonable efforts taken to make the material error-free after the consent of the author. No part of this book shall be used, reproduced in any manner whatsoever without written permission from the author, except in the case of brief quotations embodied in critical articles and reviews.

The author of this book is solely responsible for its content including but not limited to the views, representations, descriptions, statements, information, opinions and references ["Content"]. The Content of this book shall not constitute or be construed or deemed to reflect the opinion or expression of the Publisher or Editor. Neither the Publisher nor Editor endorse or approve the Content of this book or guarantee the reliability, accuracy or completeness of the Content published herein and do not make any representations or warranties of any kind, express or implied, including but not limited to the implied warranties of merchantability, fitness for a particular purpose. The Publisher and Editor shall not be liable whatsoever for any errors, omissions, whether such errors or omissions result from negligence, accident, or any other cause or claims for loss or damages of any kind, including without limitation, indirect or consequential loss or damage arising out of use, inability to use, or about the reliability, accuracy or sufficiency of the information contained in this book.

*Dedicated to the Youth and the Salesians of India
Whose Faith and Love Sustained Me through this Journey and
Continue to Inspire Me.*

CONTENTS

Acknowledgments .... *v*
Preface .... *vii*

1. Introduction 1
2. Review of Studies 12
3. Research Methodology 100
4. Data Analysis and Interpretation 117
5. Findings, Conclusions and Recommendations 186

References *196*

ACKNOWLEDGMENTS

Many individuals and groups have contributed generously to the successful completion of this book. First, I would like to express my sincere gratitude to the Triune God, The Blessed Mother Mary, St. Joseph, and St. John Bosco, helped me to complete this work, which will enrich the lives of many young people.

I would like to thank my supervisor, Dr. Riju Sharma, for her assistance, support, and persistence, with which she led me to explore the field of mental health, spiritual well-being and social support. I thank Rev. Dr. Stephen Mavely, the Vice-Chancellor of Assam Don Bosco University, Rev. Fr. Joyce Thonikuzhiyil, former Provincial, Rev. Dr. Jose Thomas Koyickal, the present Provincial of the Sacred Heart Province of Bangalore, and the Rector and community of Don Bosco College Sulthan Bathery for being a pillar of strength in the arduous endeavour in completing this book.

I am indebted to Dr. Lukose P.J., Dr. K.C. Kapoor, Assam Don Bosco University, Tapesisa, Dr. Jose Antony, Rev. Dr. Joy Kaipan SDB, Fr. Joseph T.T., and other friends who went through this manuscript and provided their unstinting support at every stage of my research.

I am incredibly grateful to Dr. J. N. Vishwakarma, the research director of ADBU, Professor Basil Koikara and Rev. Dr. Biju Michael, former Registrars and Rev. Dr. Johny Pathinanchil, the present Registrar, for their assistance and support. I thank the librarians of ADBU, NIMHANS, and District Library, Silchar, for their support and availability whenever required. I also thank my batchmate scholars at Assam Don Bosco University for their interactions and discussions, which led me to understand better various research methods.

I am greatly indebted to the principals, teachers and students of CBSE Senior Secondary Schools in Ernakulam District, Kerala, for their wholehearted collaboration, participation in the surveys, and sharing views that enriched this study. I sincerely wish them good health and happiness to live their lives positively. I would like to remember my beloved parents, family members, friends and well-wishers who have played an essential role in my life journey with their blessings, love, and prayers.

A special word of gratitude and acknowledgement to the Salesians of Don Bosco College, Sulthan Bathery Community, for their support and encouragement in publishing this book. Last but not least, Clever Fox publishers deserve my greatest gratitude for bringing out this work in an admirable way.

PREFACE

A common man's understanding of mental health is about how people handle stress, relate to one another, and make real-time decisions. When I noticed that apparently familiar people fall prey to anxiety, have attitudinal problems, and make wrong judgments, I got an impetus to study this deeply. The more I delved into mental health studies, the more I found that no one can ignore the underlying factors of spiritual well-being and social support.

Serious mental health problems lead to schizophrenia, bipolar disorders, depression, alcohol or drug abuse and even untimely deaths. School students and teenagers in general, are becoming more and more hampered in facing challenges because of the waning of family harmony and peer support and the erosion of spiritual anchorage. A conglomeration of various other personal and social factors also contributes to their unstable mental and physical health.

I have concentrated on the school students as a core group during my research. Moreover, many of the interacting factors can be dealt in detail and carefully studied. Besides, the students still have the opportunity to undertake life's journey in a new and wholesome direction. Even though mental health can be promoted and sustained in many ways, I would like to focus on spiritual well-being and social support as two undeniable factors that can bring about a quantum change in teenagers' lives in general and students in particular.

Memories of one's early days at school evoke feelings of happiness and at times nervousness among students. Sometimes these negative feelings sink in deep and lead to relationship problems displayed in unhealthy competition, conflicts and other violent acts. Children with less social support and poor spiritual upbringing tend to have poor mental health and deal with day to day problems. Students' need to improve social care and spiritual welfare becomes relevant when enhancing their mental health. The overwhelming question that guided my study was 'what are the issues contributing to the decline in the student's mental health at school, home and more significantly in society?' Two factors, namely, spiritual well-being and social support, are focused on exploring the support systems that need to be strengthened to enhance the school student's mental health.

The mixed-method was adopted for this present study keeping in mind that every theory has limitations. The term mixed method refers to an emergent research methodology that integrates quantitative and qualitative factors within a single investigation. The goal is to expand and strengthen the studies by answering the research questions. This approach helps the researcher recognise the utilities and limitation of different paradigms in spiritual well-being, social support, and mental health. Review of studies from vast literature revealed that there were many studies conducted on mental health. However, no study has been conducted on the mental health of senior secondary school students, and more specifically the CBSE New Delhi XI class students in relation to their spiritual well-being and social support.

The present study was obtained from school students of the age group 16-18 years through standardised tools and narrative case studies including questionnaire schedules, observation, and in-depth interviews. Stratified sampling was applied to select thirteen schools from Ernakulam district of Kerala. Simple random sampling was applied to select 582 respondents from the selected schools to explore the relationship between mental health, spiritual well-being and social support. A mixed-method of data collection was employed, and memos were written while reflecting on the data until the analysis and case studies were completed. And the obtained data were evaluated by using SPSS 25.0 (Statistical Package for Social Sciences).

The findings revealed that 82 per cent of the students were in the age group of 17 years, and 18 per cent were 18 years of age. Out of the 582 respondents, 309 (53.1%) were female respondents, and 273 (46.9%) were male. The computed coefficient of correlation value came out to be 0.90 between the mental health and spiritual well-being scores; 0.67 between the social support and mental health scores, and 0.74 between social support and spiritual well- being scores. From this, it was interpreted that mental health status was related to the spiritual well-being and social support of the senior secondary school-going students in Ernakulam district of Kerala. Mental health is directly related to individuals' status of spiritual well-being, and social support. The five narrative case studies suggest that parents, teachers, friends and community play an essential role in school-going children's mental health.

The research findings indicate that adolescents are viewed as persons with compassion, energy, creativity, actions and interactions rather than as problems. Hence, there is a need to strengthen spiritual well-being and social support of the senior secondary school students to enhance their mental health to bring significant and positive outcomes in the life of school students. Finally, the professional role of social workers, who can influence the school management, parents and the government to organise mental health programmes for students, cannot be overlooked.

Adolescents should be helped in understanding their abilities and interest in health-seeking behaviour so that they can work synergetically to ensure their development into healthy adults.

Chapter 1

INTRODUCTION

Earth is a unique place where living beings from tiny ants to adaptable human beings co-exist. Humans stand out in the world because of their unbeatable intelligence, an indicator of decision-making ability and propagation of moral values. These human qualities support and sustain the shared existence of all creation. The sustainability of this planet depends on the harmonious coexistence of all beings. The dynamics between human versus human and human versus environment thrives on the platform of mental, spiritual, and social well-being.

1 EMERGENCE OF THE CONCEPT

Lokah Samastah Sukhino Bhavantu is an invocation for harmony. This Sanskrit shloka means, may all beings be happy and free, and may the thoughts, words, and actions of my own life add to that joy, happiness and freedom for all. Lokakṣema or Lokakṣhema is a Sanskrit word meaning global well-being. Loka means 'world' and Kshema means 'welfare' in Sanskrit (Gopal, 2004; p. 1022). The above-mentioned ancient Sanskrit mantra's impact is far more significant than simple human kindness (Murphy, 2018 & Allinson, 1992, p. 173).

At all times in every society, there have been people who were great examples of unmatched calibre. Such gifted people later received due recognition and appreciation for their contribution to society. An analytical enquiry into their lives and practices enabled the researcher to ask the following question: What made them different from the others? The answer indicates that these were men and women of excellence and holistic health, supported by spiritual well-being and social-support right from their adolescence.

1.1 ADOLESCENT PERIOD

Adolescents, from 10-19 years, around 1.2 billion, which is (16%) of the total world population (UNICEF, 2012). In India, about 243 million (21.4%) of the population are adolescents (Population Council, 2013). The adolescent and the youth population constitutes almost one third of the country's population. This is a critical segment of the community and the state at large. The demographic, social, economic and political development of a state depends on this young population. Therefore, investing in adolescents' growth seems to be the best way to strengthen the nation's competitive advantage.

Adolescence forms one of the most significant periods in an individual's life. It is a time of immense creative energy, self-discovery and exploration. However, this period is sometimes distorted by feelings of isolation, loneliness and angst they experience in their families, schools and the community. The world-wide scenario indicates that the youth's well-being is significantly decreasing in the current days. Recent studies (UNICEF, 2012) show a rise in adolescents' problems, such as severe emotional disturbance, increased sexual activities in schools, and greater alcohol consumption. Apart from this, the use of addictive drugs and the rate of school dropouts have also increased in recent years (UNICEF, 2012).

In India, a recent growth rate in school participation shows that education access has considerably improved. Adolescents from 10-19 years makes about one-fourth of India's population and young people between the age of 10– 24 years about one-third of the population. School students spend more time in schools than ever before. Therefore, schools play a key role in bringing up adolescents in a healthy environment to maximise their potential (UNICEF, 2013).

1.2 ADOLESCENTS AND MENTAL HEALTH

As pronounced by the World Health Organization (WHO), the persons who are in the age of 10-19 years are adolescents. It is considered the most critical transition period in one's life span, marked by significant growth and potential. During this period, the adolescent's behaviour patterns have a long-lasting impact on mental health, well-being and social support. According to the WHO, mental health is "a state of well-being in which the individual realizes his or her aptitudes, can cope with the normal stresses of life, can work efficiently and fruitfully and a contribution to his or her community". (WHO, 2004, p 12). Adolescents in good mental health often experience sadness, anger and unhappiness. Furthermore, this is part of a fully lived life for every individual. Despite this, mental health has been considered a purely positive effect, marked by feelings of happiness and a sense of mastery over the environment (Lamers et al., 2011).

According to the latest Kerala State Mental Health Survey report, in Kerala, around 14.4 % of people, aged 18 and above suffer from psychic disorder once in their lifetime. Though Kerala has an improved health care system, about 11.36 % of the overall population is affected by mental disorders (Kerala Schools

Top, 2019). National Mental Health Survey of India, 2015-16, conducted by National Institute of Mental Health and Neuro-Sciences, says that anyone can have issues regarding their mental health. The majority of suicides (37.8%) in India are people below 30 years (Vijaykumar, 2007). Even though Kerala has achieved health targets for all by 2000, the state has a high suicide rate, indicating severe drawbacks in people's mental health status (Praveenlal, 2000).

According to Gosain (2020, August 25), a healthy mind resides in a healthy body. Good health is the birth-right of every human being. It is pivotal for every society's development and productivity, and vital for the happy and healthy life of a person. In 1948, the Universal Declaration of Human Rights assured equality and dignity rights to all children. It confirms that human rights begin at birth and that childhood is a period demanding special care (UNICEF, 2013). The WHO defines health as including physical, social, mental and spiritual well-being, not merely the absence of a disease or infirmity. As a result of this, mental health has been gaining importance. The World Health Day held on October 4, 2001 and the World Health Assembly held on May, 15, 2001 (World Health Report, 2001) were dedicated to mental health.

1.3 ADOLESCENTS AND SPIRITUAL WELL-BEING

Well-being refers to an experience of health, happiness and richness. It comprises of good mental health, high life-satisfaction, a sense of meaning or purpose and managing stress. Every side of life influences one's well-being. Health is multifaceted, with increasing evidence including spirituality with physical, mental, emotional and social well-being. The status of spiritual health as an essential element of general health was acknowledged and accepted officially by WHO in 1998 (Robert, 2003). "Spiritual" means having a sense that life is meaningful and has a purpose, and that we are guided in our journey. Spiritual wellness is about accepting the metaphysical and reaching beyond the physical realm of existence and experiences.

Practising spirituality by being disconnected from the world is a myth. However, people's personal experiences and a few studies show that spiritual principles give us the right way of thinking, working and living. Spiritual well-being is a powerful indicator of self-esteem. It is an ability to cope effectively with daily challenges and distresses. It indicates a positive relationship between belief in a higher being and the feelings of meaning and purpose in life (Kamya, 2000). This relationship between spirituality and mental health is being explored today in many ways (Cornah, 2006).

In the 20th and the 21st centuries, we always look for the acceptance from outside of us to make ourselves happy. Some of these belief systems support the evolution of culture, while others restrict the expansion of culture. All types of separation based on the political-model, economic-model, scientific-model and environmental-model have begun to collapse as information became readily available. Globalisation is another cause for the collapse of social structures. When an individual evaluates one's own emotions and understands that it is the past residue, the individual begins to observe them. Observing the self means, you are no longer observing the programme. However, the conscience is observing, which is the first step to change and move towards wholeness. In the past decade, researchers across various disciplines have shown great interest in exploring and even acknowledging the positive mental health contributions of spirituality. Various studies point out that spiritual wellness contains one's values, beliefs, and purpose. It can be achieved through several ways, including physical and mental aspects.

Spirituality is the science of cleansing our inner being with divine virtues and revealing the divinity inherent in the soul. Spirituality is often linked to external customs, traditions and rituals which form the religious practices in society. Religious practices are acceptable if they help us to connect to the inner world. Nevertheless, if performed without the inner connection, these practices are meaningless because the essence of religion is spirituality. Spirituality is the science of learning how to be the best one can be, do the best, and thereby, feel the best one can feel. Spirituality refers to the way individuals seek and express meaning and purpose of life, the way one experiences the self, others, nature, the sacred, the significant and one's connectedness to the moment. While religion asks what is true or what is right, spirituality asks where one can find meaning, connection and value.

Similarly, spirituality and emotional health are distinct but interconnected. Spirituality means seeking a meaningful connection with something bigger than oneself, leading to positive emotions such as peace, awe, gratitude and acceptance. This research indicates that emotional health enables human being to become aware and incorporate a connection to something larger than oneself. Spiritual well-being can be a driving force to personal stability through mental, emotional and physical health. It is one of the primary resources available to individuals who are in the process of recovering and healing. This research delves into various writings and concepts of spiritual well-being to show its several elements that must be considered. These include two dimensions; namely horizontal (existential) and vertical (religious) dimensions. While horizontal relationships are related to oneself, others and nature, vertical relationships involve a supernatural connection with a higher being. In this research, a broad concept of spiritual well-being (i.e., horizontal and vertical relationships, beliefs, the meaning of life) is used to analyse the relationship between spiritual well-being with social support and mental health of senior secondary school students in Kerala (Moberg, 1978).

1.4 ADOLESCENTS AND SOCIAL SUPPORT

According to Wilson, "No one is rich enough to do without a neighbour" (Wilson, 2011, p., 15). This Danish proverb expresses an idea fundamental to much of the current thinking about social support. Conscientious and compassionate relationships are interrelated to health and well-being at all stages of life. Social support, which has become an essential subject in the 21st century, especially in educational institutions is discussed extensively in this research to promote students well-being. Social support has direct, protective and compensatory effects on one's mental health (Cobb, 1976). The present research points out that social support makes an individual realise that he/she is cared for, loved and valued as member of a social network.

The research also gives readers an understanding about the importance of social support in students' mental health and spiritual well-being. It acts as the basis for enhancing the mental health of the students and their spiritual well-being. It plays a vital role in reducing the impact of daily hassles and mental stress of students (Bouteyre, 2007). The review of related studies on social support reveals that social support serves as a stress buster and thus enhances the individual's ability to deal with stress, thereby reducing the stressful event's impact (Skok, 2006). The results indicate that social support from friends, family members, school staff and other personnel are great stress-buffers for reducing senior secondary school students stress in Kerala.

1.5 MENTAL HEALTH AND RELATED PROBLEMS

According to Adam Ant, an English singer and musician, mental health requires special attention and it is the final taboo that needs to be managed and dealt with (Adam, n.d). Mental health problems are one of the major causes of diseases world-wide (Vos, 2013). The National Mental Health Survey of India 2015-16, points out that mental disorders are common in the age group of 13-17 in India, which was 7.3 per cent of the total population. It requires an urgent and active intervention in both genders. The mental health of adolescent school students is a matter of increasing concern even for major international organisations, including the World Health Organization (WHO, 2005). The International Association for Child and Adolescent Psychiatry and Allied Professions have published detailed arguments about the prevalence of mental health problems in young people (Okasha, 2003). Most common problems of school students are their involvement in physical fights, watching and showing pornography to others, poor academic performance, alcohol abuse, smoking, romantic relationships and so on.

1.6 ADOLESCENTS AND MENTAL ILLNESS

In the investigation, related studies indicate that half of these mental illnesses commence at the age of fourteen and suicide is the leading cause of death among 15-20 year-old youth. Often, youngsters who are unable to cope with stress use a variety of coping mechanisms like substance abuse. According to the United News of India, in the world, the number of people affected by depression has gone up by 67 per cent between 1990 and 2013. By 2025, it might rise by another 22.5 per cent (UNI, 2018).

Indian school students are burdened with exams, expectations, peer pressure, violence and social tensions. The school students of the age group of 16 to 18 years generally study in class eleven and twelve, the senior secondary school. It is the transitional stage from puberty to legal adulthood, along with physiological and psychological progress. At the same time, the adolescent brain undergoes remarkable changes and development. The individual will face new experiences and stressors, especially in a peer relationship. In this age group, they experience peer victimisation, which can have a very long-term effect on their physical and mental health if it continues for a lengthy period of time (Takizawa, 2014). Hence, adolescence is a stage which is vulnerable because they fail to evaluate complex concepts.

School students are more likely to be depressed nowadays than before. Even after having symptoms like irritability, anxiety and poor academic performance, the disorder goes unnoticed. Traumatic events in early childhood, frequent migration, adverse life events, educational setbacks, early relationship problems, stress at school and family are the main reasons for depression among children and adolescents. Early diagnosis and prognosis will help to improve the mental health and quality of life of such persons. Studies also reveal that having sympathetic and supportive relationships, managing emotions, and the willingness to ask for help aid in their recovery.

1.7 CHALLENGES OF SCHOOL STUDENTS IN KERALA

Kerala has one of the highest suicide rates among the states in India. In Kerala, one out of every five students in the age group of 12-19 suffers from psychological distress. Studies across the state have also shown that emotional and sexual abuse have triggered mental illness in school-going adolescents (The Times of India, 2018). Day after day, the number of abuse cases keeps increasing, besides the many that go unreported for various reasons. It was also noted that adolescents face the threat of abuses while travelling, while being alone at home, school and tuition places. (Dhar, 2011).

According to Jacob (2019) Kerala, a 100% literate state way back in 1991, has schools and colleges mostly run by the government, private trusts, or societies. Each school is linked with one of the following, namely the Indian Certificate of Secondary Education (ICSE), the Central Board for Secondary Education (CBSE), Kerala State Education Board or the National Institute of Open Schooling (NIOS). For this research, the researcher has selected senior secondary CBSE schools in Ernakulam district, Kerala.

Most of the schools in Ernakulam city performed well in the Class XII examinations conducted by the CBSE in 2019. The highest pass percentage was 98.2, with five students from different regions of Kerala including Ernakulam scoring 495 marks out of 500. Thus, Kerala students topped the CBSE class XII examination results announced in New Delhi in May 2019 (The Times of India, 2019). Besides the academic results, CBSE education needs to be appreciated for launching its comprehensive school health programme to create health-promoting schools.

Comprehensive School Health Programme is part of the CBSE schools in India. The board also gets involved with WHO on a Global School Health Survey. CBSE developed a decision support system called 'Saransh' to upgrade children's education by improving the interaction between school authorities and parents (Saxena, 2015). The school administration was advised to take up various initiatives as per the Health Promotion Manual. The Manual was designed explicitly for the three major age groups, classes 1-5, 6-8 and 9-12.

A detailed survey of health statistical data shows that the society and specifically the youth were facing diseases related to lifestyle. The data and its review show that the second millennium is quickly approaching the 'Smart Machine Age' (SMA). According to Hess (2017), this term describes a time when machines will be performing complex tasks and non-routine work. Moreover, once required human labour would be replaced by technologies like robotics, artificial intelligence, nanotechnology and genetic engineering, which will quickly dominate the lives of humans, both professional and personal.

In the twenty-first century, school students face a challenging adolescence period. In modern times, an adolescent is highly drifted towards emotional instability and unrealism, which leads to anti-social behaviour, drug and sexual abuse. The biological, psychological and emotional changes occurring during adolescence make the adolescents non-compatible with the family, friends, society and even one's personal life. Hence, this research is warranted to look at Kerala's senior secondary school students' mental health, with spiritual well-being and social support. Various theories on mental health enabled the researcher to apply a 21st century approach to the research.

To understand the interconnectedness of spiritual well-being, social support and mental health, we need to understand the existing concepts, definitions and various theories on each of these topics. How did the concepts of spiritual well-being, social support and mental health evolve over the years? How are each of these factors perceived internationally, nationally and on state levels? What are the policies implemented in India regarding mental health? For answers, let's move on to chapter 2.

Chapter 2

REVIEW OF STUDIES

The central purpose of this chapter is to make a conceptual review and identify the levels of spiritual well-being, social support, and mental health. Secondly, this research examines the empirical findings of spiritual well-being, social support and mental health and the relationship among spiritual well-being, social support and mental health. In this quantitative model, the researcher uses the related studies as a framework for the research questions and hypotheses. The purposes as mentioned above are explained in detail as Part 1 and Part 2.

PART 1: CONCEPTUAL REVIEW

Health is a universal matter of detail and concern to all human beings. Mental health is an essential component of health. The World Health Organisation's 1977 Expert Committee pointed out the importance of developing national programmes that encourage children and adolescents (Rahman, 2000). Subsequently, various studies revealed that the transition from adolescence to adulthood is a vulnerable stage. Mental health problems such as risk behaviours, depression, conduct disorder, and substance use are increasing in CBSE's senior secondary school students (Lerner, 2004). Studies also point out that well-being was decreasing (Goldbeck et al., 2007) and this leads to several mental health problems and mental illness in later adulthood (Gore et al., 2011).

Spiritual well-being and social support are important factors in helping young adults to handle significant life changes and supporting their mental health (Azmitia, 2013). Hence, the researcher has tried to understand the health problems of this population, the processes and the mechanisms that affect their mental health, and the importance of spiritual well-being and social support.

1.1 CONCEPT OF SPIRITUAL WELL-BEING

Empiricism thinks that spirit does not exist as it cannot be experienced or measured directly by human senses or machines. The same could be said of beauty, love, conscience, intelligence and even mind. However, some empiricists deal with these concepts as if they exist. D. Moberg points out that just because some scientists' opinions overstep the limitations of science, spiritual experiences need not be overlooked because they cannot be measured (Moberg, 2010).

Spirituality and religiosity is now being understood widely in their relationship with many commonly studied adolescent development domains, such as health risk behaviour and internalising disorders (Cotton, 2006).

Spirituality has been the basis of Indian culture. The spiritual dimension has always been an essential component in indigenous health systems (Bisht, 1985). Sri Aurobindo calls the 'Psychic Being' as the soul that develops through evolution. According to Sri Aurobindo, a spark of the Divine is present in all forms of life. This Divine element starts to evolve and grow into a psychic personality commonly known as a 'Psychic Being'. The psychic being acts as a stimulus of the Divine consciousness.

It is progressive and grows using body, life, and mind as its instruments. The psychic being is the psychological centre of our being. However, in ordinary life, it is mostly controlled by the instruments of the outer being. The psychic being remains behind the outer consciousness like a "secret witness", "a secluded king in a screened chamber" (Sri Aurobindo, 1971). The ancient Indian wisdom of health and well-being is centred on "swasth" (to be rooted in one's self), a state of positive well-being, and "arogya", a state of absence of illness (Rao, 1985). Nevertheless, there is a need to explore spiritual well-being from an Indian perspective and its relation to health.

According to Principe (1983), spirituality was based on its Latin concept. This concept appeared in studies only after the fifth century (Principe, 1983). In English, a religious or devotional sense of "spirituality" continued until the early twentieth century. Therefore, no paper on spirituality or spiritual well-being shows an agreed definition of these terms. These terms cannot be understood directly because they involve relationships. The term 'spiritual well-being' (SWB) appears to have first been mentioned at the 1971 White House Conference on Aging (Moberg, 2010). Later, the National Inter-faith Coalition on Aging (NICA) formed its "working definition". Spiritual well-being is the affirmation of life in relationship with God or Supreme Being, the individual self, community and environment that supports, nurtures and celebrates totality (NICA, 1975).

In the last couple of decades, people have been showing their interest in religion and spirituality in an attempt to enhance their physical and mental health. Before the fourth wave of transpersonal psychology, modern western psychology primarily addressed the biographical details of a patient's life. Sigmund Freud, Carl Jung, Karen Horney and Melanie Klein proposed psychoanalysis. Ivan Pavlov introduced a form of learning behaviour called a conditioned reflex. John Watson and B.F.

Skinner studied behaviourism. Carl Rogers, Abraham Maslow and Clark Moustakas introduced humanism.

The transpersonal concept developed by Carl Jung was upgraded to transpersonal psychology through Roberto Assagioli, Sri Aurobindo, Abraham Maslow, Stan Grof, Charles Tart and Ken Wilber. Studies reveal that transpersonal psychology is cosmic-centred and it is not about individuals' needs and interests. It is a detailed study of compassion and love for human nature, keeping aside disgust and indifference. Such higher psychology, the science of life, could also be a life of passion, hope for humanity, and can lead to revelation of values (Gilot, 2000).

Ken Wilber's research on 'Transpersonal Psychology' has become a specialised field of developmental studies (Wilber, 1999). This study addresses the stages of identity and consciousness. The growth of highest talent, creativity and intuitive intelligence help us reach optimal well-being. In this context, transpersonal psychology is all about mental healing. Stanislav Grof contributed to psychiatry by reaching beyond the biographical elements and including the prenatal and transpersonal elements (Grof, 1988). Transpersonal psychology involves science and spiritual tradition. It is relevant for consciousness research, developmental studies, and psychotherapy. The scientific sources of Carl Gustav Jung, Assagioli, David Émile Durkheim and Franklin have a common element; the concept of the Ego-Self axis.

In contrast, in Christian mysticism, the important concepts are humility, devotion, and surrender to God's will. Christian mysticism leads to mental silence, which is essential for the unity of the soul with the Divine. Eastern and Western streams of spirituality are complementary. The Eastern stream is based on awareness practices which help in opening the third-eye chakra, or intuitive spiritual intellect (wisdom). The Western stream is for the opening of the heart chakra (love). When the paths of love and wisdom are joined, it will lead to transpersonal development, education, and psychotherapy (Gilot, 2000).

In the late 1960s, in the United States of America, transpersonal psychology evolved in later decades as a new field of research. A revolutionary concept, joining scientific psychology and traditional wisdom, was put forward as a fresh approach to mental health theories. The word 'transpersonal' refers to the distant zones of human nature (Maslow, 1969) and states of consciousness in which the identity of an individual travels beyond the individual psyche, and cosmos (Walsh, 1993). We must look into developmental research, consciousness disciplines, education, and non-dual tradition practices for the evaluative research on transpersonal psychology and psychotherapy. It also includes purification and self-healing methods, awareness training, clinical aspects of spiritual crises, the relationship between psychotherapy and meditative practices, and Eastern and Western psychology. It is a holistic approach to modern psychology (Harris & MacDonald, 2003).

The Father of psycho-synthesis, Roberto Assagioli (1888-1974), agreed with Jung on the concept of the ego-self axis. In his view, the self is the conscious ego and it exists in the psychological phenomena and organic life. They cannot influence the person, but their influence can change the psycho-physical conditions greatly (Assagioli, 1973). Assagioli recognised that the ego has a permanent nature and it is interconnected to universal life. In other words, the self has a universal nature that goes beyond the limits of death. It is the typical core of Truth, Goodness and Beauty. The display of spiritual virtues develop from a reality called Spirit, Consciousness or *Summum Bonum* (a Latin expression which means the highest good).

Compared to Jung, Assagioli goes outside theory and puts forward a practical, experiential goal. For Assagioli, Self-realisation is connected to transformative spirituality. He considered this as the goal of psychosynthesis and the highest meaning of human development. Assagioli highlighted that Self-experience is different from Self-realisation. The growth of spiritual qualities will lead to mental purification. In a Christian perspective, humility heals intolerance, fear and competition, which are the after-effects of pride. The devotion method helps to lessen possessiveness and sets one free from the sense of separation from others. The practice of surrender to God heals both pride and greediness and releases one from every personal desire.

According to Sandhu, (2011), in his Updesh (teaching) to the Khalsa-Sarbloh Granth, courage, strength, will and creativity are the results of humility and dedication, as mental stability and lack of anxiety help the surrender to God's will. In the spiritual path, for both East and West, the suffering from ego is removed when consciousness becomes attentive to mental contents. It is the non-ego state achieved when personal importance is abandoned. Living is concentrated on the growth of virtues (Gilot, 2000 & Sandhu, 2011). The most suitable example is the 37th World Health Assembly in 1984, which decided to add spiritual dimension to the scope of health. In other words, a large number of evidence support the beneficial influence of spirituality on health. It is described by various sides of spirituality and spiritual well-being. Spirituality is the innermost thing in people, that gives direction and motivation to them. In simple words, it helps a person to become oneself, remain healthy, overcome difficulties and survive bad times. However, spirituality implies different things to different people. It is a method to understand the world, to recognise one's place in the world and to give direction to one's life. It is a belief in a higher being or a greater force. It becomes the core of human identity, giving a sense of belongingness. Spirituality can be the beginning of a quest for wholeness, hope and harmony with a sense that there is more to life than material things. Spirituality is to be seen as a broader concept than religion.

People have different ways of expressing their spirituality. Some may practice practices rituals, reading scriptures, fasting and giving up a specific food, using certain attire, using music or art to explore the highest power, yoga, meditation, spiritual retreat and even voluntary selfless social work. Others may practice spirituality by being sympathetic to nature and humanity, taking them to hardcore spirituality.

2.1.1 DEFINITIONS OF SPIRITUAL WELL-BEING

Throughout human history, spiritual quests have been an important part of human life, at both individual and societal levels. A discussion on the definition of spiritual well-being will help to bring better clarity. Ellison (1983) specifies that spiritual well-being has psycho-social and religious elements which indicate a relationship with superior power, i.e., God. Existential well-being is the psycho-social component of spiritual well-being. It indicates a persons' feeling of who he/she is, what he/she does, and why and where he/she belongs. Both religious and existential well-being is about moving beyond self.

Both spirituality and spiritual well-being have different aspects to it. According to the National Interfaith Coalition on Ageing, spiritual well-being has been described as "the affirmation of life in relationship with God, self, community and environment that nurtures and celebrates wholeness" (National Interfaith Coalition on Ageing, 1975).

According to Seaward, spiritual well-being blends concepts from several disciplines such as psychology, sociology, philosophy, and theology. Through this, a clear network expressed as emotions and behaviours is established in spirituality (Seaward, 1991).

Spiritual well-being may be defined as a feeling of communicating with others, having meaning and goal in life and having belief and relation with divine power (Hawks et al., 1995).

Spiritual well-being is the ability to find sense, value and purpose in life and feel contented, satisfied and happy (Burkhardt & Nagai-Jacobson, 2002). Shabani defined spiritual well-being as "one's ability to establish a coordinated and harmonious relationship with God, oneself and others, as well as changing and adjusting one's personal and social environment to resolve one's personal and collective inclination in a balanced manner" (Shabani, 2010).

As Moberg (cited in Ekşi & Kardaş, 2017) pointed out, spiritual well-being has two dimensions; a person's relationship with a higher power within a particular religious system and meaning and purpose in life. Thus, meaning and purpose in life is independent of religious structures.

Moberg (cited in Omar, 2018) defined spiritual well-being as "a sense of transcendence beyond one's circumstances and other dimensions such as the purpose of life, reliance on inner resources, and a sense of within-person integration or connectedness".

Spiritual well-being is a fundamental human element and a driving force for a person's stability, meaning, realisation in life and faith in self (Rovers, 2010). Spiritual well-being means the ability to find the meaning and purpose in life by connecting with self, others, art, music, literature, nature or a power greater than oneself. A person with spiritual well-being will be able to manage her problems and situations in life. Spiritual well-being includes the physical, emotional, mental, and spiritual dimensions of an individual. The four domains of human existence are personal area (relationship with oneself), social field (relationship with others), environmental domain (relationship with one's situation), and transcendent realm (relationship with a higher being) (Fisher,

2011). Appropriate amount of these domains will make a person spiritually healthy.

2.1.2 ORIGIN AND DEVELOPMENT OF THE CONCEPT OF SPIRITUAL WELL-BEING

Spirituality and spiritual development have always been linked with religiosity. However, this concept is changing as spirituality is becoming part of secular science and scientific research. Spiritual well-being includes healthy self-esteem, relationship, and acceptance of a higher power. It also includes personal principles and purpose in life. It is a principle of self-development and self-actualisation. It is about self-reflection where one can search for the meaning of life. Human beings have always tried to bring in values in societies, so that economic, intellectual and ethical development can be ensured. An individual develops spirituality through self-awareness and the choice of implications. In recent times physicians and psychologists are open to the spiritual aspect of a person. It is a positive value of the person or event (Tvorogova, 2011).

Issues of well-being were always discussed in both theoretical and empirical levels. Representatives of economics and health sciences, have always discussed about human well-being. Our opinion about the prosperity or fullness of life keeps changing. People have always considered economic richness as an important indicator of well-being in modern society. Intellectual, technological and socio-economic advancements are also considered as adding value to a modern-day person's welfare. Although these factors are without doubt, essential components of well-being, the non-material aspects of human nature and spiritual well-being are often ignored. The elements mentioned above cannot promise total well-being. Nowadays, society is falling to pieces because of crises such as crime, family disintegration and suicides. Therefore, a holistic method, joining both metaphysical and physical aspects is necessary for human well-being. The Christian anthropology states that a person is created to unite two essential components – physical and spiritual (Vaineta, 2016). Experimental data prove the importance of natural relationship with God for spiritual well-being. It also reveals the existing link between spiritual and physical health. We can assume that improvement of spiritual health on communal and environmental relationships could greatly help to reduce social-moral pathologies faced by today's humanity. Hence, personal spiritual well-being is an integral constituent of human well-being (Vaineta, 2016).

According to Abraham Maslow, supreme ideals are truth, kindness, beauty and the feeling of unity. Among them, some values greatly affect the order of importance in inner growth and personal development. Spiritual well-being helps the individual to develop in relation with all other aspects of life. However, reaching such a high level of spiritual well-being and health is a challenge because a person often prefers the advantages of physical, social, mental or spiritual values. (Tvorogova, 2011).

Experts from various branches of science have considered different aspects of human life while trying to determine what is suitable for the human body. Psychologists try to find out what is ideal for the mental health of a human being. Do sociologists consider the welfare of man as a social being who operates in the social environment? Theologians have always believed that finding converging points of view was the benefit of spirituality. It points out that a human individual is one whole being and all spheres of well-being are interrelated (Tvorogova, 2011). Over the past few decades, spirituality has appealed to many psychologists and mental health professionals (Hsiao, 2010).

These days, concerning the spiritual dimension of health, many recommendations have been presented to the WHO. As a result, WHO has included spirituality in the definition of health as one of the dimensions of health (Esfahani, 2010). In the WHO's classification system of diseases known as International Classification of Diseases-10, the mental aspect was incorporated. Just like the physical, mental, and social dimensions are interrelated, one's mental and spiritual health is linked with the other aspects of health (WHO, 2010).

2.1.2.1 Spirituality is Innate

A study conducted by Columbia and Yale University researchers points out that the parietal cortex is the region in our brains which processes spiritual experiences. Personally relevant spiritual experiences were created in a diverse group of subjects. The results showed a neurobiological home for spirituality. It means that when people feel a connection with something more significant than themselves, a particular part of the brain becomes active. Thus, the study points out that there is a universal, cognitive basis for spirituality, which could help mental health treatment (Livni, 2018).

Spirituality unifies the whole person and is an inbuilt feature of the human beings. It may develop from the beginning of an individual's life or depends on current condition. Hence, spirituality is a fundamental and vital component of being human (McCarroll, 2005; Nolan, 1997 & Oldnall, 1997).

2.1.2.2 Four Domain Model of Spiritual Health and Well-Being

Osman J. D. and Russell R. D. recommended including spiritual well-being in the concept of well-being. Later, experts accepted well-being as one of the important aspects of personal and group life. Spiritual well-being is the latest dimension of well-being, joining the physical, psychological and social aspects (Osman

& Russell, 1979). Ellison thought that spiritual well-being rises from spiritual health and is an expression of good health (Ellison, 1983). Fehring, Miller and Shaw supported this view by adding spiritual well-being as an indicator of quality of life in the spiritual measurement or merely a sign of their spiritual health (Fehring, 1997).

In 1998, Fisher put forward the four domains: personal domain, public domain, environmental domain and transcendental domain. Studies reveal that these four domains can enhance spiritual health. These include relationships with self in the personal domain, relation with others in the public domain, relation with the environment in the environmental domain and in the transcendental domain a relationship of the self with something beyond the human level. That is the ultimate concern, cosmic force, transcendent reality of God. It includes adoring and worshipping the source of mystery of the universe (Fisher, 1998).

2.1.2.3 Spirituality and Science

It is proven that there are two different levels of physical reality: the one we are familiar with (using the five senses) and second one termed as psycho-energetic science. It is a level of physical reality that can be greatly influenced by human intention. Stanford University professor and physicist William A. Tiller is associated with this finding.

The discovery includes human consciousness and human intention in the traditional science to affect both the living and non-living physical reality. Einstein and quantum physics opened the door to this concept at the beginning of the twentieth century (Jones, 2012).

2.1.2.4 The Central Features of Spirituality

Spirituality is significant in one's life. It makes sense of life's situations, deriving the meaning purpose of existence. It can have several features like values, connectivity and becomingness.

Value: It includes beliefs and standards linked with truth, beauty, worth of thought, object or behaviour beyond oneself (transcendence).

Connectivity: It means a relationship with self, others, the environment, the cosmos and God/higher powers.

Becomingness: It is an assessment of life that demands reflection and experience. It also includes a sense of who one is and how much one knows.

2.1.2.4.1 Spiritual Well-Being and Health

Dhar (2011), in his article "*Spiritual health scale 2011: defining and measuring four dimensions of health,*" points out the statement of Yach Derek. According to Yach Derek, the World Health Assembly in May 1998 felt that the four dimensions of health were absent from its definition of health. Hence, WHO Executive Board (1998) proposed to amend the definition in the Preamble of the Constitution as a dynamic state of complete physical, mental, spiritual and social well-being and not just the absence of disease (Dhar, 2011). Research has found considerable evidence showing that spirituality or religion is positively related to health (Dossey, 1999 & Ellison, 1991).

In 2005, through Bangkok Charter for Health Promotion in a Globalised World, the WHO pointed out spiritual well-being as the highest health standard.

Spirituality is connected to fatigue and pain. A study conducted in Mumbai showed spiritual well-being as a primary negative predictor of fatigue (Lewis, 2014). Spirituality develops acceptance in critically ill patients. The proven role of spiritual well-being in achieving better health must be understood at every stage of care in healthcare delivery (McClain, 2003). Spirituality helps to prevent many illnesses, to cope with disease and grief better and has reported speeding up recovery. Mental health providers should encourage the practice of spiritual well-being in a manner supported by our culture. Hence, yoga and meditation are used to prevent many chronic illnesses. Non-communicable diseases, including psychiatric conditions, have become more common due to lifestyle factors. Therefore, focus on spiritual well-being is even more required.

2.1.2.4.2 Relationship between Spiritual Well-Being and Resilience of Young People

Resilience is an individual's mental and emotional ability to cope with a crisis. Studies reveal that adolescents' resilience is the result of the relationship between personal attributes, characteristics, available social support and health-supporting environment. Increasing social capital by strengthening family, friends, school and local community helps the flexibility at the interacting level (Semo, 2011). However, strengthening the qualities of resilience can promote spiritual well-being.

Australian and international research identified the relationship between spiritual matters and their positive results. Regularly attending religious and spiritual activities strengthens social networks, connectedness to family and friends and lead to life satisfaction (Smith, 2005 & Stoll, 2012). Meyers (2006) found that people who were part of religious activities experienced greater happiness and reported low depression and recovered faster after loss and life crises than non-religious individuals. However, in his study on "Resilience in adolescents: The development and preliminary psychometric testing of a new measure" Gartland argues that evidence linking religion and spiritual behaviour to resilience are still doubtful (Gartland, 2009). Furthermore, Vilchinsky & Kravetz (2005) in their study "How are religious belief and behaviour good for you? An investigation of mediators relating religion to mental health in a sample of Israeli Jewish students," points out that spiritual well-being's association with health is weak (Vilchinsky, 2005).

Spiritual well-being is often derived from the subjective interpretation of an experience. Several studies have tried to examine the relationship between spiritual substances and health results. For example, adolescents with a high spiritual well-being level showed fewer depressive symptoms and engaged in less risk-taking behaviours (Cotton et al., 2005). These empirical findings show the need for further investigation and the importance of spiritual well-being.

2.1.3 MAJOR ASSERTIONS ON SPIRITUAL WELL-BEING

Spiritual well-being has been the topic for discussion in psychology, education, health care and social development (Tacey, 2004). Many studies have been conducted about its nature, as it is often understood in different ways by different people. In general, the term refers to diverse approaches for discovering, experiencing, and living an authentic human life (Muldoon, 1995). Various theories on spiritual well-being reveal many points to think about the nature of spirituality.

2.1.4 VARIOUS THEORIES ON SPIRITUAL WELL-BEING

In 1902, William James, one of the early fathers of psychological science, published his important work on religion. In humanity's history, we can see that spiritual experience evolved into great religions through different cultural traditions approved by society. Subsequently, spirituality became the subject of scientific psychology. In the following decades, other prominent psychologists studied spirituality and its relationship with physical health and mental health theoretically. They include Adler & Jahn, 1933; Erikson, 1958; Freud, 1928, and Jung, 1921. Later, existential and humanistic psychologists such as Maslow, 1954; Frankl, 1964; Rogers, 1961 came out with their views on religion and spirituality. Others who spoke extensively on religious experience include Allport, 1937,1967 and Bucke, 1923. Recently, the religious and spiritual phenomena have attracted the attention of transpersonal psychology due to authors like Grof, 1993 and Wilber, 1995 and the emergence of positive psychology of Seligman 1998.

From the above details, it is clear that there are several psychological models and theories on religious and spiritual experiences. Theoretical background and the methods for crucial concepts of some authors are discussed below.

2.1.4.1 Psychoanalytical Approach

This model is developed from Freud, Jung, Fromm, Erikson, Bowlby, and others. In the *Totem and Taboo*, Freud reported the projection of omnipotence as a characteristic of the infantile thinking is a phylogenetical characteristic of the magical and later on religious thinking (Freud, 1928). Sigmund Freud (1930), in the "*Civilisation and its Discontents,*" openly developed his theory of religion. According to him, religion is a universal, obsessive neurosis of humankind. It is identical with the obsessive neurosis in children, which develops from Oedipus Complex (a boy aged between 3 and 6, becoming unconsciously sexually friendly to his mother). In other words, according to Sigmund Freud, the projection of all-powerfulness is a characteristic of magical and religious thinking. Religion is deemed to be a universal obsessive neurosis rooted in the Oedipus complex.

However, Jung treated religious beliefs as a by-product of the archetypal system (Jung, 1969). According to him, the archetypes of God, the devil, salvation and other ancient religious images are part of the collective human unconscious. A particular psychological function enables us to know the archetypal contents and symbols. From the latest psychoanalytically influenced interpretations of religion, one can explain the relational models inspired by object-relation theory. In this respect, the religious experience reflects the child-mother relationship with its attachment or separation dynamics. In other words, religion is intricately connected with our collective unconscious. The archetypal system consisting of God, the devil and salvation has been adopted by natural human ability.

2.1.4.2 The Relational Theories

Two theories, John Bowlby's psychoanalytic attachment theory and Erik Erikson's physiological theory development discuss the bond significance of infants with caregivers. This theory points out that children are born with a tendency to be attached to caregivers. Trust is important in an infant's psychological development. Bowlby points out that attachment is a "lasting psychological connectedness between human beings." Attachment, communication, and interaction with the infant are important to the child's psychological need to maintain the relationship and the physical need of survival. Such a child has less fear and the confidence remains somewhat unchanged for the person's entire life because of the attachment a child had developed between infancy and adolescence (Karen, 1998).

Erikson's psychosocial development theory emphasises the ego and various development stages from infancy (0 to 1½ years) to maturity (above 65 years). Erikson explained eight psychosocial stages. According to Erikson's psychosocial development theory, trust and mistrust occurs in the first year of life. An infant learns to trust the primary caregiver to meet the basic needs. If this stage is successful, hope is established which enables the infant to develop trust in a time of crisis. Otherwise, the infant will fear and start to mistrust, which affects the development of the other seven psycho-social stages. These stages are (a) autonomy versus shame and doubt (1½ to 3 years), (b) initiative versus guilt (3 to 5 years), (c) industry versus inferiority (5 to 12 years), (d) identity versus identity confusion (12 to 18 years), (e) intimacy versus isolation (Erikson, 1963).

Berger & Calabrese (1975) offered a theoretical point of view for dealing with interpersonal interaction's entry. Uncertainty was standard by proposing the uncertainty reduction theory. This theory attempts to explain how human beings use passive, active, and interactive communication approaches for reducing uncertainty regarding other human beings. A passive strategy is observing someone from a distance and arriving at conclusions based on those observations. A more active strategy might be the 'act' of collecting data about someone to get information. An interactive strategy happens when information is exchanged directly in person. Different sources can be used when collecting information through verbal and non-verbal communication, including familiarity or mutual benefit. This information-seeking behaviour reduces their uncertainty.

2.1.4.3 Humanistic Psychology

Humanistic psychologists Allport, Maslow and Rogers through crucial concepts, i.e., projection of the superior (supreme) presence being patterned originally in early child object (mother) relation. A problem in a relationship points out the opinions and feelings of the individuals in that relationship. Psychologists have applied this concept in the clinical and empirical approaches to self-actualisation (Maslow, 1969).

2.1.4.4 The Existential Psychology and Logotherapy

Existentialist Viktor Frankl (1962), the proponent of logotherapy, believed that to resist difficulties, one needs to have the motivation or the will to find a sense of meaning in life. The basic concept of logotherapy is that human beings are most motivated to search for meaning in life. It takes place through one's own acts, interaction with others and the choice of one's attitude under any circumstance. This theory's basic concepts are religiosity and spirituality, which are important factors in forming a purpose and rational reason. Three techniques are used in logotherapy, which includes (a) helping someone to change the focus from themselves to other people, (b) Paradoxical Intention, the technique of helping the person wish for the thing that he/she was most worried about and (c) Socratic dialogue, a way to support a patient helping him/her to self-discover through one's own words (Frankl, 1962).

2.1.4.5 Transpersonal Psychology

Stanislav Grof and Ken Wilber are the proponents of the transpersonal approach in psychology. Transpersonal psychologists join the spiritual and other-worldly aspects to involve wider dimensions of humankind, life, psyche or cosmos (Grof, 1993). This theory's basic concept is that religion and spirituality connect the individual with the transcendental reality.

In the last decades, the experimental research on spirituality and religion and related phenomena is increasing, as mentioned before. A religious and spiritual experience includes cognitive, affective and motivational sides related to genetic, developmental and socio-cultural factors. The research on religious and related phenomena is defined as hypotheses representing religious and spiritual issues. It includes faith, hope, fear of death, religious experience, religiosity and spirituality.

The experimental research of religion and spirituality has only a short tradition. Nevertheless, it is progressing quickly and we are challenged with related phenomena like meditation and near-death experiences.

2.1.5 DIFFERENT PROGRAMMES FOR SPIRITUAL WELL-BEING

Based on the observation and research data, professionals in social work, psychology and education are now aware of the commonness of depression, addiction, suicide and psychological suffering in modern society. Subsequently, more schools across the western world are introducing spirituality into curricula to encourage holistic well-being in children, which will be reflected in the child's school-experiences and the quality of life (Karstens, 2010).

Over the years, schools worldwide are trying for health-promoting school programmes in reply to the World Health Organisation's focus on health. The focus has now changed from individual's behaviour to healthy settings. (Mũkoma, 2004). A health-promoting school strengthens its role as a setting for good health and holistic educational outcomes. Such schools use an approach wherein the school supports teaching and learning experiences, which involve the whole school (Mũkoma, 2004).

2.1.6 CULTURAL PRACTICES ON SPIRITUAL WELL-BEING

Human health has multiple sources, such as material, social, cultural and spiritual. Human beings are social creatures that need traditions to make life worthwhile. Language, knowledge, beliefs, assumptions and values that gives meaning to life are exchanged between individuals, groups and generations. Humans' sense of spirituality is sublimely connected to the world. Spirituality brings a sense of connectedness to the world, even though it is not always consciously expressed. Religion is the most common, cultural representation of spirituality. It is a system of beliefs and rituals that usually focuses on a god or gods (Eckersley, 2007).

Socio-cultural messages can create misunderstanding, disagreement and hostility within individuals and groups when they oppose the religious beliefs and teachings. This gives religion little place in their peaceful co-existence. This can lead to an adjustment and compromise within religions, leading to a higher tolerance of consumerism and self-gratification and thus removing any need to choose between "God and mammon" (Pargament, 2009). Spirituality includes practices, beliefs and experiences. All these sides of spirituality receive attention from authors who discuss various practices such as meditation, mantra repetition, mindful practice, non-attachment and many other beliefs about happiness and the nature of human beings. Lots of experiences in meditation and many other facets of spirituality are mentioned in several articles. The four classical Indian approaches to spiritual exercises include meditation (dhyāna yoga), devotion (bhakti yoga), action (karma yoga) and knowledge (jñāna yoga). Each yoga has different practices. It includes selfless action (nishkāma karma) in the yoga of action and differentiation between the changing and the changeless (nitya-anitya-viveka) in the yoga of knowledge.

2.1.7 CHALLENGES AND CONCERNS OF SPIRITUAL WELL-BEING

In recent years, there have been several attempts from various people to link spirituality and health within the idea of spiritual well-being. For example, Hateley (1983) wrote about spiritual health as the relationship to self, empathy in the community and relationship with God. Goodloe & Arreola, in their article "Spiritual health: out of the closet," points out the interrelatedness of mind, physical body and spirit in a state of inner peace (Goodloe & Arreola, 1992).

2.1.8 ASSESSMENT OF SPIRITUAL WELL-BEING

The Spiritual Well-Being Scale (SWB) is used to assess individual and congregational spiritual well-being. The scale focuses on twenty items, of which ten estimate religious well-being, which is the self-evaluation of an individual's relationship with God. The other ten items estimate existential well-being, giving a self-evaluation of an individual's sense of life purpose and overall life satisfaction. These elements are used to evaluate the overall opinion of an individual's spiritual quality of life.

2.1.8.1 Studies Related to Spiritual Well-Being

Tvorogova (2011), in his article "Spiritual well-being," considers the role of personal and social values in the regulation of human behaviour. These values could be the reason for habits and rules. Since these reasons are not always explained, they give rise to beliefs, tenets, social mindsets, patterns, personal and social behavioural targets and regulate the decision-making procedures at all stages of societal activity. The study concludes by stating that the spiritual component should be included in comprehensive research on public health.

Phenwan & Peerawong (2019) in their article "The Meaning of Spirituality and Spiritual Well-Being among Thai Breast Cancer Patients: A Qualitative Study", point out that spirituality is the essence of a human being. However, health-care providers usually under-estimate this aspect due to a lack of practical guidelines.

2.1.9 STATUS OF SPIRITUAL WELL-BEING IN THE INTERNATIONAL, NATIONAL AND STATE SITUATIONS

Several professionals are accepting spiritual well-being as a link to good health. They can be measured by the rise in the number of discussions, journals and books on spiritual well-being over the past few decades.

2.1.9.1 International Level

Marian (2009) in his editorial "Spirituality and well-being" for the 8th International Conference on Children's Spirituality, held in Australia in January 2008, used the theme 'The role of spirituality in education and health: finding meaning and connectedness to promote well-being' (Marian, 2009). World Health Organization suggests the physical, psychological, social and spiritual characteristics as core aspects of human reality that helps in human society's development (Crisp, 2005). It offers stability in life, peace, harmony and coordination, feeling close relationship with oneself, God, society and the environment (Azarsa, 2015). According to studies, spirituality is posited at the heart of human experience (McCarroll, 2005) and experienced by everyone (Nolan & Crawford, 1997). Spirituality can be fundamental and vital component of being human.

2.1.9.2 National Level

Research has initiated the idea of joining spiritual well-being into that of religiousness and spirituality. Both are strongly linked to health and well-being in various ways (Wagani & Colucci, 2018). In India, the linkage between spirituality and well-being is an ancient practice. But only limited efforts have been made to know the impact of spirituality and religion on (a person's) well-being, including the prevention of suicide. A sense of meaning in life can give people higher levels of psychological and physical well-being. It can be the most important factor in preventing suicidal behaviour (Reker, 1994).

In India, most of the parents focus too much on refining their children's cognitive excellence and academic achievements. Schools are struggling to attain 100% results, curricular and co-curricular achievements and maintain linguistic standards, so that the children could get admissions in top colleges. However, unintentionally they are ignoring the inner, personal and social lives of their children. Lack of role models, difference in elders' words and acts, the adverse influence of social networking, over-loaded curriculum and the use-and-throw attitude divert adolescents from a truly value-oriented life.

Numerous instances of psychological and pedagogical research show that the age of 14 to 18 years is very important for education and development of spiritual values in an individual. This is the stage where children start shaping their interests and basic requirements. It could be the starting point for either spiritual wealth, emotional generosity and moral strength or spiritual poverty, narrowed down interests, insensitivity and uncontrollable will power. During these years, a person re-valuates the experience gained up to that point. This helps them to develop the foundation for life philosophy and builds attitudes towards people, society, the world and their place in it. The life philosophy of a senior high school student is inseparable from the world view as the social value of a person is determined by the contribution made to society's progress. A teacher must explain the moral motive for action and raise awareness regarding its original purpose.

2.1.9.3 State Situation

A survey that was conducted to examine the influence of religion, religious behaviour and understanding about spirituality on positive mental health (PMH) in Kerala revealed that religious differences are mostly explained by behavioural restrictions and occasions for socialisation, that religion does or does not provide (Nima, 2012). Another study by Gnanaprakash (2013) indicates the level and coping ability of post-graduate university students in their spirituality and resilience. The results revealed that students who had scored high in spirituality had a better ability to manage their stressors, better adaptability and a positive point of view towards their problems. So, religion and spirituality can play an essential role in enhancing students' mental health and their overall development as good human beings and civilized citizens.

2.1.10 SPIRITUAL WELL-BEING OF ADOLESCENTS

Spiritual growth could be a turning point in child and adolescent development. The public imagination is ready to discuss social changes that challenge young people spiritual lives (Roehlkepartain, 2006). The period of growth during adolescence lasts from about 13-15 years to 20-22 years. This period is the beginning and the peak of physical and sexual maturation. By completing physical development at about 25 years, adolescents become socially and emotionally mature personalities. According to Macek (2003), adolescence can be separated into three phases: early adolescence (10-13 years), middle adolescence (14-16 years), and late adolescence (17-22 years). Adolescents face rapid cognitive, social and physical variations. This makes them the main subjects for the study of development and well-being. Over the last three decades, there is an increasing interest shown for evaluating the spiritual health and well-being of late adolescents. However, evaluating the spiritual health of younger adolescents has received little attention (Macek, 2003).

According to Saraswati Swami (2018), many factors influence spirituality. Any single definition will not be enough as they differ from individual to individual and from religion to religion. Empirical research has highlighted religious values, ethics, personal beliefs and societal values that influence spirituality. Some factors indicate that spirituality begins with a relationship with oneself and develops relationships with others, thus encouraging the purpose in life. Three factors are found to have an influence in spiritual growth; educators, school and parents.

2.1.10.1 The Role of the Educator

Majority of educators identify themselves as role-models of acceptable behaviour and attitudes including tolerance, forgiveness, kindness and love. Besides, educators are also aware of their role in promoting spirituality and laying the foundations of religion, its knowledge and experience. A general view was that educators have to persuade the students to be careful in their choice of freedom, belief and practice.

2.1.10.2 The Role of the School and the Curriculum

School management and governing bodies are the primary authorities who decide how spirituality may be included in the school curriculum and what additional programmes may be given to students to promote their spiritual well-being. Participants acknowledged that educators in public schools do not favour any specific religion above the other. The education policy in the National Curriculum is about Sarva Dharma Samanvaya, the core of the Gandhian perspective about Indian secularism. It is practised to encourage religious harmony by celebrating all the major festivals in schools and including some facts about every religion's textbooks (Rao, 1989).

2.1.10.3 The Role of Parents

The majority of educators expect children to learn spirituality and religion from their parents. It is the parents' responsibility to encourage children's spiritual well-being. Besides, educators expressed a desire to be "partner(s) with the parents" to develop the students' spiritual well-being.

2.1.11 STATUS OF SPIRITUAL WELL-BEING WITH ADOLESCENTS IN THE CBSE SCHOOLS

Adolescence is perhaps the most important phase in an individual's journey of life. It is characterised by creativity, curiosity about oneself and the universe, rapid growth in the physical body, mood swings and increased need for communication. The period also faces identity crisis, feelings of isolation, anxiety, alienation and confusion. Health is a significant concern of senior secondary school students of CBSE. Obesity or thin body, mental and emotional stress are also important concerns. Therefore, in CBSE schools, there is an urgent need to create a health-oriented syllabus. Health and Wellness Clubs, which is already part of CBSE schools, can become the centre point of enhancing mental health.

2.2 CONCEPT OF SOCIAL SUPPORT

Health is a concept influenced by a large number of biological, psychological, social, cultural, economic, mental and spiritual factors. Social attachment has an important role for psychological adjustment and mental health (Sarason, 1983). Psychotherapists motivate their clients to engage in self-examination and self-awareness to promote self-acceptance. Similarly, soldiers develop strong, reinforcing ties with one another, essential for their success and survival. The attention and verbal expressions of physicians have useful effects on their patients' well-being and rapid recovery from illness. Social support offers physical and psychological advantages to students facing crisis in their lives by giving positive adjustment and personal development against stress (Sarason, 1983).

The study of social support originated from the epidemiological and public health models of diseases connected with psychological phenomena (Bloom, 1965). A fundamental concept for these models was the multi-factorial causation (Price, 1974). The etiologists viewed it as a result of multiple risk factors, such as a pathogen interacting with both a host organism amid noxious or protective environmental factors (Sanford, 1972).

2.2.1 DEFINITIONS OF SOCIAL SUPPORT

Social support denotes the amount of support that a person believes to have obtained. Social support is about interactions of people offering good attention and quality of social relationships, such as the availability of help or support received. It is selfless, conveying a sense of obligation and the understanding of reciprocity (Schwarzer, 1992). The understanding and actuality are that the one cared for has assistance available from other persons. More commonly, one is part of a supportive social network. Social support is increased through emotional encouragement, companionship, information assistance and quantifiable aid from others.

Social support is usually the availability of people upon whom one can trust, people who create a feeling of being cared for, valued and loved (Sarason, 1983). According to Cohen (2008), social support is defined as the qualitative roles performed for the individual by significant others. It includes the number and frequency of contacting friends/family, marital and parental status/group along with membership.

According to Malecki (2002), social support is an individual's understanding of general support or specific supportive behaviours that enhance their functioning and safeguard them from negative outcomes.

Costello (2001) in his manuscript "Social supports for children and families: A matter of connections" explains a broad definition of social support by Reid which provides four specific kinds of support:

1. Instrumental support which is direct support to an individual in the form of financial assistance, skill training, health services and transportation.
2. Informational support which includes providing information about a need or referrals for help, including health-related information;
3. Affiliative support which means simply being with other individuals who have mutual interests.
4. Emotional support means close friends or family members, or professionals, who fulfil emotional needs or help at the time of personal crises.

2.2.2 ORIGIN AND DEVELOPMENT OF THE CONCEPT OF SOCIAL SUPPORT

Social support denotes various types of support. It is assistance or help that people receive from others. Social support is an important factor that can influence mental health. For the last 30 years, researchers have shown great interest in social support, mostly regarding health. Previous research works have found that those with high quality or quantity of social networks have a reduced risk of mortality than those with a lower quality or number of social relationships (Berkman, 2000). Social support has both positive and negative sides; each of which is connected with mental health outcomes. This research joins various roles of social support on the mental health of senior secondary school students. The review discloses that social support can help school students adjust and prevent psychological distress and the access and care social support provides enhances mental health.

Social activity is said to involve social support. Perceived support, also known as operational support, is the subjective belief that family and friends would give enough assistance against future stressors. People with high perceived support believe that they can count on their family and friends at any time. A person may develop perceived support through the various roles of their lives. However, perceived support can also develop from ordinary socialising and companionship more than the experiences of getting help in a stressful situation (Procidano, 1983).

The primary component of perceived support is not known currently. However, this primary component can be the increased self-esteem got by evaluating others' views of the self (Gecas, 1982 & Rosenberg, 1981). Another important component of social support is the stress-related interpersonal interactions in which network members provide help for a problem or dilemma. In this sense, social support can be viewed as a coping technique (Procidano, 1983).

2.2.2.1 The Influence of Social Support on Health Behaviours

Although many earlier studies consider health behaviours as confusing, recent models of support points to its potential role as mechanisms (Uchino, 2006). The importance of positive social support is best understood from married couples with long-term healthy behaviour and relationship.

According to Cobb (1976), the concept of social support is an important subject in the 21st century, especially in educational institutions. Furthermore, it has direct, protective and compensatory effects on mental health. The theoretical issues of social support is discussed in the next chapter, based on reviews. The study focuses on the possible mechanisms through which social support may impact school students' psychological well-being.

2.2.2.2 Positive and Negative Dimensions of Relationships

In an individual's life, he/she involved in various social relationships with immediate families, spouses, friends, co-workers and neighbours etc. These social bonds differ widely in their positive and negative qualities (Rook, 2015). Positive characteristics of relationships include the support provided, companionship, affection and social control. Negative aspects are unsuitable support, unwelcome support, criticism, demands, irritations and conflict. Ambivalent relationships are optimistic and pessimistic at the same time. In this respect, it is important to focus on social factors influencing mental health and perceived social support. Social support alone is not enough, but what is important is the belief in social support (Marmot & Wilkinson, 2008).

Social support offers physical and psychological support for individuals facing stressful physical and psycho-social events. It reduces psychological distress even when faced with stressful events (Brummett et al., 2005). Much research has been done on the impact of social support on health, quality of life, and especially mental health during recent decades. However, each study has been conducted on a different population and has used different instruments, sampling methods, and statistical people, which have resulted in mixed results. For instance, Afrooz &Taghizadeh (2014) and Shakerinia (2012) found a strong connection between social support and mental health, while Pahlevanzadeh (2011) found that the connection was weak. Since the conclusions are varied and sometimes opposites, to get quick and correct information, resources must be used systematically.

The results joined to achieve a tangible and overall effect. It helps to minimise bias in these studies, and also to reduce errors.

2.2.3 VARIOUS THEORIES ON SOCIAL SUPPORT

Social support theory emerged from the writings of Don Drennon-Gala and Francis Cullen. They drew insights from many theoretical traditions (Kort-Butler, 2017). The social support theory puts forward that instrumental, informational and emotional support decreases crime. Different social support views give importance to different operational mechanisms. However, Lakey & Cohen (2000) discussed three important theoretical point of views in social support research, which are presented below.

2.2.3.1 Stress and Coping Perspective

Lakey & Cohen (2000), in their article "Social support theory and measurement," point out that Richard Lazarus, a psychologist, established the Transactional Theory of Stress and Coping (TTSC). It presents the transaction between a person and his or her complex environment. This view put forward the concept that support contributes to health by protecting people from the adverse effects of stress. Coping refers to a process by which a person continuously changes the cognitive and behavioural efforts to manage external and internal demands even though it is beyond the person's abilities. Hence, it is important to focus on particular threats that a student is experiencing at a specific time rather than focusing on the illness in general.

2.2.3.2 The Social Constructionist Perspective

Berger and Luckman (1991) in their book, *The Social Construction of Reality*, regard individuals as connected with cultural, political, and historical evolution at particular times and places. Similarly, social support proponents Lakey & Cohen (2000) believe in the social constructionist perspective. The social constructionist perspective abandons the idea that an individual's mind has a mirror of reality. Constructionism believes that individual maps are formed from their personal experience and how they see those realities. Hence, every student creates his or her own world by viewing the actual world. Social constructionism gives central role to language, communication and speech in the interactive process through which individuals understand the world and themselves.

2.2.3.3 The Relationship Perspective

Relationship perspective says that effect of social support on health cannot be separated from relationship processes. It includes companionship, intimacy and low social conflict. Relationship perspective points to a positive, stable and secure relationship that may fulfil a basic, biological need (Baumeister, 1995). Support is related to health only because it joins in a common cause with other related processes. For example, the prediction that persons with low backing are more likely to have poor health only because less support is associated with social conflict. From the above discussion, social support theories and its influence on mental health are very vibrant. Hence, more research is needed on factors of social support as from social support arises supportive action. However, these concepts do help to show that it is possible to conduct theoretically based research on social assistance. This theory points out that health is related to social support and low support can lead to students poor health.

2.2.4 ASSESSMENT OF SOCIAL SUPPORT

The hypothesis of social support has been useful in understanding mental and physical health, including mortality and some illnesses. The most standard measure of social support is perceived support. In general, this measure shows steady and strong relations to mental health. It is often related to many indices of physical fitness.

Although researchers have tried to evaluate social support through behavioural observation, only a small number of such measurements have been developed. One promising observational calculation is the Social Support Behaviour Code (SSBC). The SSBC has a good inter-rater agreement, but it has not yet been used widely in research. There is comparatively little information about its validity (Cutrona, 1997). Hence, the researcher has used the Social Support Questionnaire (SSQ) established by Sarason et al. (1983), consisting of 27 items.

2.2.5 SUB-FACTORS OF SOCIAL SUPPORT OF ADOLESCENTS

Social support should be evaluated in terms of quantity and quality. That is how the type of relationship is linked with how satisfied a person is with those relationships. Social support is a complex concept about interpersonal relationships' structural and functional aspects (Cohen, 1985). Structural elements refer to the existence of interconnections in social groups. Perceived and received support typically share only 12 per cent common variance and may have different relationships with outcome variables (Haber, 2007). Operational elements relate to the particular functions served by interpersonal relationships. Practical support is divided into perceived support (Cohen, 1988).

2.2.6 DIFFERENT PROGRAMMES FOR SOCIAL SUPPORT

Fairbrother (2011), in his article "Social support", points out that for adolescents, social support is the physical and emotional comfort given by family, friends, teachers, classmates and others.

It realizes that adolescents are part of a school or community of people who love, care and value one another. Adolescence is commonly viewed as the period in life when the individual attains the skills and attributes necessary to become a creative and reproductive adult. Nearly all cultures recognise this phase in life by acknowledging these aspects of young people, most of the world's adolescents make it through this phase without much difficulty. However, some research shows that adolescents' regulating tasks are becoming more difficult because of reduced social control by families. (Frydenberg, 1997). Programmes in South-East Asia accessed for this document reported that changes in the social structure and the economy – including an increase in educational attainment, increasing urbanization and increased modern-sector employment opportunities for young women – have led to a weakening of the traditional familial support.

Involving adolescents in health-related issues through the school is useful for improving adolescent health and attracting adolescents to existing health services. Creating linkages between the public health sector and the school will greatly encourage adolescents to seek help. Information, education, communication (IEC), or media campaigns were carried out to increase awareness about the use of existing sources of support for adolescents. Information booths or centres have been started to give youth information on sources of help, health services, job training and recreational activities in the United Kingdom (U.K.), and to a limited extent in Colombia and the United States (Barker, 1996).

Reproductive and Sexual Health Issues (TARSHI) Delhi, India, which operates a telephone help-line from Delhi, offers free and confidential information, counselling and referrals on sexuality and reproductive issues to adolescents. Necessary information on sex conception and contraception are some of the adolescent's main concerns (Barker, 2007). Life-skill development is a useful support system for adolescents at the school and community level. It helps adolescents take positive actions and improve their coping skills towards stress and problem-solving ability. Life skills are used to choose friends and career, to develop or break habits, to make and break relationships, follow discipline, understand one's needs, solve problems and to communicate better with teachers and parents (Michael, 1999). Life-skill education enhances mental well-being in young people and prepares them to face the realities of life. This helps the individual to behave in a pro-social way, additional to healthy living (Jamali et al., 2016).

Consequently, life-skills education can empower adolescents to take more responsibility for their actions, enhance competence in young people as they face life's realities, take positive actions to protect themselves, and improve health and meaningful social relationships.

2.2.7 CULTURAL PRACTICES ON SOCIAL SUPPORT

School culture points out how teachers and other staff members work together on the basis of common set of beliefs, values and assumptions. A vibrant and encouraging school atmosphere enhances the students' ability to learn. Understanding social support within a cultural context requires knowledge of that culture. Learning is an important feature of one's identity because it defines, prescribes, directs and gives meaning to life. Using Keith's definition, culture is "a design for living, the shared understanding underlying a shared way of life. The essential attribute of culture is that it is shared and provides a vocabulary of symbols to express and assign meaning to various aspects of social life" (Keith, 1991). Culture can influence students' beliefs, attitudes, expectations and responses. Therefore, a student's culture becomes the ground for social support to be given and received. This contextual ground helps to express specific needs that would require social support. Although numerous factors such as social class, gender and age, can impact giving and receiving social assistance in different families, cultural context is also important. The context in which these supportive behavior happen help us to understand how cultural norms, attitudes, beliefs and practices support networks in families (Mutran, 1985).

2.2.8 CHALLENGES AND CONCERNS ON SOCIAL SUPPORT

Social support is an important aspect of an adolescent's life. The experiences help to understand what actions could be taken to support adolescents during this vulnerable stage. The important changes experienced during adolescence are independence from parents and family, close relationship with peers, physical maturation, start of romantic relationships and stressful events which occur repeatedly (Hankin, 2007). These sudden changes may lead the adolescents to unhealthy behaviour and problems, including depressive symptoms (Byrne, 2007) and anxiety symptoms (Adewuya, 2007).

Most of the research results show that girls experience a higher level of stress with parents, peers and romantic partners than boys (Moksnes 2010). Hankin (2007) found that interpersonal events (i.e., relationship with peers, intimate partners or family members) cause depressive symptoms among girls. At the same time, boys react more to achievement-related events (i.e., sports performance). Some have even claimed that girls respond more negatively when facing similar levels of distress. (Mezulis, 2010).

2.2.9 MAJOR DECLARATIONS AND POLICIES ON SOCIAL SUPPORT

Unlike the signed declaration and policies of mental health, social support has no significant policy to explain guidelines and programmes. However, restrictive discipline is being increasingly used in activities focused on improving students' mental health and well-being in schools.

2.2.10 STATUS OF SOCIAL SUPPORT IN THE INTERNATIONAL, NATIONAL AND STATE SITUATIONS

According to *Encyclopaedia Britannica*, support networks are made up primarily of nongovernmental organisations (NGOs). Still, they include people from the public or private sector. Internationally, nationally and regionally, support networks focus on the mobilisation, explanation and distribution of information to bring change in the behaviour of governments, private firms or even international organisations. These networks support many of the characteristics of social movements. They expanded quickly across international borders, starting in the 1990s. In both domains, support networks have become active causes of social and political change.

Disaster management is also called crisis management. The student community joining with groups of teachers, made its presence in helping communities to deal with difficulties. Supporters of social care are independent of the local authority and national health services. They are trained to help the students understand their rights, express their views and wishes and make sure that their voice is heard.

2.2.11 SOCIAL SUPPORT STATUS WITH THE ADOLESCENTS IN THE CBSE SCHOOLS

Social support, a protective factor, reduces the effect of stress by working on the risk factors, thus helping in the healthy development of an adolescent. These factors contribute to resistance, which ensures mental health, irrespective of the problems experienced. Life skill education and training recommended by the World

Health Organization form a part of the school mental health programme in CBSE schools in Kerala (CBSE & NPSC, 2019).

2.3 CONCEPT OF MENTAL HEALTH

The concept of mental health does not have clear-cut borders because of its polysemic nature. The concept has a historical point of view that needs to be better understood. What is broadly understood by "mental health" has its origins in developments in public health in clinical psychiatry and other branches of knowledge (Bertolote, 2008).

The origin of the current concept of mental health is generally attributed to the work of Clifford Beers. They formed the mental hygiene movement in the USA in 1908. Based on his personal experience of being admitted to three mental hospitals, Clifford published a book titled *A Mind that Found Itself* that was highly influential. Similarly, at the same time of the year, a Mental Hygiene Society was established in Connecticut in the New England region of the north-eastern United States.

The term "mental hygiene" had been suggested to Beers by Adolf Meyer. In 1909, this led to the creation of the National Commission on Mental Hygiene. From then on, the worldwide activities of this commission led to the establishment of many national associations concerned with mental hygiene in France, South Africa, Italy, and Hungary. From these national associations, the International Committee on Mental Hygiene was created. Later, this committee was replaced by the World Federation of Mental Health (Bertolote, 2008). The mental hygiene movement was mostly concerned with humanizing the care for people with mental disorders, thus removing the abuses and cruelties. Subsequently, the committee developed its program to include the minor forms of mental weakness and more significant concern for preventive effort (Bertolote, 2008).

The justification behind this change was the belief that "mental disorders frequently have their beginnings in childhood and youth while preventive measures are most effective in early life". Furthermore, environmental conditions and modes of living produce mental illness (Beers, 1937).

In 1937, the US National Committee for Mental Hygiene put forward to achieve its objectives by promoting early diagnosis and treatment, developing suitable hospitalization, motivating research, securing public understanding and support of psychiatric and mental hygiene activities, instructing individuals and groups in the application of mental hygiene principles and collaborating with government and private agencies whose work touches at any point in the field of mental hygiene (Bertolote, 2008). Thus, the mental hygiene movement keeps in mind of not a single patient, but a whole community and looked at each member of that community as an individual whose mental and emotional status was determined by several causes and who needs prevention rather than cure. Eventually, both psychiatrists and mental hygienists became more than ever conscious of their objectives. They needed one another to carry out their everyday tasks (Bertolote, 2008).

From its very start in 1948, the WHO always had an administrative unit dedicated to mental health and requests from its member states. Later, the administrative section was called "Mental Health" in the English version (WHO, 1951). In 1948, the First International Congress of Mental Health was organized in London by the British National Association for Mental Hygiene from 16 to 21 August. Even though it started as an international conference on mental hygiene, it ended with a series of recommendations on mental health. After the congress, the International Committee on Mental Hygiene was replaced by the World Federation for Mental Health. Thus, in 1949 the

National Institute of Mental Health started its activities in the United States of America (Bertolote, 2008).

More than half a century of mental health activities and nearly a century of mental hygiene movements, reasonable progress can be viewed in these areas. WHO's concept of health has been recently questioned as it was created half a century ago, thus not suitable to the current situation (Frenk, 1997). Mental health continues to be used to denote a state or a dimension of health. It refers to the movement derived from the mental hygiene movement, corresponding to psychiatry's application to groups, communities and societies.

However, improvement in the standards of mental health care and the removal of abuses faced by people with mental disorders are still important causes for promoting mental health worldwide (Bertolote, 2008). The concept of mental health takes a complete evaluation of the individual through his/her personality traits and behaviours. A mentally healthy person shows desirable attitudes/values, and moral self-concepts and scientific view of the world. Several psychologists (Erickson, 1936; Rogers,1961 & Hurlock, 1972) have expressed their view in a similar way. A mentally sound person is a lively and conscientious person who is reasonably rational in choosing his or her pious destinations (Anand, 1988). Therefore, mental health is an attitudinal concept toward oneself and others (Lehner, 1962). It also presents a humanistic approach and attitudes towards self, positive feelings, attitudes towards self, and others.

2.3.1 DEFINITION OF MENTAL HEALTH

Mental health generally refers to the cognitive, behavioural, emotional and social well-being of people. It is often used as an additional for mental health ailments such as depression, anxiety and schizophrenia.

Med Lexicon's Medical Dictionary explains mental health as emotional, behavioural and social maturity or normality. It is a state of psychological well-being in which one has made the natural drives acceptable to both oneself and the social environment as well as an appropriate balance of love, work and leisure pursuits.

Sigmund Freud gave a minor but a significant definition of mental health that "a person is said to be mentally healthy if the person could love and work" (Freud, 1900).

Shah A.V. has specified mental health as "the most essential and inseparable component of health" (Shah, 1982).

According to the WHO, mental health is defined as a state of well-being where the individual understands his or her abilities and manage everyday stresses of life to work productively to contribute to the community (WHO, 2004). Mental health can have an impact on daily life, relationships and even physical health. It also means the person's ability to enjoy life, attain a balance between life activities and achieve psychological resistance.

2.3.2 SUBFACTORS OF MENTAL HEALTH OF ADOLESCENTS

Mental health forms an important part of an individual's health. It interacts in a complex manner with physical health and abilities to succeed in school and society. Sound mental health is needed for an individual to overcome imaginary threats and fears (Punia & Berwal, 2015). Six indices of mental health have been selected for this research from the manual for mental health battery (MHB), such as emotional stability, over-all adjustment, autonomy, security- insecurity, self-concept, and intelligence (Singh, 2013). Each dimension is explained below as follows.

2.3.2.1 Emotional Stability

Emotional stability means the ability to manage challenging situations, handle difficulties and remain productive without becoming anxious, nervous, tense and emotionally upset. Behaviours of a person with emotional stability are stable emotions and self-image. Different circumstances are successfully dealt with a strict schedule is followed to feel in control, feeling content with life and accepting one's situation and building a safe living environment (Singh, 2013).

2.3.2.2 Over-all Adjustment

Over-all adjustment refers to adaptability. It means adjusting to life in various situations, such as in the field of education and health. It helps in maintaining balance between needs and problems. The characteristics related with overall adjustment are adapting to various areas of life like education and social health, at home, school or society, maintaining balance in different life situations, positive attitude towards life, the balance between work and family, tackling fear, anxiety, and stress, forming a positive relationship dealing with the challenges of life (Shaffer, 1948).

2.3.2.3 Autonomy

Autonomy is the state of being independent, self-determined and free. It is explained as the ability of an individual to be governed by his principles and laws. It can respond freely to any situation (Bordages, 1989).

2.3.2.4 Security-Insecurity

The concept of security and insecurity was introduced by W. I. Thomas and Alfred Adler. Although different writers have given different definitions for the term, in the present study, security refers to safety, confidence, stability, pleasantness and satisfaction. At the same time, the term insecurity is associated with the feeling of threat, uneasiness, anger, frustration, unpleasantness created under threatening and unsupportive environment (Cameron & McCormick, 1954).

2.3.2.5 Self-Concept

Self-concept is the belief about one's strengths, weaknesses, status, cognition and achievements. In general, it refers to how one thinks about oneself or one's self-image. Self-concept's defining characteristics are self-image, relationships with friends, understanding about one's abilities, cognition, good self-image, self-esteem and abilities to meet basic needs (Adler &Towne, 1981).

2.3.2.6 Emotional Intelligence

The term emotional intelligence originated from the works of Peter Salovey and John Mayer. However, the term got more popular when Dan Goleman wrote a book on emotional intelligence in 1996. Salovey and Mayer (1990) defined emotional intelligence as the capacity to observe one's own and others' moods and emotions and to use this information appropriately (p. 189). Goleman (1996) described emotional intelligence as a group of positivity. It includes political mindfulness and self-confidence, including awareness of self and self-regulation, upholding the balance between relationships, motivation, and understanding others' emotions.

2.3.3 ORIGIN AND VARIOUS STAGES OF DEVELOPMENT OF MENTAL HEALTH

Early experiences faced by the developing brain are the basis of sound mental health. Any disturbance to this developmental process can damage a child's ability to learn and to relate to others for a lifetime. Some of these important factors which affect children's mental health are explained below:

0-4 years: Good mental health includes well-being and cognitive development, shaped in the womb. It is affected by multiple, complex genetic and environmental factors. Both mother and father act as safeguards against stress, enabling babies to adjust to the environment. Parental approval and warmth help the children to have high self-esteem. Toddlers face the highest risks of poor mental health, including the parents' mental health problems, addiction or misuse of substances and poverty (Centre for Mental Health, 2019).

5-10 years: Schools are the most important influence on a child's mental health after their family. Schools can either enhance or weaken a child's mental health, and they must know how to help (Centre for Mental Health, 2019).

11-15 years: Adolescence is a period of neurodevelopment. It is also the peak period for developing mental health problems. Young people in this age group mostly do not know where to get help for emotional breakdown and stigma. Informal sources of support, like friends and family help them (Centre for Mental Health, 2019).

16-25 years: Many adults suffer from a diagnosable mental health problem by the age of 24. Common mental health conditions that first happen in adolescence have a higher chance of happening again if not quickly treated and contained. It is the peak period for the beginning of psychosis (Centre for Mental Health, 2019).

2.3.4 VARIOUS THEORIES ON MENTAL HEALTH

Theories are important in social work practice because they help to justify the processes followed, the ideas created and used by the researcher or practitioner. Theories also provide a guideline about how a social work researcher should view an issue or a problem and take appropriate techniques to correct them. It gives social workers a standard for being accountable for their actions (Nash, 2005). It is also about self-esteem and the ability to have meaningful relationships with others. The concept of mental health is better developed in psychology literature. Ryff in the article "In the eye of the beholder: Views of psychological Von Franz" has provided an extraordinary account of 'happiness', that uses mainly the concepts of Maslow, Rogers, Jung, and Allport to develop a multidimensional construct of psychological well-being (Ryff, 1989).

Different researchers have collected evidence that supports theories. In psychology, theories are used for understanding human thoughts, emotions and behaviours. A psychological theory has two key components: First, it must describe a behaviour and second, it must make predictions about future behaviours. Several theories have been proposed to explain and predict various human behaviours. Some of these theories underwent many tests and finally are well-accepted at present. To understand mental health and mental illness using Western science and philosophy, we need to identify which theories have been used to understand mental health problems. To explore how the different approaches to understanding mental health have influenced treatment options. An effort is also made to consider how different mental health views influence our interactions and our response to mental health. The beginning of mental health theories dates back as far as the Greek philosophers, Plato and Aristotle's time in 500 BC. For Aristotle, the heart was necessary for intelligence, not the brain. Aristotle published his first known text in the history of psychology, called *Para Psyche*. He laid the first principles of the study of reasoning, which became the basis for modern approach to mental health. Hsün Tzu (ca. 312–230 BC), a Chinese Confucian philosopher, explained that the regularity and orderliness of nature is achieved through opposite and complementary energies, namely Yang (associated with power, hardness, heat, dryness and masculinity) and Yin (associated with weakness, softness, cold, moistness and femininity). They concluded that it is the balance between Yang and Yin that brings physical and psychological health.

Thus, the Chinese opened the door to physiological psychology, a belief that mental processes are greatly related with the physical body. Egyptian psychology gave importance to immortality and life after death. They often viewed the heart as the seat of mental life. Meanwhile, the Hebrews thought that mental disorders are caused by the anger of God for human disobedience. Zoroastrianism considered mental and physical disorders as the work of the devil.

However, Ayurveda, the ancient Indian science of medicine, engaged in positive health goals according to the social, religious, seasonal, climatic and regional contexts. It is known as Ashtanga Ayurveda because of its eight disciplines. Bhoot vidya, one of them, is the study of psychological and emotional disorders (Verma, 1965). Several concepts are considered important in mental health theories, such as psychodynamic theory, behavioural theory, cognitive theory, social theory, humanistic theory and biological theory.

2.3.4.1 Psychodynamic Theories

Psychodynamic theories are based on Sigmund Freud's psychoanalytic theory. During the late nineteenth century, Freud indicated that the mind is divided into two major components:

the conscious mind and the unconscious mind. The conscious mind includes awareness of events, thoughts and feelings that can be remembered. The unconscious mind consists of thoughts and feelings that are not accessed by the individual's conscious or subconscious awareness. For Sigmund Freud, personality has multiple parts, namely Id, Ego and the 'Super Ego. The 'Id' is the irrational and impulsive part, consisting of the primal animal desires. Ego is the rational self that bridges the gap between the Id and Super Ego. Super Ego is the moral self. It is judgmental and a representation of the society. Freud also put forward the idea that the conscious and unconscious parts fight each other, producing a repression phenomenon. He described this as a state where an individual is unaware of certain troubling motives or wishes (Freud, 1900). According to Vinney, mental illness is caused by mental tensions. It could be cured by making this repressed motives conscious and developing a coping strategy called defence mechanisms (Vinney, 2020). Other psychodynamic theorists include Alfred Adler, Carl Jung and Viktor Frankl. They separated Freud's initial principles, identifying other theories and strategies for understanding effective treatment of mental health conditions. Other leaders like Erik Erikson, Karen Horney broke off from old Freudian psychoanalytical concepts and joined the concepts from behavioural, social and biological theories.

2.3.4.2 Behavioural Theory

John B. Watson supported the behavioural theory of behaviourism. This theory says that observable, measurable and objective criteria are important to understand human behaviour and effect behavioural change. It centres on the idea that all behaviours are the result of conditioning (Schwarzer & Frensch, 2010). Ivan Pavlov is credited with discovering the behavioural theory of classical conditioning forces comprised of genetic factors and the environment through association or reinforcement (Rilling, 2000).

2.3.4.3 Cognitive Theory

The major proponents of cognitive theory, Tolman, Piaget and Chomsky, studied how people think, perceive, remember and learn. Several self-help books have been written from the cognitive viewpoint, each tells people the ways to adjust, change the way how the people think about themselves and the world. This theory believes that by changing our thoughts, we can change our mood, reduce our anxiety or improve our relationships (Friedenberg, 2006).

2.3.4.4 Social Theory

Proponents of this theory include Bandura, Lewin and Festinger. This theory focuses on explaining social behaviour including group behaviour. It also looks at social perception, leadership, non-verbal behaviour, conformity, aggression and prejudice. This theory point out that social psychology is not just about looking at social influences but also to understand social behaviour (Elliott, 1999).

2.3.4.5 Humanistic Theory

In 1960 the humanistic approach was developed by Carl Rogers, Maslow, Fredrick Perls and Victor Frankl. The humanistic theory was developed as a reaction to the technical importance of both psychodynamic and behaviourist learning approaches. This theory focused on the whole person, including mind, body and spirit, which are important to well-being (Bühler, 1971).

2.3.4.6 Biological Theory

In 1859 Charles Darwin put forward the biological theory. First, he proposed that genetics and evolution contribute to many human qualities, including personality. This theory clearly states that mental disorders can be gradually understood biologically. These explanations make patients less responsible for their disorders (Batson, 2011).

To sum up various mental health theories, it may be said that the ideas from the psychodynamic theory clearly state that the human mind is not straightforward and may instead play a trick. Adult behaviour is shaped by early relationships. These techniques help people to become more conscious of unconscious habits and patterns. The behavioural theory believes that a person's behaviour is the result of learning, that is, a response to a stimulus. This response can be researched scientifically without using inner mental states. Humanistic theory encourages the client to take an active role in healing.

Nevertheless, bio-psychologists have focused on abnormal behaviour and have tried to explain it in physiological terms. The theories mentioned above are vital and authoritative. Every theory may help to enhance the school students' mental health.

2.3.5 CULTURAL PRACTICES ON MENTAL HEALTH

Mental illness is a universal phenomenon. Cultural relativists say that the causes of mental illness are related to the individual's social and cultural context (Siewert, 1999). India is an ethnically and culturally diverse country (Srivastava, 2002).

India is known as a home of religions and cultures. In India, culture plays an important role in directing, shaping and modelling social behaviour of an individual and a group of individuals (Pandey, 1998). Culture includes the social skills, ethics, attitudes, values and ways of life which are spread informally, rather than geographically. Ethos and values are passed on from generation to generation through members of the society.

Generally, mental health is considered as a very personal matter affecting only the particular individual. However, studies reveal that mental illnesses and mental health, in general, are caused by biological and genetic factors, psychology and society. Hence, society and its diversity in cultures and backgrounds affect an individuals' mental health-related experiences. There are many ways in which culture shows its influence. For instance, culture affects how people describe their symptoms, such as whether they choose to describe emotional or physical symptoms.

Similarly, mental illness can be more present in certain cultures and communities. But this can be caused by either genetic or social factors—for example, the occurrence of schizophrenia. Cultural and social factors are the important reasons for illnesses like depression, post-traumatic stress disorder and high suicide rates.

People's decision on how they will manage the mental illness and seek treatment depends on these cultural influences and ideals. For instance, some Asian groups have been shown to avoid upsetting thoughts regarding personal problems rather than accepting and expressing that distress. African American groups are more likely than whites to handle personal problems on their own or to turn to spirituality for support (Kramer et al., 2007). Culture has a role in determining the amount of social support people get from their families and communities. Therefore, culture affects the quality of life of a person who seeks help for mental illnesses. It can cause severe distress and secondary health effects. Different cultures in India control mental health practices as a country and Kerala as a state. India is yet to give importance to mental health services. Very few mental health professionals are working in India. Mental illness is considered a shame, taboo or stigma in India. Hence, it is important to bring awareness among the people and advise them to follow mental health services (Hosman & Jane-Llopis, 1999).

2.3.6 CHALLENGES AND CONCERNS ON MENTAL HEALTH

In India, mental health problems affect at least one in four people. One of the most distressing results of mental health problems is suicide. Suicide is the second leading cause of death among those aged between 15 and 35 years (WHO, 2005).

Governments now recognize the importance of mental well-being for all citizens. However, worldwide, most of those who need mental health care do not get high-quality mental health services. Challenges such as shame, shortage of human resources, broken service delivery models and lack of research for implementation and policy change contribute to the current mental health treatment gap. To bring down this gap, the WHO developed the Mental Health Gap Action Programme Intervention Guide (Wainberg, 2017). However, propagation and implementation of these guidelines and converting scientific findings into health policy has been lagging (Thornicroft, 2012).

2.3.7 ASSESSMENT OF MENTAL HEALTH

A mental health assessment is for diagnosing people's mental health conditions, anxiety, depression, schizophrenia, postnatal depression, eating disorders and psychotic illnesses. This evaluation separates mental and physical health problems. A mental health assessment tries to build up a clear picture of the needs of the individual. During an assessment, various points will be considered, ranging from mental health symptoms and experiences to hopes and aspirations for the future. It encourages the individual to be frank and open, but only if he/she is ready and willing to discuss them. Keeping a diary to record the progress of the assessment may be helpful. It may also help to bring in a friend or family member who can describe the individual's mental illness symptoms from their viewpoint. If the assessment is for school children, it might help asking their teachers if they have observed any symptoms. A complete record of the medicines taken by the student may be useful as some drugs can affect the thinking or reasoning processes.

A mental health examination should have a mix of questions regarding the physical examination and possibly in the form of a written questionnaire. The doctor will observe how the patient looks, stares, gazes, expressions and mannerisms. The doctor would subtly enquire about the patient's personal history, including work and marital history. Mental health assessment gives the doctor a comprehensive picture of the individual's emotional state and how well the individual can think and remember.

2.3.8 MAJOR DECLARATIONS AND POLICIES ON MENTAL HEALTH IN INDIA

In India, the laws regarding persons with mental disorders (PMI) was made from the British period (Narayan, 2013). Attending to the mentally ill in the asylums was also a British discovery (Sharma, 1984). After the takeover of the administration of India by the British crown in 1858, The Lunacy (District Courts) Act, 1858, The Indian Lunatic Asylum Act, 1858 (with amendments passed in 1886 and 1889) and The Military Lunatic Acts, 1877 helped for the establishment of mental asylums and procedure to admit people with a mental health condition. Till the middle of the 19th century, these laws served as the background of lunacy legislation in India (Narayan, 2013).

In the first part of the 20th century, the miserable conditions of mental hospitals got public attention. The Indian Lunacy Act, 1912, Mental Health Act 1987 and National Trust Act-1999 enabled and empowered the persons with autism, cerebral palsy, mental retardation and multiple disabilities to live independently. India was one of the first nations to recognise the need to join mental health services with general health services at the primary care level. The Indian Constitution, under Article 21, clearly indicates that no individual shall be deprived of his or her life or individual liberty except according to procedures established by law. In 1982, the National Mental Health Programme (NMHP) was launched. The aim was to treat mental disorders using the existing primary health centre and community health centre staff. These staff members were given special training for this purpose. Unfortunately, the implementation of this programme was not satisfactory (Agarwal et al., 2004). On 7 July 2018, the Mental Health Care Act of 2017 came into effect.

In 2006, the UN's Convention on the Rights of Persons with Disabilities (CRPD) was passed. Moreover, India became its signatory in 2006, which was approved in 2007. It postulates persons who have long-term physical, mental, intellectual or sensory impairments. Subsequently, the 2013 Bill was planned to bring India to fulfil the Convention's requirements on the Rights of Persons with Disabilities (Kelly, 2011).

2.3.8.1 Government Policies Outside the Health Sector Which Influence Mental Health

Many macrosocial and macroeconomic factors are affected by the mental health policies that lie outside the traditional health sector. Governments can influence many of these factors at the policy level.

2.3.8.2 Poverty

Poverty is one of the factors affecting mental health. Poverty has become a cause and the effect of mental illnesses in many countries. Underprivileged persons are more likely to have mental disorders (Patel, 2001). They face barriers to mental health services. The departmental services are unavailable to people with mental disorders, especially those with chronic conditions, homelessness, unemployment and social exclusion. The government's timely interventions with good policies are likely to impact mental disorders (WHO, 2003) significantly.

2.3.8.3 Urbanization

Urbanization increases mental disorders. Urbanization increases the risk of environmental issues, such as pollution. It also breaks the traditional patterns of family life, leading to reduced social support (Desjarlais et al., 1995). In developing countries, urbanization has caused economic development due to the formation of formal market economies and industrialization. Government policies promoting housing facilities must respect and protect human rights.

2.3.8.4 Homelessness

Mental disorders often result in homelessness. People living in poor housing conditions are more likely to have psychological problems. (Sullivan, 2000). Housing-related legislation and national housing policies, which lessen homelessness and raise the quality and availability of houses in a country, may help reduce mental disorders.

2.3.8.5 Good Employment

Acceptable service practices are essential for promoting and upholding mental health to maintain the mental health of a country's labour force, service practices must be made acceptable to the employees. Although employment has a protecting impact on mental health, it does not guarantee good mental health. As working conditions are important factors for mental health, labour laws can endorse safe working environments. Occupational and safety legislation should address mental health and substance abuse (Harnois et al., 2000).

2.3.8.6 Unemployment

Unemployment has a strong two-way connection with mental disorders. The unemployed are at increased risk for depression and higher rates of suicide and self-harming behaviour (Kposowa, 2001). Unemployment can especially trouble the older adults' mental health who have little chances of re-entering the job market. Many developing countries have started economic modifications and restructuring in the last decade.

2.3.8.7 Education

Education is an important factor for future mental health. Schools give a chance to identify behavioural and emotional problems in children before it grows into major mental disorders. Promotive and preventive activities in mental health can be conducted through schools. Absence of secondary education can cause mental health problems. By reducing the number of students who drop out of secondary school, mental disorders can be prevented greatly. Other preventive activities include training programmes that promote problem-solving abilities, coping skills, assertiveness and interpersonal skills, and programmes for preventing alcohol and drug abuse among adolescents (Shastri, 2009).

2.3.8.8 Criminal Justice System

It is more likely that individuals with mental illnesses come into contact with the criminal justice system than the general population. Policies are needed to prevent the unacceptable imprisonment of people with mental disorders. The misery of the children and youth in detention centres and prisons should be changed through legislation. Policy changes in one area will have influence on other areas, impacting the original initial area. The mere presence of mental health legislation does not guarantee respect and protection of human rights. Paradoxically, in some countries, mental health legislation has resulted in abuse, rather than the advancement of human rights of persons with mental illnesses (Lurigio, 2011).

2.3.8.9 Mental Health of Adolescents

Adolescence is a crucial formative period in which individuals begin their transition from childhood to adulthood. Mental health problems create a significant burden of disease for adolescents globally. It is observed that one in five adolescents will experience mental disorder each year. Furthermore, self-harm is considered the third leading cause of death for adolescents, followed by depression. (WHO & Partners, 2017). Despite this, adolescent mental health is yet to receive its importance in global health programmes.

2.3.9 WORLD HEALTH ORGANIZATION AND THE INTERNATIONAL CONGRESS OF MENTAL HEALTH

The importance of human rights is gradually being recognized in general, and mental health in particular. Various declarations and policies act as influential factors for change in areas such as mental health care. Mental health law in India has changed with time and requirements over the past few decades. There has been growing attention on a person's human rights and privileges (Raveeshetet et al., 2019).

2.3.9.1 Major Declarations and Policies on Mental Health in the World

An important objective of the UN was to make an intellectual and legal framework that would support and promote a culture of human rights all over the world.(United Nations, 1948). According to Ross (2018), the first article of the Universal Declaration of Human Rights (UDHR) points out that every person is eligible to all the rights and freedoms mentioned in the Declaration, without distinction of any kind. This was made more visible by the UN in 1991. In short, it pointed out that every person with mental illness can have all civil, political, economic, social and cultural rights as documented in the Universal Declaration of Human Rights.(United Nations, 1991).

UDHR further explains that the rights of the individual are based on the principle of liberty, including the right to life (Article 3).This is particularly relevant to the mentally, because of their lengthy, involuntary detention in various institutions. According to Kelly (2016), the right to liberty was strongly re-emphasized in 1991 in the UN's Principles for the Protection of Persons with Mental Illness and Mental Health Care Improvement.

Historically, people with mental disorders have often been not given human rights, including the rights to liberty and treatment (Kelly, 2015). According to Kelly (2016), the first comprehensive statement of persons' rights with mental illness was UN's Principles for the Protection of Persons with Mental Illness and the Improvement of Mental Health Care in 1991.

To support these goals, the Universal Declaration of Human Rights was adopted by the UN General Assembly at Palais de

Chaillot in Paris on 10 December 1948. Though there are many ways to improve school children's mental health, one important way is to carry out declarations, policies, plans and programmes.

The right to health is detailed, either directly or indirectly, in several human rights documents. It includes the International Covenant on Economic, Social and Cultural Rights (art. 12), the Convention on the Rights of the Child (art. 24), the Convention on the Rights of Persons with Disabilities (art. 25) and the Convention on the Elimination of All Forms of Discrimination against Women (arts. 10). According to Asanbe et al. (2018), it is a comprehensive right focusing on timely and appropriate health care and the fundamental aspect of health. In mental health, the factors include low socioeconomic status, violence and abuse, adverse childhood experiences, early childhood growth and whether there are supportive and tolerant relationships in the family, the workplace and other situations.(United Nations High Commissioner for Human Rights, 2017).

The World Health Organization has declared ten basic principles of mental health care law in 1996. Later, these principles were developed further in 2005 in the WHO Resource Book on Mental Health, Human Rights and Legislation which presents a detailed statement of human rights issues which need to be addressed at the national level (Duffy, 2017).

2.3.9.2 Declaration of Caracas

According to Itzak Levav (1994), the Declaration of Caracas (1990) was accepted by legislators, mental health professionals, human rights leaders and disability activists convened by the Pan American Health Organization (PAHO/WHO). This declaration concluded that outdated mental health services put patients' human rights at risk. The declaration aims to encourage community-based and upgraded mental health services through changed psychiatric care. It states that resources, care and treatment for persons with mental disorders must safeguard their dignity and human rights, provide rational and appropriate treatment, and try to maintain persons with mental disorders in their communities (Itzak, 1994).

2.3.9.3 Declaration of Madrid

International associations of mental health professionals have attempted to protect the human rights of persons with mental disorders by issuing their own sets of guidelines for professional behaviour and practice. An example of such guidelines is the Declaration of Madrid (1996) adopted by the General Assembly of the World Psychiatric Association (WPA) in 1996. Among other standards, the Declaration gives importance to treatment with the permission of persons with mental disorders. They also suggest that involuntary treatment must be carried out only under exceptional circumstances (WHO, 2005).

2.3.10 INDIAN POLICIES WHICH INFLUENCE MENTAL HEALTH

Universal mental health is the international point of view which includes study, research and practice that give importance to improving mental health and attaining equality in mental health for all people worldwide (Patel, 2010). The overall aim of global mental health is to support mental health worldwide by providing information and identifying mental health care needs to develop cost-effective methods to meet those needs.

There was also a growing realization that promoting mental health was possible in 1982 through the primary health care system. Still, India had been facing a shortage of qualified mental health professionals even for the District Mental Health Programme (DMHP). Recognizing this, the Government of India formulated workforce development schemes under the National Mental Health Programme to solve this issue. Opening of more mental health care centres, establishing departments dedicated for mental health specialities, adding psychiatric departments to medical colleges, and the overall modernization of state-run mental hospitals were some of the government's actions (Patel, 2010).

Further, the National Mental Health Programme tries to make sure minimum mental health care is available for all by spreading mental health awareness into the general health care system, joining mental health with general health services, encouraging community participation and ensuring a balanced distribution of resources. However, this programme has failed due to the absence of a national mental health policy. Currently, people in all income groups are using private health care system than the public ones.

2.3.11 DIFFERENT PROGRAMMES FOR MENTAL HEALTH

Kerala's mental health features include higher suicide rates, alcohol use, breakdown of marriage and family, problems of ageing, stress due to mismatch between parental hopes and children's achievements in studies, high rates of migration and single-parent families (Praveenlal, 2013). Therefore, Kerala's mental health projects include district-based suicide prevention schemes, school mental health programmes, old age, treatments and palliative care.

In principle, a mental health program will deal with the transmission and control of mental disorders in different countries, considering their cultural differences and country-specific conditions. It will study about their treatment options, mental health education, structure of mental health care systems, human resource in the field of mental health, political and financial aspects and human rights issues. Access to mental health service is a significant barrier in adolescents' mental health services. Children who need mental health services rarely seek it by themselves, because they are dependent on adults, such as parents, teachers or other referral agents. They will need the help of these adults to even recognize such a need and to enquire which institute to contact. Another problem is that human service agencies are not well coordinated with educational institutions, child welfare or other community institutions that interact with adolescents (Armbruster, 1997).

2.3.12 STATUS OF MENTAL HEALTH IN THE INTERNATIONAL, NATIONAL AND STATE SITUATIONS

There has been increased attention on improving adolescent mental health services in different countries around the world (Vandenbroeck et al., 2013). International health is now trying to achieve its objectives through a mix of global, national and local policymaking and action (Lai et al., 2020). One in four persons in the world suffers from mental or neurological disorders at some point in their lives. Around 450 million people are currently affected by mental disorders. Mental disorders are among the leading causes of ill-health and disability worldwide (WHO, 2001).

According to Premkumar (2020), over 90 million Indians, which is 7.5% of the country's population, suffer from some form of mental disorder. WHO, without expecting a corona virus pandemic, had earlier predicted that by 2020, roughly 20 per cent of the population would suffer from mental illnesses. During the lockdown, 66 school-age children committed suicide in Kerala since March 25, 2020. Then the state government launched programmes to address the mental and emotional well-being of children. Premkumar (2020), in his article, points out these programmes, including 'Chiri' (Smile). A programme called 'Ottakkalla, OppamUndu' (You are not alone, we are with you) has resulted in over a lakh phone calls being made by school counsellors to students. School counsellors often provide initial support and recommend further course of action (Premkumar, 2020). Almost one million people die due to suicides every year and it is the third leading cause of death among young people. Depression is the leading cause of years lost due to disability worldwide and is projected to rank first in 2030.

2.3.13 RECENT DEVELOPMENTS IN MENTAL HEALTH

International community has now accepted that invisible disabilities, such as mental health problems, are the most neglected. Yet ,these issues are the main cause for not reaching the internationally agreed development goals. The Declaration of Alma-Ata (WHO, 1978) affirmed, for the first time, the important role of primary healthcare for all. The early establishment of the WHO's Mental Health Division and the World Federation of Mental Health in 1948 gave importance to global mental health via research, policy, training and advocacy over the later decades (Jenkins, 2019).

Mental illnesses create one-sixth of all health-related disorders. 15 per cent of the global mental and neurological sicknesses and substance abuse disorders are from India. Over 70 per cent of people with mental disorders do not get treatment or get a late treatment. The scarcity of funding and the low priority given in the healthcare budget are the reasons why people suffering from mental health issues do not receive timely treatment. Only 0.06 per cent of India's health budget is devoted to mental health. In 2011, there were only 301 psychiatrists and 47 psychologists for every 100,000 patients suffering from a mental health disorder in India (NIMHANS, 2016 & Kler, 2020).

According to the Kerala State Mental Health Authority and National Health Mission, in Kerala, about 9% of people belonging to different age groups are suffering from mental depression, schizophrenia, bipolar disorder and alcohol-related mental disease. It was pointed out that one in every eight persons, (12.43%) of people covered under the survey, required psychiatric attention. (Mental Depression High Among People of Kerala, 2016).

2.3.14 STATUS OF MENTAL HEALTH WITH THE ADOLESCENTS IN THE CBSE SCHOOLS

In school mental health programs have helped in enhancing the psychological well-being of school-going children. WHO promotes school mental health along with psychosocial competence. There is a growing awareness about the need for implementation of school mental health programs (Agarwal, 2004.). For example, the Central Board of Secondary Education (CBSE) has emphasized reducing stress in children and encouraging a positive attitude through programs in schools (CBSE, 2008). The CBSE recommended all senior secondary schools to employ a counsellor and carry out programmes for enhancing students' self-concept, self-image, ability to withstand pressures, and sense of enterprise. The CBSE board has started to include life-skills training in its curriculum as it helps the learner to face life with a sense of confidence and conviction (CBSE, 2008).

2.4 SHORT SUMMARY

It is apparent that spiritual well-being is associated with religiosity and a link to good health. It influences adolescents' self-esteems and their ability to manage challenges and distress (Kamya, 2000). The review further points out that the health-care providers usually under-estimate the role of spiritual well-being due to the absence of practical guidelines. Many studies on spiritual well-being indicated a universal cognitive basis for spirituality. It is now featuring as topics for discussion in many fields, including education and health care (Livni, 2018). Hence, the review points out that along with adolescents' health promotion programmes, family members and school teachers, with the help of adequate training or practical guidance, should try to spread knowledge on spiritual well-being. Thus, the conceptual analysis of spiritual well-being enhances adolescents' understanding of spiritual well-being and its role in their family and school life.

Similarly, concepts from various theories on spiritual well-being boosts school-going students' mental health. In the past decade, scholars across various disciplines have accepted the positive contribution of spirituality to mental health and its relationship with social support. Since spiritual well-being contains an individual's values, beliefs and purposes, it can be achieved in several ways including physical, social and mental levels.

Social support includes the structural and functional aspects of interpersonal relationships that have its origin in public health (Bloom, 1965). It displays the function and quality of social relationships. Quality social relationships can influence mental health and reduces the risk of mortality compared to those who have a low number of quality social relationships (Berkman, 2000). More importantly, the review revealed that social support could help school-going students adjust and prevent psychological distress and provide access and care that can enhance their spiritual well-being and mental health.

Social support theory emerged from the writings of Don Drennon Gala and Francis Cullen. They drew insights from many theoretical traditions. (Kort-Butler, 2017). Perceived support can develop from ordinary socialising and companionship more than the experiences of getting help in a stressful situation (Procidano, 1983). It can be viewed as a coping technique which provides adolescents physical and psychological advantages for facing stressful, physical and psychosocial events. It reduces psychological distress even when faced with stressful events (Brummett et al., 2005). Similar studies have been performed on adolescents for understanding the effects of social support on health, quality of life and especially mental health during recent decades.

The review on the concept of mental health revealed that mental health has its origin in public health, in clinical psychiatry and other branches of knowledge (Bertolote, 2008). It refers to the movement derived from the mental hygiene movement, and psychiatry's application to groups, communities and societies. Since 1948 mental health is treated as a state or a dimension of health. It is also clear that mental health generally points to people's cognitive, behavioural, emotional and social well-being. The six mental health indices include emotional stability, overall adjustment, autonomy, security-insecurity, self-concept and intelligence. It points out the importance of mental health in daily life, relationships and even physical health. It means the person's ability to enjoy life and be happy, attain a balance between life activities and work towards achieving psychological resilience. Subsequently, Sigmund Freud (1900) explained that a person is mentally healthy if the person could love and work.

The conceptual review of mental health is considered a very personal matter that has to do only with the individual. However, various theories and studies reveal that mental health is affected by biological and genetic factors, psychology and society. Society and its diversity in cultures and backgrounds do affect an individual's mental health-related experiences. All governments propose to give importance to mental health and well-being as necessary to all its citizens. However, most of those who require mental health care worldwide experience difficulty getting high-quality mental health services, including adolescents in the schools. During the Covid-19 pandemic lockdown, 66 school-going children committed suicide in Kerala since March 25, 2020. The state government then launched a few initiatives to address children's mental and emotional well-being, including 'Chiri' (Smile). A programme such as this has enhanced the psychological well-being of school-going children. In the school, students come across challenges such as stigma and human resource shortage. Hence, there is a need for mental health projects which need district-based suicide prevention schemes, school mental health programmes, old age, treatments and palliative care. The WHO pronounces mental health as a state of well-being. Individuals know their capacities and utilise them for the use of their respective communities. The review points out that mental health is influenced by a set of complex factors such as spiritual well-being and social support.

Hence, it should be acknowledged that health and mental illness have biological or psychological aspects and have parallel spiritual, ecological and social dimensions. Nature can play an essential part in creating, sustaining, promoting health, and preventing diseases. The researcher investigates further various studies based on empirical knowledge.

PART II: EMPIRICAL REVIEW

2.5 STUDIES RELATED TO EMPIRICAL KNOWLEDGE

Empirical studies based on direct observation and describes what is happening in the mental health of the senior secondary school students. For the better understanding of students' mental health, the researcher has examined studies related to spiritual well-being, social support and mental health. This section discusses the studies conducted both abroad and in India regarding how the senior secondary student's mental health was enhanced through spiritual well-being and social support.

2.5.1 STUDIES RELATED TO SPIRITUAL WELL-BEING

The empirical research on spiritual well-being was first mentioned in 1971 at the White House Conference on Aging. Numerous researchers and theorists have tried to understand and explain how spirituality enhances wellness and growth. The association between spiritual well-being and mental health was first understood by William James in the early 20th century (Hodges, 2002). Others, such as Peck (1998), realised that overall well-being resulted from a mix of social, emotional, physical and spiritual sides of human life. Patients who have good spiritual well-being (SWB) will also have a better quality of life.

Several sociological and developmental theories put forward the positive role of religion in the lives of adolescents. Durkheim's theory of social integration says that involvement in a religious organization will be connected with well-being. Durkheim suggested that commitment to the activities and rituals of a group or community would help to increase the ethical standards. In addition to this, his theory proposes that religion plays a central role in legitimizing and strengthening a given society's norms, thus giving individuals guidelines for positive behaviours (Durkheim, 1915). Wilkinson et al., (2018) studied the connection between frequency of personal prayer or worship attendance and spiritual wellbeing among 468 students attending fourth, fifth and sixth classes within 18 Church of Ireland schools diocese in the Republic of Ireland. The findings agree with the opinion that personal prayer is an important factor in forming individual spirituality.

Mathad & Rajesh (2017) in their article "Spiritual well-being and its relationship with mindfulness, self-compassion and satisfaction with life in baccalaureate nursing students: a correlation study" aimed to study the role of spiritual well-being among nursing students. One hundred and forty-five BSc nursing students were recruited from three nursing colleges in Bangalore. The results showed a connection between self-compassion, mindfulness and satisfaction with life on personal, communal, environmental and transcendental spiritual well-being domains. Pandya (2017) examines in his article, titled "Spirituality for Wellbeing of Bereaved Children in Residential Care: Insights for Spiritually Sensitive Child-Centred Social Work Across Country Contexts", the effect of spiritual programmes. Data include pre and post-tests from 1689 orphaned children in residential homes across 13 countries. The study results suggest that spiritual programmes work for such children and these programmes should be customized and focused, consider diversity, emphasize positive thinking, futuristic attitude and self-practice.

Kimura et al., (2016) describe in their article, "Depressive symptoms and spiritual well-being in Japanese university students", the causes of depressive symptoms and spiritual well-being of Japanese university students. Results presented that, female students had higher total SS-25 scores. An analysis of covariance used for gender and age indicated that students who believed in religion had higher total SS-25 scores.

Muñoz-García & Herrera (2014) in their study on "Effects of academic dishonesty on dimensions of spiritual well-being and satisfaction: a comparative study of secondary school and university students" pointed out that no gender differences were observed in any of the variables. In the study, university students considered dishonest behaviour less severe and more common than secondary school students indulging in more dishonest behaviour. The study revealed that students showed greater spiritual, personal, community, environmental well-being and greater satisfaction with learning. Tvorogova (2011) in the article "Spiritual well-being" reflects the role of personal and social values in the regulation of human behaviour. The article also points out that spiritual component study should be included in research on public health. Thus, the above studies and articles show the formation and the significance of spiritual well-being in the life of a human being and its relationship with health.

2.5.2 STUDIES RELATED TO SOCIAL SUPPORT

Since the mid-1970s, empirical research on social support began and has become a focus of research. Yolak (2019) in the article, "The contribution of remedial courses on the academic and social lives of secondary school students" investigates the effect of informal education, namely remedial courses, on students' lives. The findings revealed that such courses had academic, social, psychological, economic and career development impacts on the students' lives. Moreover, as students' school success improved, they learned how to spend their free time effectively in a secure environment. This increased their self-confidence and helped them to realize their potential.

Camara & Bacigalupe (2017) in their study on "The role of social support in adolescents: are helping me or stressing me out?" indicated the importance of interpersonal relationships which protected them from psychological distress. The study indicated that adolescents depend on support sources that were familiar, mature, friendly and most importantly, worthy of trust. The study pointed out that their most valued type of support was emotional, although there should be a match between the needs and the help offered. Peltzer (2008) in the study "Social support and suicide risk among secondary school students in Cape Town, South Africa" examined social support in a sample of secondary school students in Cape Town, South Africa. The analyses showed low suicide risk among students who had significant teacher support, peer support, parental support and personal control. Among eight different activities, girls who lacked social activities had high suicide risk. Hence interventions must be made to enhance social support resources and personal life skill competencies.

Boulton (2005) in the article "School peer counselling for bullying services as a source of social support: A study with secondary school pupils" shows the individual interviews conducted for secondary school pupils' views on peer counselling service for bullying in their school. The study pointed out that around a third of the students expressed a preference for seeing a counsellor of a particular gender. A similar number of participants showed a preference for seeing one of a specific relative age.

Tierney & Dowd (2000) in the article "The use of social skills groups to support girls with emotional difficulties in secondary schools" discussed about social skills for group work to help female students with emotional problems. The groups consisted of students from 3 secondary schools identified by their teachers as unhappy and friendless. The groups had six sessions which included speaking, listening to know themselves and each other. The sessions also discussed about friendships and bullying. Teacher and student questionnaires showed that this short-term programme was effective for girls whose emotional development was of concern to teachers. The findings indicated that while social skills group can provide support for young people, schools also need to support secondary school students.

Diener & Fujita (1995) discussed in the article "Resources, personal strivings, and subjective well-being: a nomothetic and idiographic approach", the covariation of resources such as money, family support, social skills and intelligence with subjective well-being. The study assessed 195 college students. The results of the study concluded that resources taken together are moderately strong indicators of subjective well-being. Furthermore, the conclusion pointed out that life satisfaction was more related to resources than affective well-being. Social and personal resources were, in general, more strongly related to subjective well-being than material resources. The findings supported the hypothesis that resources are more related with subjective well-being when they are relevant to an individual's idiographic personal inclinations and interest. Thus, the empirical study on social support indicated that social support is an essential element in adolescents' life helping their confidence and mental and emotional maturity. However, there is a gap in the empirical study on adolescents' social support. There is no study done on mental health and social support of Class XI CBSE syllabus students in Kerala.

2.5.3 STUDIES RELATED TO MENTAL HEALTH

Guerra & Rajan (2019) in the article "The implementation of mental health policies and practices in schools: an examination of school and state factors" explained that poor mental health outcome is common among adolescent youth. Secondary schools play an important role in encouraging positive mental health by implementing policies and practices supported by evidence. However, the factors associated with this implementation are unclear. The study stated that health and safety coordinator in mental health and suicide prevention had positive effect on schools' implementation of mental health policies and practices. The study concluded with recommendation that health-related programmes must be carried out for the better implementation of mental health policies and practices in schools and provide better support for youth in their mental health outcomes.

Holen et al. (2018) investigated the teacher-student relationship as a possible solution to reduce mental health problems and were assessed in the study through students' self-reports in the 10th grade. Further, in the study, a dual-factor serial mediator model was used, allowing the effect of mental health problems on school dropouts to be mediated by teacher- student relationship. The study results indicated that the teacher-student relationship is a potential solution to reduce the negative associations between mental health problems and later non-completion of school. Students with mental health problems seemed to experience less supportive teachers. The patterns were similar between genders. Therefore, interventions aiming teacher-student relationships may be required.

According to Odenbring (2017) in the article "Mental health, drug use and adolescence: meeting the needs of vulnerable students in secondary school" pointed out an increasing number of students were suffering from different kinds of mental health problems. However, very little information was available on how professionals in secondary schools and the other professionals in the society handled these issues. The findings in the study make an essential contribution to the research field regarding professionals' efforts to meet students' needs. The study depends on semi-structured interviews with the professionals and observations made during students' welfare team meetings. The findings revealed that in the absence of a good mentor and guidance, the use of pills or drugs or both has become quite common among adolescents to solve their mental health problems.

Brännlund & Strandh (2017) conducted a study on "Mental Health and Educational Achievement: the Link between Poor Mental Health and Upper Secondary School Completion and Grades" pointed out that education greatly affects an adult's socioeconomic status. Hence, it is important to ensure that all children have the capability and opportunity to achieve educational goals. The study examines the connection between mental health during adolescence and upper secondary school completion, which has received little attention to date. Results of the study showed a negative relationship between mental health problems and educational outcomes. Only small variances between the sexes were identified. The study concluded that poor mental health during childhood was connected with low education and suggested to give more resources to support children with mental health problems.

Ninaniya (2017) in his article on "Attitude towards modernization of senior secondary school students" points out the modernization of senior secondary school students of Hisar district of Haryana, India. Modernization is the process of social change and adoption of new values and practices in organizations. According to the author, adolescence is an important stage of development, as adolescents face internal crises because of cognitive, social and biological changes. Results observed that girls had a more positive attitude in all the modernisation components than their counterparts except politics, where boys possessed a higher percentage than girls.

Helen et al., (2015) in their study on "Mental toughness in education: exploring relationships with attainment, attendance, behaviour and peer relationships" points out the relationship between adolescents mental toughness and various aspects of their secondary school experiences; namely social inclusion, confidence in abilities, confidence and interpersonal relationships. The result shows that mental toughness is also a useful construct within secondary schools.

Lester (2013) in the study on "The relationship between school connectedness and mental health during the transition to secondary school" pointed out the relationship between school connectedness and mental health during the change from primary to secondary school. This change resulted in a reduced sense of connectedness, which has been linked with symptoms of depression and anxiety. The study investigated the relationship between feeling connected to the school and mental health before and over the transition period. Data were obtained from 3,459 students in a study of adolescents' knowledge, attitudes and experiences of bullying victimisation during the transition from primary school to secondary school. The findings suggested that increased connectedness to the school was associated with decreased depression and anxiety. Subsequently, increased depression and anxiety is associated with decreased connectedness to the school.

Dogra (2012) in the article "Nigerian secondary school children's knowledge and attitudes towards mental health and illness" speak about children, who are likely to hold negative attitudes towards mental illness. The study aimed to establish the views and knowledge of students about mental health and illness. It was found that students lacked the knowledge regarding mental health problems. Educational programmes need to be carried out to improve mental health literacy, which will influence attitudes and social distance. However, the schoolchildren were optimistic about recovery.

Mariu et al., (2012) in the article "Seeking professional help for mental health problems, among New Zealand secondary school students" explain that the study is aimed to investigate whether secondary school students sought help from general practitioners for mental health problems and also to investigate whether mental illness type, socio-demographic variables, family, school and community factors were associated with seeking help. It was found that school students with mental health problems did not get the help they needed from general practitioners. The study also found that given the commonness of mental health problems, "it is essential to find ways of identifying adolescents with difficulties and encouraging them to seek help".

Kutcher & Wei (2012) in a review "Mental health and the school environment: secondary schools, promotion and pathways to care" indicated that it was important that educators, mental health experts, researchers and other related service providers understand the most current research findings to influence policymaking. The review also showed the preceding year, studies on school-based mental health programs adopting mental health promotion, prevention, early identification and intervention or treatment. Hence, the study pointed out that needs are to be done to develop and evaluate programmes which are proven effective, safe and cost-effective.

Arora & Jasdeep (2010) in their study on "Effect of self-concept and mental health on academic achievement of secondary school students" attempt to study the effect of self-perception and mental health on the academic accomplishment of secondary school students. For this study, 600 students studying in senior secondary classes were considered. Self-Concept Questionnaire (SCR) by Saraswat and Mental Health Battery (MHB) by Singh & Gupta were used to collect data. This study showed that mental health, gender and location of schools (urban or rural) have a significant effect on academic achievement of secondary school students, but the effect on self-concept was insignificant. According to Kalashian (2009), mental health services in secondary schools pointed out that students who have mental health issues shows poor academic performance. This investigation aimed to examine teachers' and students' knowledge of current mental health services and identify which services they indicated as the most crucial and beneficial to the student body.

Myer et al., (2009) in the study on "Impact of common mental disorders during childhood and adolescence on secondary school completion" pointed out how mental disorders in childhood and adolescence might influence different socio-economic positions and educational attainment. Dhuria et al., (2009) in their study on "Assessment of mental health status of senior secondary school children in Delhi", pointed out that school children undergo quick mental, emotional and social changes and are likely to have psychiatric disorders. The study concludes that mental health requirements of schoolchildren need to be addressed by the school health services. Burke & Kerr (2008) in their study on "Male secondary school student's attitudes towards using mental health services" indicated that the rate of suicides among young men was rising. However, they were reluctant to use mental health services. Results indicated that students held opposing views on mental health services. Many students did not recognise depression as a mental illness and could not separate depression and feeling sad as two different concepts. Hence, the study points out that the absence of knowledge about mental illness and prejudice against mental health professionals are preventing young men from accessing mental health services.

Ola & Morakinyo (2008) in their study on "Mental health and attitude towards education of secondary school students in Nigeria", explained that mental health is very important for community health. Features related to students' mental health, success in school and the students' attitude towards education were also investigated in the study. Results of the study pointed out that about four out of ten students had psychopathology. Two out three students with psychopathology had a negative attitude towards education (odds ratio of 3.7; 95% confidence interval = 2.982-4.592). This study suggested that the largeness of mental illness among students seems high and it is associated with a negative attitude towards education, low parental educational level and poor socio-economic status.

Ng & Tsang (2008) in their study on "School bullying and the mental health of junior secondary school students in Hong Kong" found that verbal bullying was the most common form of school bullying behaviour. Boys were significantly more involved than girls in direct physical bullying as bullies, victims and bully-victims. The study pointed out that girl victims suffered more in mental ways. Regression analysis indicated that bullying and gender contributed notably to the students' mental health variances.

Hamburg et al., (1972) in the article "Peer counselling in the secondary schools: A community mental health project for youth" indicated that peer counselling program trains high school and junior high school students to help other students with personal problems or situational stress. Training is carried out in small groups in weekly sessions. It includes behavioural principles, issues of relevance to adolescents and guided practical experience. Criteria are suggested for judging the suitability and effectiveness of students in the counselling role. Yuang (2000) determines in the study on "Correlation between Self-esteem and Mental Health of Secondary Normal School Students" found that the correlation coefficients were significant. The scores and esteem levels indicated that Secondary school student's mental health status is thoroughly related to self-esteem levels.

2.5.4 STUDIES ON INTER CONNECTIVITY OF SPIRITUAL WELL-BEING, SOCIAL SUPPORT AND MENTAL HEALTH CONCEPTS

2.5.4.1 Spiritual-Wellbeing and Social Support

Ibrahim & Che Din et al., (2019) in their study on "The role of social support and spiritual wellbeing in predicting suicidal ideation among marginalized adolescents in Malaysia" discussed about the adolescents and young adults having suicidal thoughts. The study aimed to examine the connection between social support and spiritual wellbeing in predicting suicidal thoughts among Malaysian adolescents. The Spiritual Wellbeing Scale (SWBS) was used to measure the religious well-being (RWB), the existential wellbeing (EWB) and the overall score of spiritual wellbeing (SWB). The study found that both RWB and EWB presented a negative correlation with suicidal ideation, i.e., students with high RWB and EWB had low suicidal thoughts. Likewise, support from family and friends also showed a negative correlation with suicidal thoughts.

Further analysis using multiple regressions showed that RWB and SWB and family support predict suicidal thoughts in adolescents. Thus, the study concluded that spiritual wellbeing and family support play an important role in predicting suicidal thoughts. Therefore, encouraging spirituality and social support such as family support may positively help suicidal adolescents.

Park & Lee (2019) in their study on "Unique effects of religiousness/spirituality and social support on mental and physical well-being in people living with congestive heart failure" pointed out that people living with congestive heart failure often experience increased levels of depressive symptoms. Their quality of life were found to be reducing with disease progression. The study also revealed that religiousness/spirituality (R/S) might help them. The study examined four mental and physical outcomes and found depressive symptoms, positive states of mind, mental health-related quality of life and physical health-related quality of life. Further, the study revealed that basic health status and social support increased positive states of mind; only social support predicted improved physical health-related quality of life. Furthermore, only spiritual peace predicted reduced levels of depressive symptoms.

Alorani & Alradaydeh (2017) in their article "Spiritual well-being, perceived social support, and life satisfaction among university students" identified the connection between spiritual well-being, perceived social support and life satisfaction among the university students in Jordan. The study was based on a sample of 919 students at the University of Jordan. The study presented that university students were with moderate levels of spiritual well-being and perceived social support. The study displayed significant connection between spiritual well-being with perceived social support and life satisfaction (r = .49, .53, p .53, p <.001). Perceived social support was positively connected with life satisfaction (r = .46, p < .001). It was found that spiritual well-being is positively connected with all sources of perceived social support. Hence, the study concluded that relationships between spiritual well-being and perceived social support should be considered in university health programs.

2.5.4.2 Spiritual Well-Being and Mental Health

Zare et al., (2019) in their study on "The relationship between spiritual well-being, mental health and quality of life in cancer patients receiving chemotherapy" investigated the relationship between mental health and spiritual well-being. The study results revealed a positive connection between spiritual well-being and mental health (P = 0.001) and QoL (P = 0.01) in cancer patients receiving chemotherapy.

Deb et al., (2016) in their study "Spirituality in Indian university students and its associations with socioeconomic status, religious background, social support and mental health" The result indicated that female students were significantly more spiritual than male students, especially in spiritual practice and a sense of purpose. The study suggested an opportunity for open conversation on spirituality for university students to enhance their mental health, adopt a positive mindset and enhance resistance through support services.

Unterrainer et al., (2014) in their paper on "Religious/spiritual well-being, personality and mental health: a review of results and conceptual issues" provided information about the development of the Multidimensional Inventory for Religious/Spiritual Well-being and then summarised findings from its use with other measures of health and personality. The study showed important evidence for religiosity/spirituality being positively related to mental health, including subjective well-being and personality aspects. Moreover, the study also indicated that religiosity or spirituality can help recovery from mental illness and protect against addictive or suicidal behaviours.

Jafari et al., (2010) in the article "Spiritual well-being and mental health in university students", pointed out that there was a significant relationship between spiritual well-being and mental health. The research sample has consisted of 223 university students (110 males and 113 females). Spiritual well-being scale and the general health questionnaire were used to collect the data. The spiritual and existential well-being in females was significantly higher than males. The study indicated that spirituality promotes mental health by providing a sense of integrity and existential connection. Individuals with spiritual experience and religious beliefs could manage their stress and psychological problems. Thus, the study pointed out that spiritual well-being has a protective effect and could act against stress.

Eckersley (2007) in the article "Culture, spirituality, religion and health: looking at the big picture" make some observations about the cultural expression of spirituality and its relationship with well-being. The article points out that religion offers positive health and well-being, including social support, existential meaning and a sense of purpose. Therefore, maintaining the spiritual aspect of life is essential for good health.

2.5.4.3 Social Support and Mental Health

Ford et al. (2018) explained that children with poor mental health often struggle at school. The relationship between childhood psychiatric disorder and exclusion from school has not been frequently studied. However, both will affect the person's life when he/she becomes an adult. Results indicated that weak general health is linked with learning disability among parents with poor mental health.

Brännlund (2017) in the article "Mental-health and educational achievement: the link between poor mental-health and upper secondary school completion and grades" explains that education greatly affects adult socioeconomic status. Therefore, all children must be given the chance to reach educational goals. Results of the research pointed out that more resources are needed to support children with mental health problems.

Iachini et al., (2016) in the article "Exploring the Principal perspective: implications for expanded school improvement and school mental health" explained that principals have an important role in improvement efforts at school. Yet, very few studies have been carried out to upgrade their point-of-view on what contributes to teaching, learning and broader school improvement. The study results indicated that principals accept mental health as one of the most important needs of students, teacher and school staff. The article concludes with suggestions for school social work research and practice, particularly school improvement and school mental health.

2.5.5 Studies related to Senior Secondary School Students

Yuen (2017) in the article "Spiritual health, school engagement and civic engagement of secondary students in Hong Kong" investigates more than 15,000 secondary students. The results of the investigation indicates that spiritual health links positively with school engagement and civic engagement.

Seth (2016) in the study on "Study of mental health and burnout in relation to teacher effectiveness among secondary school teachers" investigated the cases of mental illness and burn out among school teachers. The goal was to find out what service a country could expect from her future citizens when guided by teachers who were frustrated, stressed and strained. A sample of 60 secondary school teachers was taken from five schools of Kaithal district of Haryana for the study. The result of the investigation indicated a significant positive relationship between different sides of mental health. It includes positive self-evaluation, view of reality, integration of personality and autonomy. Thus, the study pointed out the importance of school psychologists and counsellors, who could identify and assess mental health issues in the organization and proposed different solutions for enhancing teachers' mental health.

Bashir & Liyaqat (2016) in their study on "Investigating the relationship between self- regulation and spiritual intelligence of higher secondary school students" tried to find out any significant difference on spiritual intelligence and self-regulation among higher secondary school students. The investigation results revealed that no difference was found between urban and rural students on self-regulation. But, a significant difference was found between urban and rural students on spiritual intelligence.

Dowdy et al., (2015) in their investigation, suggested universal experiments to move school-based psychological services from the back of the service delivery system to the front. This will encourage prevention, early intervention and promotion. Hence, multidisciplinary team of school psychologists used these experimental data to engage in preventive consultation with the administration. This also helped them to decide the refinement and expansion of mental health service delivery options. The role of the school psychologist and multidisciplinary team members were pointed out as important parts of this approach to service delivery change.

In his article, Ellen (2015) points out the pressures faced by young people in schools, the fear of discussing any mental distress and the need for therapists who could give a safe environment for young people to talk about their problems. The author points out the need for a generalised education in positive mental health to reduce the number of undiagnosed young people.

Dumbili (2015) points out that the use and misuse of psychoactive materials among adolescents are increasing quickly in Africa. In Nigeria, there are no written policies to regulate alcohol production or availability. This led to heavy drinking among adolescents there. The results of the study revealed lifetime alcohol use among males than females. The findings showed that the motives for using alcohol include staying awake to study at night, drinking to forget one's problems, to reduce anxiety and to enjoy festivals. The author also discussed the possible re-orientation of Nigerian adolescents to make effective alcohol policies and suggested further research.

Wolters & Knoors (2014) in their article "Social adjustment of deaf early adolescents at the start of secondary school: the divergent role of withdrawn behaviour in peer status" examined the peer relationships and social behaviours of deaf adolescents in the first two years of secondary school. For deaf mainstream students, quiet behaviour was the most important and negative indicator of peer status. In unique education settings, prosocial behaviour was the most important and positive indicator of peer status.

Saini & Punia (2013) in their article "Academic stress in relation to self-efficacy and mindfulness among senior secondary school students" pointed out that academic stress is the result of a mixture of academic-related demands that exceed the capabilities of an individual. If a student could not manage academic stress, then his/her psycho-social-emotional health will be affected.

Raufelder & Jagenow (2013) in their article "Social relationships and motivation in secondary school: four different motivation types" examined a large sample of adolescent students to identify whether social relationships in schools are important for motivation. The findings pointed out the need for learning programs that support students on a more individualized level.

Briggs et al., (2011), in their article titled "Assessing and promoting spiritual wellness as a protective factor in secondary schools" pointed out the importance of a multidimensional protective factor for students. This article reviewed the studies which discussed how spiritual wellness is connected with succeeding in the adolescent population. The article also suggested programmes in secondary school to promote spiritual wellness.

Patton et al., (2000) in their article "The Gatehouse Project: a systematic approach to mental health promotion in secondary schools" points out the importance of the programmes for mental health promotion in secondary schools. This study indicated that healthy attachments to peers and teachers promote a sense of security and trust. This would enable the students with effective communication and a sense of positive self-regard. Finally, the intervention encourages linkage between the school and the broader community, particularly emphasising young people needs at high risk of school drop-out.

2.6 SHORT SUMMARY

The experimental research on the term spiritual well-being points out the effort made by many researchers and theorists to understand and explain how spirituality enhances wellness and growth. The above-discussed studies and articles indicate a correlation between self-compassion, mindfulness and satisfaction with life on personal, communal and transcendental domains of spiritual well-being. It also indicates the significance of spiritual well-being in adolescence and its relationship with mental health.

William James first explored the relationship between spiritual well-being and mental health in the early 20th century (Hodges 2002). Later, others realised the overall well-being resulted from a combination of social, emotional, physical and spiritual aspects (Hodges 2002). Phenwan (2019), in his article, pointed out that spirituality is the essence of a human being. Studies also pointed out that patients who had good spiritual well-being also had a better quality of life. Durkheim's theory of social integration emphasizes that involvement in a religious organisation is connected with well-being. He recommended that commitment to a group and participation in community rituals might help people to increase the ethical standards of the society felt by the individual.

The concept of social support began in the mid-1970s and has become an essential subject in the 21st century in educational institutions (Bloom, 1965). The use of social skills for group work to help students with emotional problems was useful in providing support for young people (Diener & Fujita, 1995). Hence, there is a need in the schools to develop various social skills to enhance the confidence of the students and to widen their social support. This is also important for their mental and emotional maturity.

Social support enhances the interpersonal relationship, which helps adolescents cope with stressors, protecting them from psychological distress. The experimental research on mental health has its roots in public health, clinical psychiatry and other branches of knowledge (Bertolote, 2008). Studies further point out the importance of the teacher-student relationship, which could help reduce the negative associations between mental health problems and educational outcomes. Thus, the experimental review on mental health indicates the secondary school students' mental health status is related to mental toughness, attitude towards education, parental educational level and socioeconomic status.

2.7 SUMMARY OF THE CHAPTER

Several studies show that the transition from adolescence to adulthood is a vulnerable stage. The senior secondary school students of CBSE syllabus had an increase in several mental health problems, including risk behaviours, depression, conduct disorder and substance use (Lerner, 2004). The review in this chapter discloses some essential discussions and explanations on the spiritual well-being, social support and mental health of adolescents. Further, it validates the significance, relevance and logic of this research study.

Hence, it may be said that spiritual well-being points to a shift towards healing. Social support help adolescents facing stressful physical and psycho-social events such as emotional, behavioural and social maturity or normality. The critical analyses of spiritual well-being, social support and mental health give theoretical references and helps to form the questions and problems for the study. The studies discuss mental health and its relationship with spirituality, social support and well-being. There is a general agreement among various researchers that spirituality and social support reduces mental stress and support mental health.

Some studies reveal that spirituality and social support are related to adolescents mental health and mental health is related to spiritual well-being and social support. Nevertheless, the researcher has identified various gaps and realized that there had not been an adequate study about the spiritual well-being, social support and mental health of senior secondary school students. Hence, these gaps permit the researcher to investigate more into the spiritual well-being, social support and mental health of senior secondary school students in Kerala.

Further, to date, the researcher could not find any other specific research work that investigated the mental health of senior secondary school students in Kerala in relationship with spiritual well-being and social support. Therefore, these attempts encouraged the researcher to make a few questions to himself as a researcher. Hence, this study is academically, theoretically and empirically warranted.

However, what was the process through which this study was conducted? How was the data collected and what were the tools used? What is the logic and objectives of the study? What are the hypotheses on which the entire study is based? These are enumerated in the following chapter.

Chapter 3

RESEARCH METHODOLOGY

This chapter deals with the methodological part of the research on mental health, spiritual well-being and social support. It contains the statement of the problem, the logic of the study, the significance of the study, research questions, objectives, hypotheses, definition of key concepts, pilot study, ethical issues, delimitation, research design, sampling size, tools for data collection, pre-testing, statistical application, problems faced, and the synchronisation of the research.

3.1 THE STATEMENT OF THE PROBLEM

In recent decades health education has increased and researchers have accepted the importance of mental health, spiritual well-being and social support. However, there are many gaps, undiscussed concepts and unanswered questions in this area. The researcher perceives two problems by looking at the studies: Firstly, while there have been various studies conducted on spiritual well-being, social support and mental health, till recently, there has been no study conducted on the mental health of senior secondary school students in Kerala in relation to spiritual well-being and social support. Secondly, according to Kerala Mental Health Report (2017), the Institute of Mental Health and Neuroscience, under the guidance of experts from NIMHANS has conducted a survey. The results showed that Kerala has a better health care system.

Nevertheless, about 11.36 % of the total population in India is affected by mental disorders. The survey showed that 4.4 per cent of the population aged 18 and above in the state had suffered psychic disorder once in their lifetime NIMHANS (2016). However, there is a gap in the survey. It had considered only three districts in the state, Thrissur, Palakkad and Pathanamthitta, which are situated close to Ernakulam district. Hence, the researcher selected Ernakulam district of Kerela to conduct the study.

Yan & Xian (2014), in their study, concluded that improving social supports in families and neighbourhoods may reduce distress and encourage hope in adolescents living in very economically distressed areas. Hence, the researcher preferred to study the level of mental health, the interrelationship between gender, socio-economic status, physical health and the tools that contribute to better spiritual well-being, social support and mental health among senior secondary school students in Kerala. Given this discussion, the scholar has taken the following research problem in hand, "A study on the Mental Health of Senior Secondary School Students in Kerala in Relation to Spiritual Well-Being and Social Support". Questions formed are based on the problem.

The bulletin of the World Health Organization (WHO, 2001) points out that in most of the nations, more than one in three people suffer from at least one type of mental disorder in their life. According to NIMHANS (2016) National Mental Health Survey of India, 2015-16, anyone could have mental health issues. Even though Kerala has achieved targets for health for all by 2000, the state has high suicide rate which indicates a severe drawback concerning the people's mental health status (NIMHANS, 2016 & Praveenlal, 2000). Similarly, Kerala State Mental Health Authority revealed that 10% of the state's population is suffering from psychiatric disorders, 2% have severe psychiatric disorders such as schizophrenia and manic depression, 2-3% suffer from psychosomatic disorders and neurosis and one in every 100 kids below six years of age are mentally disabled (Radhakrishnan, 2011).

Yogesh (2004) points out that William Sweetser, in the mid-19th century was the first person to coin the term "mental hygiene" and later Dorothea Dix (1802-1887), a schoolteacher, developed mental hygiene movement and endeavoured throughout her life to help people with mental disorders. In her thesis, Nancy (2011), stated that at the beginning of the 20th century, Clifford Beers founded the Mental Health America – National Committee for Mental Hygiene (Nancy, 2011). In 2001, the WHO dedicated its annual report (The World Health Report - Mental health: new knowledge, new hope) to mental health (WHO, 2001). According to National Institute of Mental Health and Neuro Sciences' (2016) report of the National Mental Health Survey of India, 2015-16, 7.3% people in the age group 13 -17 years suffered from a mental disorder, nearly equal in both genders. This points out the need of active interventions.

Spirituality was already recognised as an important element of well-being in the 1970s. Moberg's (1971) theory was very useful in this respect. In his theory, spiritual well-being is interpreted as a lifelong search and an affirmation of living life in connection to God, self, the community and the environment (Moberg, 1990). Spiritual well-being has also been discussed as a part in a wellness model approach to work-adjustment and rehabilitation counselling (Spitznagel, 1992). The author emphasised that the concept of working with clients is generally centred on faith, belief and values. Ellison & Smith (1991) point out that spiritual well-being can be experienced as an expression of spiritual maturity. In recent years, the WHO has considered spirituality an important aspect of health and physical, psychological and social health (Yogesh, 2004).

Paloutzian (2012) developed a scale to measure spiritual well-being that included two subscales: religious and existential well-being. Though religion and spiritual beliefs were dismissed as "neurotic obsession" by Freud (1928), Jung (1969) in his theory of 'personality' includes physical, mental and spiritual selves, which is unity and wholeness within each person. The spirit was considered an important archetype which is called as 'universal unconscious ideas'. (Rovers, 2010). Their study concluded that spiritual well-being is a core human component that provides the energy to a person's stability, meaning, fulfilment in life and faith in self.

Social support is regarded to be one of the most important protective factors for students. It includes social resources that individuals view to be available which are offered to them to protect against psychological problems (Tao & Dong, 2000). Hays argued that social support is an important component of college students' successful change to the college environment (Hays, 1986). Dollete & Matthews (2004) pointed out social support as care, value and guidance provided from family, peers and community members to an individual. Canty-Mitchell & Zimet argued that 'the significant other and friends' are a strong complement to the family because it gives a different support source for the adolescent, such as a boyfriend, girlfriend, teacher and counsellor (Canty-Mitchell, 2000).

James & Julie (2006) pointed out the alarming increase in youth's mental health needs today. Traditional training programs for school-based personnel in the area of mental health are becoming insufficient. Michael & Clapp-Channing (2005) recommend that children of depressed parents are at greater risk of psychiatric disorders than children of non-depressed parents. Similarly, Itai & Christine (2009) argued that the studies on spirituality had explored almost every aspect of humanity. Research on spirituality and religion reveals that religion and spirituality positively relate to psychological well-being.

Pillai & Patel (2009) believe that higher secondary school education is a critical turning point in students' academic lives. At this stage, the adolescents' academic performance plays a crucial role in deciding about the next stage of education, and probably career. Rosa & Preethi (2012) argued that youth go through many changes physically, emotionally and socially.

Darvyri & Galanakis (2014) point out that spiritual well-being can be an important companion to the concept of spirituality. It is not synonymous to mental and physical health, but it is likely to be associated with these two variables. According to MacDonald (2014), the college is a time of development where lifelong opinions, beliefs and thought processes are formed.

Social support can be viewed as care, value and guidance provided from family, peers and community members (Dollete, 2004). Research says that social support is an important factor that describes the physical and emotional well-being given to persons by their family, friends and other significant individuals in their lives (Israel, 1990). Maya (2018) reported that according to the NITI (National Institution for Transforming India) Aayog's report and ranking of the States as per Performance in Health Outcomes Index, Kerala is on top as the overall best-performing state. However, the state is at rank 21, when the annual incremental progress was measured.

3.2 LOGIC OF THE STUDY

Many studies were conducted on spiritual well-being, social support and mental health such as Hodges, (2002), Peltzer (2008), Lester (2013) and Ninaniya (2017) but with many gaps and opportunities for the researcher for further action. The researcher also realised that no study was done until the date on senior secondary school students' mental health in Kerala in relation to spiritual well-being and social support. These gaps need to be studied. Hence, this research is warranted.

3.3 SIGNIFICANCE OF THE STUDY

From the lived experience, it is learned that well-balanced mental health is vital for an individual's full functioning. The knowledge received from this study will be of great help for the school managements, teachers and students. Kerala is considered to be a state with a high literacy level and empowered people. Hence, it will be an added advantage for the people to understand spiritual well-being, social support and mental health and use psychiatric services to improve. The students of this investigation are in their teens. They undergo biological, physical, mental and emotional changes and their roles in society are also changing. Hence, this research is significant.

3.4 RESEARCH QUESTIONS

1. What is the socio-demographic profile of the students of senior secondary school in Kerala?
2. What are the levels of spiritual well-being, social support and mental health of senior secondary school students in Kerala?
3. What is the relationship between spiritual well-being and social support of the senior secondary school students in Kerala?

4. What is the relationship between spiritual well-being and mental health of the senior secondary school students in Kerala?
5. What is the relationship between social support and mental health of senior secondary school students in Kerala?

3.5 OBJECTIVES OF THE STUDY

1. To analyse the socio-demographic profile of the students of senior secondary school in Kerala with their gender, religion and settlement.
2. To assess the levels of (i) spiritual well-being, (ii) social support and (iii) mental health of senior secondary school students in Kerala.
3. To find out the relationship between the spiritual well-being and social support of senior secondary school students in Kerala.
4. To find out the relationship between the spiritual well-being and mental health of senior secondary school students in Kerala.
5. To find out the relationship between the social support and mental health of senior secondary school students in Kerala.

3.6 HYPOTHESES OF THE STUDY

Hypothesis (1)

a) (Ha): There is a significant relationship between spiritual well-being and social support of senior secondary school students in Kerala.
a) (Ho): There is no significant relationship between spiritual well-being and social support of senior secondary school students Kerala.

Hypothesis (2)

b) (Ha): There is a significant relationship between spiritual well-being and mental health of senior secondary school students Kerala.

b) (Ho): There is no significant relationship between spiritual well-being and mental health of senior secondary school students in Kerala.

Hypothesis (3)

c) (Ha): There is a significant relationship between social support and mental health of senior secondary school students in Kerala.

c) (Ho): There is no significant relationship between social support and mental health of senior secondary school students in Kerala.

3.7 LIMITATIONS OF THE STUDY

1. The study is limited to Ernakulam district of Kerala.
2. The study is limited to CBSE schools in Ernakulam district of Kerala.
3. The study is limited to class XI students of CBSE schools in Ernakulam district of Kerala.
4. The study is limited to gender, religions and settlements of the selected sample of students.

3.8 CONCEPTUAL AND OPERATIONAL DEFINITION OF KEY CONCEPTS

Terminologies related to spiritual well-being, social support and mental health have been repeatedly used in this research. It is essential to know the meaning of these terms. Therefore, this section attempts to define these terms mostly from a psychological, spiritual and sociological point of view.

3.8.1 MENTAL HEALTH: For this study mental health is defined as "a state of well-being in which every student understands his /her potential, can manage normal stresses of life, can work productively, thereby, contributing to the community with his/ her positive feelings".

1.1.2 SPIRITUAL WELL-BEING: For this study, spiritual well-being is defined as "the student's relationship with the Divine which encourages him/her to search for purpose within or outside one's faith, as measured by inner well-being".

1.1.3 SOCIAL SUPPORT: For this study social support is defined as "the understanding of being valued, esteemed, cared (for) and loved by diverse sources which include family, friends, teachers, community, or any social groups to which one is associated".

1.1.4 SENIOR SECONDARY SCHOOL STUDENTS: For this study, senior secondary school students are middle adolescents from 16-18 years. They are studying in the senior secondary schools under the Central Board of Secondary Education (CBSE) in Kerala. It is the stage before tertiary education.

3.9 PILOT STUDY

The researcher conducted a trial study as a preliminary step to get familiar with the topic. A questionnaire was made with necessary details and some students were interviewed to start the study. At the initial study, the researcher visited four schools and had a detailed discussion with the schools' management, target population and key informants. Keeping in mind the students' conditions, the researcher held discussions with school administrators, teachers, and parents. A pre-test was conducted to review the questionnaire in terms of the relevance of the study, assess the language used, test whether the time was enough to fill-up the interview schedule and find out the difficulty and ambiguity of any of the questions. The preliminary test was conducted along with four school students in Ernakulam. On average, about 45 minutes was taken to collect data from each student.

3.10 ETHICAL ISSUES

The research procedure was obtained from the ethics committee of the Assam Don Bosco University, Tapesia. All participates were told the objective and the goal of the study as well as the nature of their participation. Additionally, the participants were educated about their rights during the study participation, including their right to leave at any point of the study period. Confidentiality was ensured and maintained. The researcher has acknowledged the research instruments used in the study.

3.11 RESEARCH METHODOLOGY

The research methodology is the detailed procedures or techniques used to identify, select, process and analyse information about a topic. For this study, the investigator has taken a mixed approach, using quantitative (answering specific questionnaire) and qualitative methods (data from observation, focused groups and specific interviews) to gather the required data. Further, the investigator adopted descriptive cum survey method of research.

3.12 RESEARCH DESIGN

The research design in a study refers to the overall strategy that the researcher chooses to logically mix the study's different components. It is the blueprint for the data collection, measurement and analysis of data. For this study, the researcher has followed a cross-sectional study of adolescents in Kerala. The research attempts to describe the levels of spiritual well-being, social support and mental health of the senior secondary students in Kerala and attempts to justify the correlations. This description will be of great relevance in making the new generation strong and mentally healthy.

3.13 THE STUDY AREA

The study area of this investigation is the Ernakulam district of Kerala. Based on geographical, historical and cultural similarities, the state's fourteen districts are generally grouped into north Kerala, central Kerala and south Kerala. For this study, the researcher has selected central Kerala, which has four districts, Palakkad, Thrissur, Ernakulam and Idukki. Following a simple random sampling method, the researcher selected Ernakulam district as the research study area. Spanning about 2,407 km, Ernakulam district is home to over 12% of Kerala's population.

3.14 UNIVERSE OF THE STUDY

The study universe is Ernakulam district of Kerala and 115 CBSE schools in Kerala Ernakulam district. Although CBSE has 195 schools in Ernakulam district, only 115 schools are affiliated to the Senior Secondary Level, which has a total number of 6700 students studying in class eleven.

3.15 POPULATION OF THE STUDY

To proceed with the research, the researcher divided all these 115 CBSE schools into three strata: urban, semi-urban and rural, using random sampling method and selected thirteen schools as four schools from urban, four schools from semi-urban and five schools from the rural area. Then the researcher contacted concerned managements and departments to obtain the name lists of the students.

3.16 SELECTION OF SAMPLE

The investigator selected a sample of 582 students of class eleven from these 13 schools. The sample has been selected using a random sampling technique. It came out 11.5% of the total population or universe of the study.

In the first stage, the researcher selected the region of study through the lottery method following a simple random sampling procedure. In the second stage, the researcher selected thirteen schools from Ernakulam district based on the three strata, namely rural, urban and semi- urban. This selection also has followed the lottery method. Then the researcher followed the simple random sampling to select students from these schools giving space for both boys and girls representation. A maximum of between 43-45 students was taken from each school, and a total of 582 students were selected who were between 16 to 18 years of age. The procedure was depending on the attendance register. Thus, this study used a multi-stage sampling method for data collection.

3.17 TOOLS USED FOR DATA COLLECTION

The essential data collection tools were interviews and spot observation. Socio-demographic sheet and other instruments were used, namely, "Mental Health Battery" (for measuring mental health) developed by Singh and Gupta (1983) and manual for the spiritual well-being scale (for measuring spiritual well-being) developed by Paloutzian and Ellison (1982). Social Support Questionnaire (SSQ) developed by Sarason, Levine, Basham & R.B., et al. (1983) is used to collect the data on social support.

3.17.1 MENTAL HEALTH BATTERY

Mental Health Battery (MHB) was developed (1983) and validated by Arun Kumar Singh and Alpana Sen Gupta. MHB evaluates the mental health of a person in the age of 13-22 years. The scale consists of 130 statements. The battery is divided into six categories with several items, namely, emotional stability (15 items), overall adjustment (40 items), autonomy (15 items), security-insecurity (15 items), self-concept (15 items) and intelligence (30 items). A student with normal mental health takes only 25 minutes to complete the test. Both temporal stability reliability and internal consistency reliability of Mental Health Battery were computed. The details are given in tables 1 & 2.

Reliability: Table 3

Reliability Coefficient of MHB Part of MHB	Test-retest Reliability	Odd-even Reliability
Part I: Emotional Stability	.876	.725
Part II: Overall Adjustment	.821	.871
Part III: Autonomy	.767	.812
Part IV: Security-Insecurity	.826	.829
Part V: Self-Concept	.786	.861
Part VI: Intelligence	.823	.792

Validity: Table 3.1

Validity Coefficients of MHB Part of MHB	Concurrent Validity	Part of MHB	Construct Validity
Part I: ES	.673*	Part III: AY	.681*
Part II: OA	.704*	Part V: SC	.601*
Part IV: SI		.821*	
Part VI: IG		.823*	

3.17.2 SPIRITUAL WELL-BEING SCALE

Spiritual Well-being Scale (SWB) was developed by Paloutzian & Ellison (1982). It includes a 20-item measure that evaluates perceptions of the spiritual quality of life. The measure has two subscales: (1) Religious Well-Being and (2) Existential Well-Being. For measuring spiritual well-being, the variable spirituality, defined as having achieved a sense of meaning and purpose in life, was measured. The SWBS is a Likert-type format, ranging from 1 to 6, with a higher number representing greater well-being.

The scale also provides sufficient validity data (e.g., positive correlations of SWBS with self-esteem and social skill and negative correlations as a measure of loneliness) to view the spiritual well-being as an indicator of quality of life. Spiritual Well-Being Scale was developed as a general indicator of the subjective state of well-being. It provides an overall measure of the perceived spiritual quality of life, as understood in two senses – a religious sense and an existential sense (Moberg, 1979). The RWBS, EWBS, and SWBS have good reliability. For the RWBS, test-retest reliability coefficients across four studies, with 1-10 weeks between testing, are .96, .99, .96 and .88. For the EWBS, the coefficients are .86, .98, .98 and .73. For total SWBS, the coefficients are .93, .99, .99 and .82. The SWBS has good face validity as is apparent by the content of the items. SWB, RWB, and EWB are correlated positively with a positive self-concept, a sense of purpose in life, physical health, and emotional adjustment. They are negatively correlated with ill health, emotional maladjustment, and lack of purpose in life (Bufford, Paloutzian, & Ellison, 1991).

3.17.3 SOCIAL SUPPORT QUESTIONNAIRE

Social Support Questionnaire (SSQ) is developed by Sarason et al. (1983) consisting of 27 items. Each item asks a question for which a two-part answer is needed. Firstly, the item requests the subject to list the individual whom they can depend on given sets of conditions. Secondly, the item indicates the level of satisfaction on a 6-point Likert Scale (very satisfied, fairly satisfied, a little satisfied, a little dissatisfied, fairly dissatisfied and very dissatisfied). The Social Support Questionnaire (SSQ) yields two scores: (a) perceived availability of the number of supportive persons (SSQN) and satisfaction with available support (SSQ-S). The number (N) score for every Social Support Questionnaire (SSQ) items is the number of support persons listed. The social support available to deal with a given problem is rated on a scale ranging from "very satisfied" to "very dissatisfied". It gives a satisfaction (S) score for each item that ranges between 1 and 6. The overall N and S scores are attained by dividing the sum of N or S scores for all items by 27. The number of items included in the social support questionnaire. The number scores for the 27 items ranged from 2.92 to 5.46, with a mean of 4.25. The mean number of persons listed as supported for the entire SSQ was 114.75. The inter-item correlations ranged from .35 to .71, with a mean interitem correlation of .54. The correlations of items with the total score (minus the item being correlated) ranged from .5 I to .79. The alpha coefficient of internal reliability was .97. The S scores for the 27 items ranged from 5.12 to 5.57, with a mean of S.38. The mean S score for the entire SSQ was 145.26.

The inter-item correlations ranged from .21 to .74, with a mean inter-item correlation of .37. The correlations of items with the total score (minus the item being correlated) ranged from .48 to .72. The alpha coefficient for scores was .94. The SSQ seems to have several desirable properties. It was found to have (a) stability over four weeks and (b) high internal consistency among items. The modest correlation of .34 between SSQ-N and SSQ-S provides a strong basis for analysing social support into its components. The perceived availability of support, reflected by the SSQ-N score, and the satisfaction with the available support, reflected by the SSQ-S score, each appear to be worthy of study and analysis.

3.18 DATA COLLECTION PROCESS

The researcher directly went to the schools and collected the primary data from the selected students using the data tools such as the tests, questionnaires and in-depth interviews. This study used a self-report format of data collection. Subjects received a survey which they were asked to complete as honestly as possible.

3.19 DATA ANALYSIS AND INTERPRETATION

Data analysis and interpretation refer to a process of assigning meaning to the collected data, which would include making the conclusions and significance of the findings.

3.20 CHAPTERIZATION

The present study comprises of five chapters. It is an attempt to understand how the mental health of senior secondary school students of CBSE in Kerela is related to spiritual well-being and social support.

The first chapter provides an introduction to the thesis. It also gives a comprehensive understanding of their variables and their significance.

The second chapter is the overview of studies from the available sources. The first part provides a brief conceptual review of spiritual well-being, social support and mental health. Part two explains the empirical studies on the interconnectivity of spiritual well-being, social support and mental health concepts.

The third chapter provides the statement of the problem, the logic of the study, and the significance of the study's study and methodology. It provides research questions, objectives, hypotheses, research design, tools and the methods adopted to collect data and to interpret. Further, this section also deals with the researcher's role, ethical issues, tools used for data, and the study's validity and reliability.

The fourth chapter indicates the analysis and interpretation of data. In this chapter, altered data is analysed based on the objectives and hypotheses.

The fifth chapter presents the findings, conclusions of the study and recommendations for further research in the light of the present research. The chapter concludes by stressing the scope of mental health among adolescents by enhancing spiritual well-being and social support of the senior secondary school students.

3.21 THE SUMMARY OF THE CHAPTER

A research methodology is a systematic way to solve the research problem and has many aspects. This chapter uses the research methodology, which consists of specific scientific steps for successful implementation and objectivity. In this chapter, the research design and sampling technique are given in detail. The procedure for construction and finalisation of the tool is also described in detail. The collected questionnaires are scored properly and suitable statistical analysis is carried out.

How is the collected data processed so that they make sense in accordance with the hypotheses of the study? What is the importance of narrative case studies in this research? For understanding the existing scenario regarding spiritual well-being, social support and mental health through case studies, let's move on to the next chapter.

Chapter 4

DATA ANALYSIS AND INTERPRETATION

After the data collection, the researcher organised the data to be analysed by appropriate statistical techniques. The modified data is analysed based on the objectives and hypotheses. This chapter is divided into three parts: Part 1: The analysis and narrative case studies. Part 2: The tenacity of hypothesis and Part 3: The data interpretations.

The first part, the primary analysis, includes the arranged data based on the objectives, followed by the statistical treatment. Finally, the results are presented in the tables and diagrams. It includes breaking down the complex factors into simple ones and joining them into general interpretation trends. Subsequently, the percentages are analysed, and important trends are identified. The relevance of the hypotheses to verify the research hypotheses relevance, to accept or reject them. The third part includes interpreting the analysed data with major trends explained based on available theories, established findings and other significant documents. These scientific interpretations are further seen in accepting or rejecting the hypothesis to make the findings and conclusions.

4.1 PART: 1. A: DATA ANALYSIS

In the first part of the data analysis, the researcher has arranged the tabulated data based on the study's specific objectives. Subsequently, the preliminary data are given in the tables. The initial data are further analysed, giving some trends and indications about the collected data.

In the beginning, the investigator presents some selected socio-demographic variables. It includes gender, religion and settlement, followed by descriptive statistics like means and standard deviations. Statistical Package was obtained for inferential analysis of all the variables and sub-variables for the Social Sciences (SPSS) calculation. Then the arithmetic mean scores and standard deviation of low, average and high groups are presented.

OBJECTIVE 1:
TO ANALYSE THE SOCIO-DEMOGRAPHIC PROFILE OF THE STUDENTS OF SENIOR SECONDARY SCHOOL STUDENTS IN KERALA WITH THEIR GENDER, RELIGION AND SETTLEMENT

Table 4 Socio-Demographic Profile of the Students with their Gender, Religion and Settlement

Sl No.	Socio-Demographic Variables	Students (N:582)	Percentage
1.	**Gender**		
	Male	273	46.9
	Female	309	53.1
	Total	582	100
2.	**Religion**		
a)	Hindu	260	44.7
b)	Muslim	91	15.6
c)	Christian	231	39.7
	Total	582	100
3.	**Settlement**		
a)	Rural	210	36.1
b)	Urban	143	24.6
c)	Semi-Urban	229	39.3
	Total	582	100

120 *Data Analysis and Interpretation*

Figure 4 Socio-Demographic Profile of the Students with their Gender, Religion and Settlement

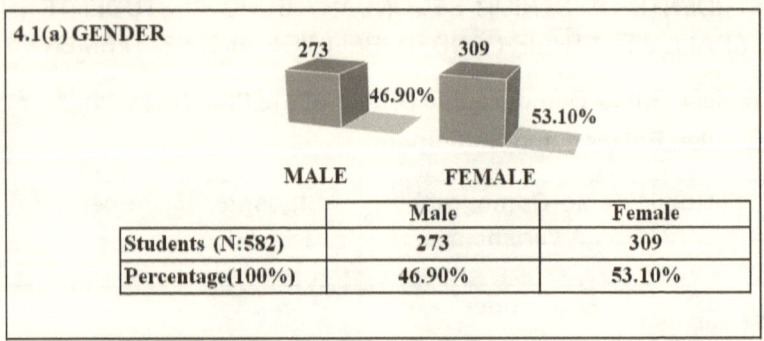

	Male	Female
Students (N:582)	273	309
Percentage(100%)	46.90%	53.10%

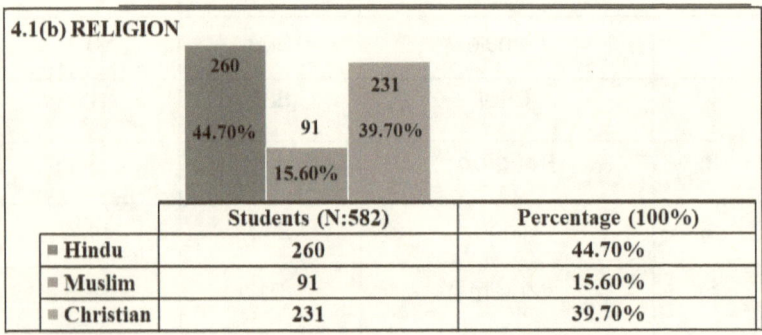

	Students (N:582)	Percentage (100%)
Hindu	260	44.70%
Muslim	91	15.60%
Christian	231	39.70%

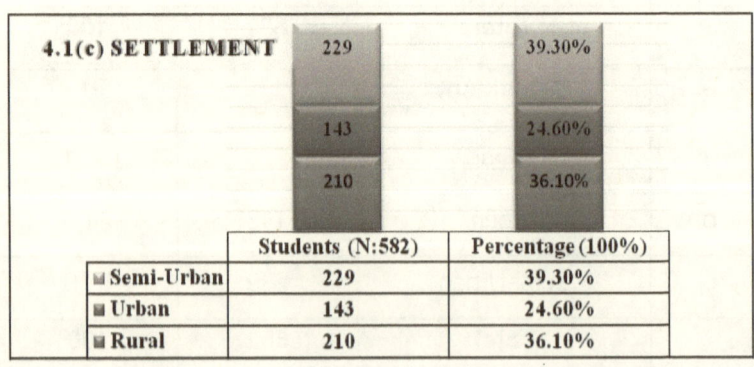

	Students (N:582)	Percentage (100%)
Semi-Urban	229	39.30%
Urban	143	24.60%
Rural	210	36.10%

Table no. 4 shows the distribution of socio-demographic profiles of the students with their gender, religion and settlement. Gender-wise, 309 (53.1%) of the students are females and 273 (46.9%) are males. Simultaneously, the religion-wise distribution shows that the majority (260, 44.7%) of the students are Hindus. In comparison, 231 (39.7%) of the students are Christians and the remaining 91 (15.6%) are Muslims. Settlement-wise, 229 (39.3%) of the students come from the semi-urban settlement. 210 (36.1) of the students come from the rural settlement, while 143 (24.6%) come from the urban settlement.

The over-all trend indicates that an equal number of male and female students participated in the research. However, the percentage of female students is slightly higher than the percentage of male students in the study. Furthermore, most senior secondary school students belong to the Hindu religion, and they come from semi-urban and rural settlements.

Table no. 4.2, no. 4.2.1, no. 4.2.2 and no. 1.1.3. show the levels of spiritual well-being, social support and mental health of senior secondary school students in Ernakulam district, Kerala.

1) For achieving Part 1 to Part 4 of the second objective of the present study, the investigator collected the required data relating to spiritual well-being by using the Spiritual Well-Being Scale developed by Craig W. Ellison and Raymond F. Paloutzian (1982). The data collected from the sample of 582 senior secondary school-going students in the Ernakulam district of Kerala was put into three categories by computing P33 and P66 of the scores. The students' frequency distribution in high, average and low levels of spiritual well-being is shown in tables.

2) For achieving Part 1 to Part 4 of the second objective of the present study, the investigator collected the data relating to social support by using the Social Support Scale developed by

Sarason, I. G., Levine, H. M., Bahsam, R. B., & Sarason, B. R. (1983). The data collected from the sample of 582 senior secondary school-going students in the Ernakulam district of Kerala is put into three categories, i.e., high, average and low by computing the P33 percentile and P66 percentile.

3) To attain Part 1 to Part 4 of the second objective of the present study, the investigator collected data relating to the mental health of 582 senior secondary school-going students, using Mental Health Battery (MHB) developed by Singh and Gupta in the year 1983. The score categorised as high, average and low based on the P33 and P66 scores of student mental health.

OBJECTIVE 2:
TO ASSESS THE LEVELS OF (I) SPIRITUAL WELL-BEING (II) SOCIAL SUPPORT AND (III) MENTAL HEALTH OF SENIOR SECONDARY SCHOOL STUDENTS IN KERALA

To investigate the levels of spiritual well-being, social support, and mental health of senior secondary school students in Ernakulam district, Kerala, the investigator organised

2.0 frequency distribution of the levels of low, average and high of the spiritual well-being, social support and mental health of the students. 2.1 is the means, standard deviations, S.E., and t-value of spiritual well-being, social support and mental health scores of male and female students of Ernakulam district of Kerala. 2.2 is the distribution of spiritual well-being, social support and mental health of senior secondary school going students as per their religion in Ernakulam district of Kerala and 2.3, the distribution of spiritual well-being, social support and mental health of senior secondary school going students as per their settlement in Ernakulam district of Kerala.

PART 1: FREQUENCY DISTRIBUTION OF THE LEVELS OF LOW, AVERAGE AND HIGH OF THE SPIRITUAL WELL-BEING, SOCIAL SUPPORT AND MENTAL HEALTH OF THE STUDENTS

Objective 2:
To Assess the Levels of the Spiritual Well-Being of Senior Secondary School Students in Kerala

Table 4.2 The Levels of Low, Average and High of the Spiritual Well-Being of the Students

LEVEL	FREQUENCY	PERCENTAGE
HIGH	77	13.23%
AVERAGE	453	77.84%
LOW	52	8.93%
TOTAL	582	100

Figure 4.2 Levels of Low, Average and High of the Spiritual Well-Being of the Students

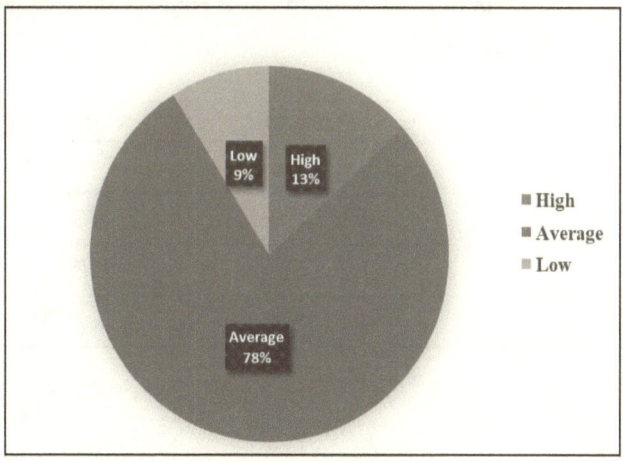

Table no. 4.2.0 shows the distribution of low, average and high scoring groups' spiritual well-being of senior secondary school students in Ernakulam district of Kerala. The table indicates that (13.23%) students came out to be in the category of high level, which refers to P66 percentile or above to it. On the other hand, 8.93 per cent came out to be in the low level of spiritual well-being which refers to P33 percentile or below. The majority of the students (77.84%) came out to be in the average level of spiritual well-being. Moreover, around 91% of students were observed to have average and above average spiritual well-being.

According to the data presented in this table, the high level is less than the average level. Thus, the general trend shows that most students came out to be in the average level of spiritual well-being. The above figure no. 4.2.0. further help in the analysis of the students' spiritual well-being.

Objective 2.1:
To Assess the Levels of Social Support of Senior Secondary School Students in Kerala

Table 4.2.1 Levels of Low, Average and High of the Social Support of the Students

Level	Frequency	Percentage
High	96	16.32 %
Average	428	73.54 %
Low	59	10.14 %
Total	582	100

Figure 4.2.1 Levels of Low, Average and High of the Social Support of the Students

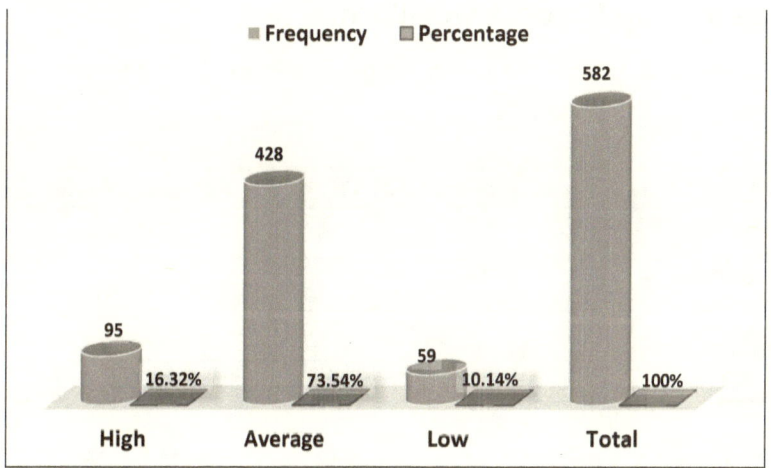

The above table no. 4.2.1 shows the distribution of low, average and high scoring groups regarding social support of senior secondary school students in Ernakulam district, Kerala. The table shows that 16.32 per cent of students fall into the category of high-level social support which refers to P66 percentile. 10.14 per cent of students were found in the low level of social support, which refers to P33 percentile value or below to it. The average level of social support has the percentile value between P33 to P66 under which the majority (73.54 per cent) students are found.

The general trend found in the table is that a significant number of 89.86 per cent of students were found above P33 percentile. It shows a status of adequate social support among the senior secondary school going students in Ernakulam district of Kerala. The above figure (no. 4.2.1) further analyses the students' levels of social support.

Objective 2.2:
To Assess the Levels of Mental Health of Senior Secondary School Students in Kerala

Table 4.2.2 Levels of Low, Average and High of the Mental Health of the Students

LEVEL	FREQUENCY	PERCENTAGE
HIGH	157	27.0 %
AVERAGE	393	67.5 %
LOW	32	5.5 %
TOTAL	582	100

Figure 4.2.2 Levels of Low, Average and High of the Mental Health of the Students

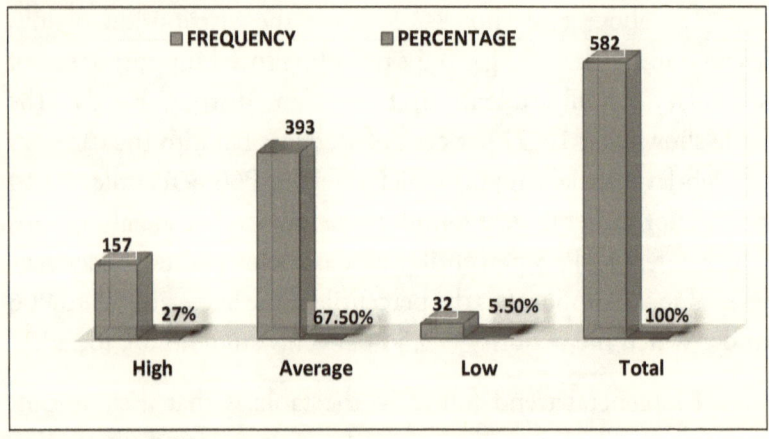

The above table no. 4.2.2 indicates that 27 per cent of students scored above P66 percentile score (86.66) out of 130 marks of the mental health scale.

5.5 per cent of students scored below P33 percentile. Furthermore, the remaining 67.5 per cent of students were found between P33 and P66 percentiles.

These levels indicate that most senior secondary school-going students in Ernakulam district are average and above average in their mental health. It is a matter of satisfaction that only 5.5 per cent of students have been found inadequate in their mental health, and 94.5% happened to be in their mental health. The above figure (no. 4.2.2) further helps analyse the students' mental health levels.

PART 2: THE MEANS, STANDARD DEVIATIONS, S.E., AND T-VALUE OF SPIRITUAL WELL-BEING, SOCIAL SUPPORT AND MENTAL HEALTH SCORES OF MALE AND FEMALE STUDENTS OF ERNAKULAM DISTRICT OF KERALA

To investigate the Means, SDs, S.E., and t-value of spiritual well-being, social support and mental health scores of male and female students of Ernakulam district of Kerala, the investigator organised the collected data in table no. 4.2.3, table no. 4.2.4, table no. 4.2.5 and table no. 4.2.6.

Table 4.2.3 Means scores, Standard Deviations, S.E. and t-value of Spiritual Well-Being of Male and Female Students

Level	Frequency	Percentage
High	157	27.0 %
Average	393	67.5 %
Low	32	5.5 %
Total	**582**	**100**

Figure 4.2.3 Means Scores and Standard Deviations of Spiritual Well-Being of Male and Female Students

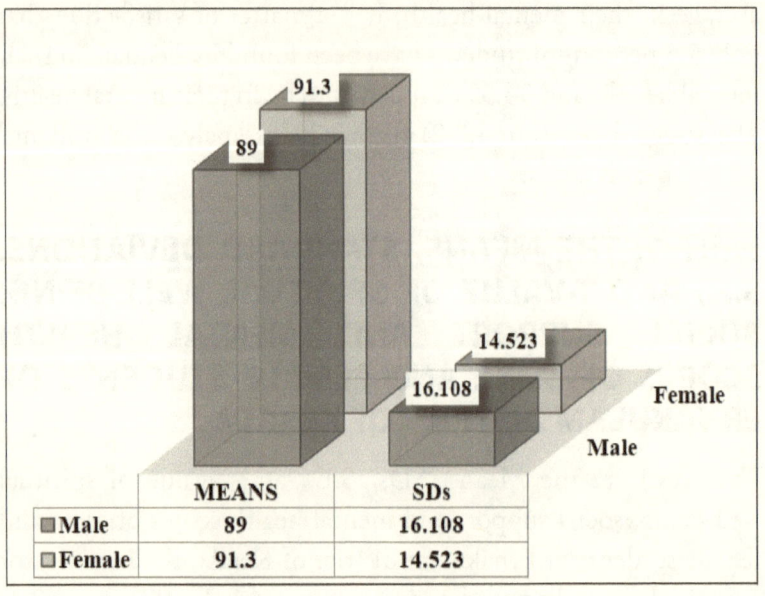

The above table 4.2.3 shows the mean scores and standard deviations of male and female students' spiritual well-being. The male mean score is 89 and SDs are 16.108. The female mean score is 91.3 and SDs score is 14.523. The SE of the gender is 975 and t-value is 1.812, which has been found lesser than the table t- value (1.96) at 0.5 level of significance for 582 df.

This preliminary analysis indicates that the senior secondary school-going male and female students do not differ greatly in their spiritual well-being scale. These students possess equal status in their spiritual well-being irrespective of their gender. The above diagrammatic representation presented in figure (4.2.3) further helps analyse the students' spiritual well- being.

Table 4.2.4 Means scores, Standard Deviations, S.E. and t-value of Social Support Scores of Male and Female Students

Gender	N	Means	SDs	S. E	T-Value
Male	273	3.61	0.757	0.062	0.031
Female	309	3.61	0.739		

Figure 4.2.4 Mean Scores and SDs of the Social Support of Male and Female Students

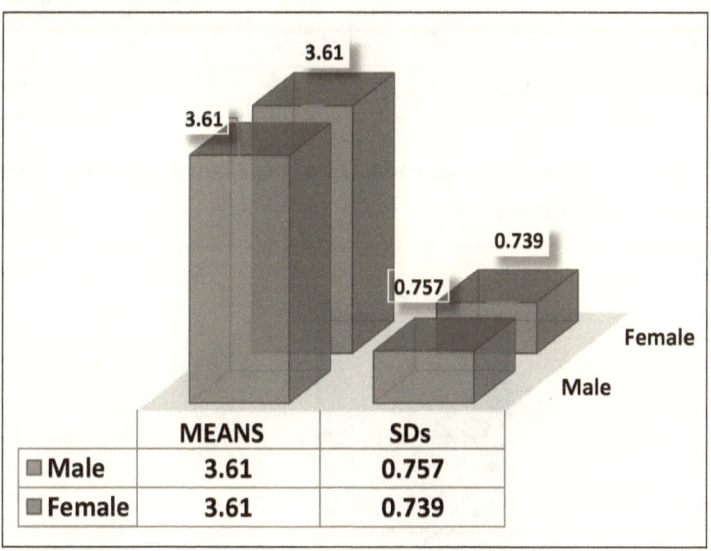

	MEANS	SDs
Male	3.61	0.757
Female	3.61	0.739

Table no. 4.2.4, specifies mean scores, standard deviations, S.E. and t-value of social support scores of male and female students. The computed t-value came out to be 0.031, which has been found lesser than the table t- value (1.96) at 0.5 level of significance for 582 df.

The diagrammatic representation of the data presented in the above bar chart no. 4.2.4 further helps in the analysis of the mean scores, standard deviations, S.E. and t-value of social support scores of male and female senior secondary school-going students in Ernakulam district of Kerala.

The overall trends of this preliminary analysis indicate that the social support mean scores of male and female students do not differ significantly.

Table 4.2.5 Means scores, Standard Deviations, S.E. and t-value of the Mental Health of Male and Female Students

Gender	N	Means	SDs	S. E	t-Value
Male	273	84.26	12.85	1.021	1.416
Female	309	85.70	11.77		

Figure 4.2.5 Means Scores and S.D.s of the Mental Health of Male and Female Students

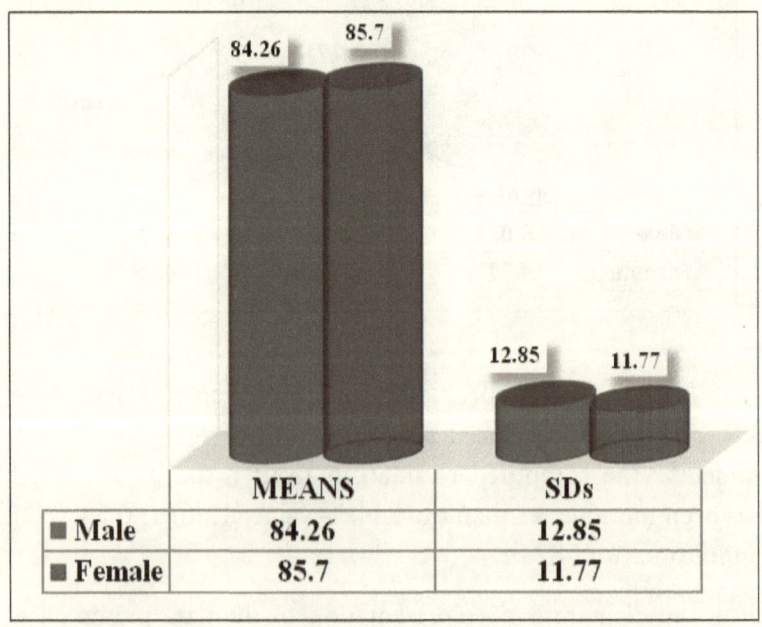

The above table no. 4.2.5 indicates that the computed t-value of the male and female mental health came out to be 1.416, which is lesser than the tablet-value (1.96) at 0.05 level of significance for 582 df. Therefore, the computed t-value (1.416) has not been considered significant.

The diagrammatic representation of this data presented in the above figure no. 4.2.5 further helps in the analysis of the levels the Means, SDs, S.E. and t-value of mental health scores of male and female senior secondary school-going students in Ernakulam district of Kerala. The general trend indicates no significant difference between the mental health mean scores of male and female senior secondary school-going students of Ernakulam.

PART 3: LEVELS OF SPIRITUAL WELL-BEING, SOCIAL SUPPORT AND MENTAL HEALTH OF SENIOR SECONDARY SCHOOL GOING STUDENTS AS PER THEIR RELIGION

To investigate the deviations of spiritual well-being, social support and mental health of senior secondary school going students as per their religion in Ernakulam district of Kerala, the investigator organised the collected data in table no. 4.2.6, table no. 4.2.7 and table no. 4.2.8.

Table 4.2.6 Levels of Spiritual Well-Being of the Students as per their Religion

Religion	Low	Average	High	Total
Hindu	19 (7.30%)	184 (70.76%)	57 (21.92%)	260 (44.67%)
Muslim	7 (7.69%)	53 (58.24%)	31 (34.06%)	91 (15.63%)
Christian	6 (2.59%)	156 (67.53%)	69 (29.87%)	231 (39.69%)
Total	32 (5.49%)	393 (67.52%)	157 (26.97%)	582 (100%)

Figure 4.2.6 Levels of Spiritual Well-Being of the Students as per their Religion

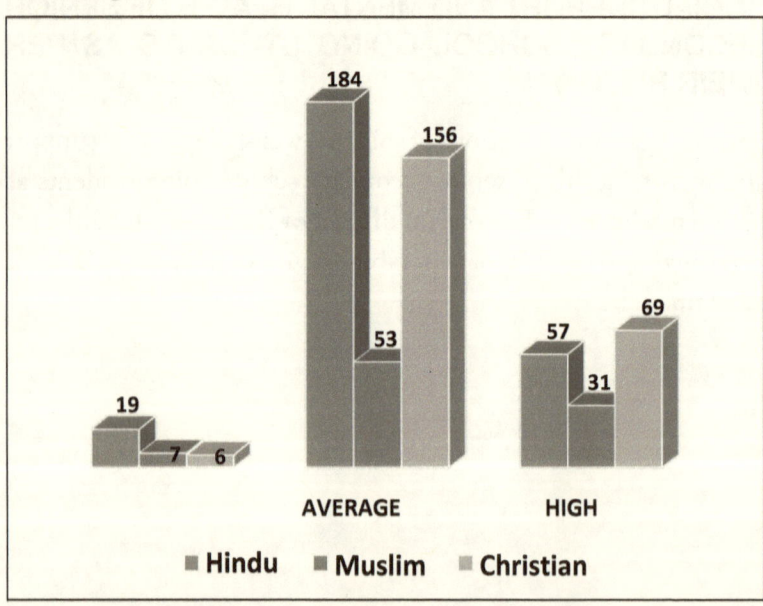

Table no. 4.2.6 shows the distribution of spiritual well-being of the respondents based on their religion. 44.67% senior secondary school-going students in the Ernakulam district of Kerala belong to Hindu families. A total of 15.63 per cent are Muslim and 39.69 per cent belong to Christian families. The senior secondary school-going students' spiritual well-being scores were categorised into three categories by computing P33 and P66 percentiles' values, i.e., high, average and low categories of students in terms of their spiritual well-being scores.

Religion-wise, 7.30 per cent, 70.76 per cent and 21.92 per cent students were found under low, average and high spiritual well-being levels respectively, belonging to the Hindu religion. Senior secondary students belonging to the Muslim community came out to be 7.69 per cent, 58.24 per cent and 34.06 per cent under low, average and high spiritual well-being categories, respectively. Similarly, the students belonging to the Christian community were found to be 2.59 per cent, 67.53 per cent and 29.87per cent under low, average and high categories of spiritual well-being, respectively. While comparing the spiritual well-being of the senior secondary school-going students, a total of 7 (7.69%) Muslim students were found in the low category of spiritual well-being as compared to Hindu and Christian students. In the average category of spiritual well-being with their religious background, an almost equal number of students were found from Hindu and Christian religions than the Muslim religion's low average. Nevertheless, in the high category of spiritual well-being, the students from the Muslim community (34.06%) marked a high percentage of students compared to the Hindus and the Christian students.

From this analysis, it is interpreted that the senior secondary school-going students in the Ernakulam district of Kerala belonging to Hinduism were found average in their spiritual well- being compared to Muslim and Christian students. The diagrammatic representation of this data is presented above in the bar chart no. 4.2.6.

Table 4.2.7 Levels of Social Support of the Students as per their Religion

Religion	Low	Average	High	Total
Hindu	30 (11.54%)	203 (78.07%)	27 (10.38%)	260 (44.67%)
Muslim	9 (9.89%)	60 (65.93%)	22 (24.17%)	91 (15.64%)
Christian	20 (8.66%)	165 (71.43%)	46 (19.91%)	231 (39.69%)
Total	59 (10.14%)	428 (73.54%)	95 (16.32%)	582 (100%)

Figure 4.2.7 Levels of the Social Support of the Students as Per their Religion

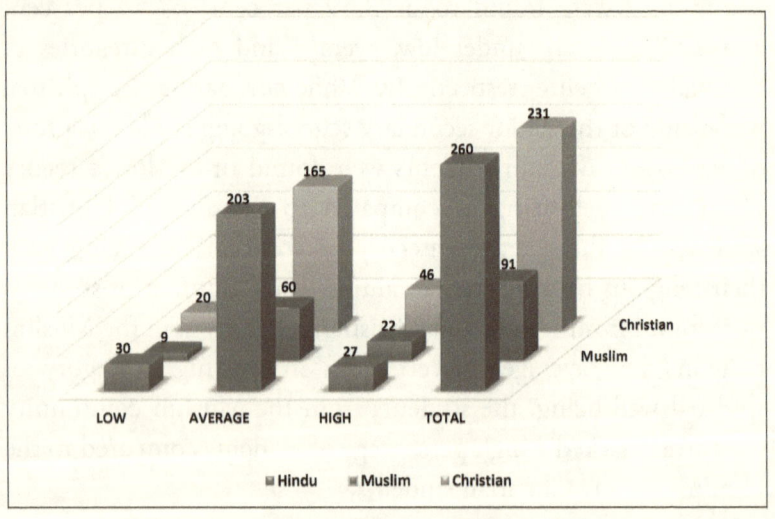

Table no. 4.2.7 indicates the distribution of social support of the students as per their religion. It came out to be 44.67 per cent senior secondary school-going students in the Ernakulam district of Kerala belonging to the Hindu community. On the other hand, 15.64 per cent and 39.69 per cent of students belong to Muslim and Christian communities.

The senior secondary school-going student's social support score were categorised into three categories, by computing the values of P33 and P66 Percentiles, such as high, average and low. Religion-wise, 11.54 per cent, 78.07 per cent and 10.38 per cent of students were found in low, average, and high social support levels belonging to the Hindu community, respectively. Students belonging to the Muslim community came out to be 9.89 per cent, 65.93 per cent and 24.18 per cent in law, average and high social support levels, respectively.

Similarly, the students belonging to the Christian community were 8.66 per cent, 71.43 per cent, and 19.9 per cent in low, average and high levels of social support, respectively. By comparing the social support of the senior secondary school-going students, it was found that high percentage (11.54%) of students belonging to Hindu community came in low level of social support as compared to the students belonging to Muslim and Christian communities. The investigator did not find any significant variation among the students in case of an average social support level. The majority of students were found under the average category of social support.

In the case of a high social support level, the students belonging to the Muslim community (24.18%) were found in this category. Hindu students happened to be 10.38 per cent which was marked very low percentage as compared to the other two communities. Finally, it was concluded that the students belonging to Hindu communities need to have more social support than Muslim and Christian communities who come under minority and get enough support from the central and state governments as compared to the students belonging to Hindu community in Ernakulam district.

The diagrammatic representation of this data presented in the above bar chart no. 4.2.7. further help in the analysis of the distribution of social support of senior secondary school students as per their religions in the Ernakulam district of Kerala.

Table 4.2.8 Levels of Mental Health of Students as per their Religion

Religion	Low	Average	High	Total
Hindu	31(11.92%)	204 (23.14%)	25 (9.61%)	260 (44.67%)
Muslim	6 (6.59%)	70 (76.92%)	15 (16.48%)	91 (15.63%)
Christian	15 (6.49%)	139 (60.17%)	77 (13.23%)	231 (39.70%)
Total	52 (8.93%)	413 (70.97%)	117 (20.10)	582 (100%)

Figure 4.2.8 Levels of Mental Health of the Students as per their Religions

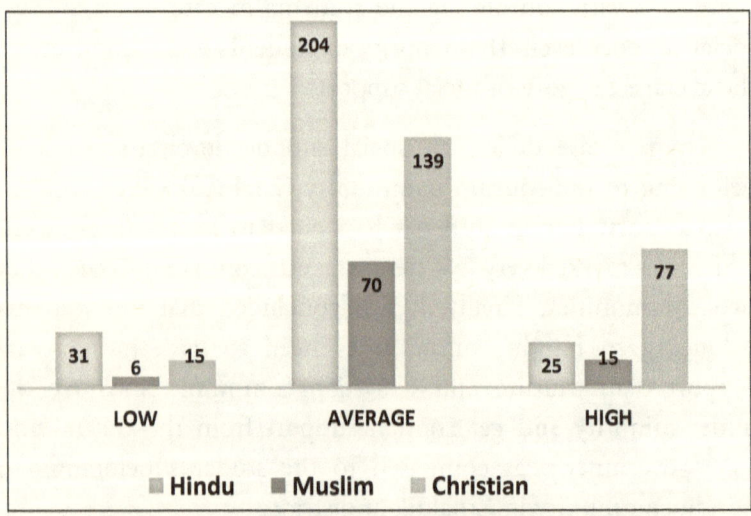

Table no. 4.2.8 shows the levels of the sample of students based on religion. 44.67 per cent senior secondary school-going students in the Ernakulam district of Kerala belong to Hindu families, and 15.63 per cent and 39.70 per cent belong to Muslim and Christian families, respectively. The mental health scores of the senior secondary school-going students were divided into three categories by computing P33 and P66 percentiles values, i.e., high, average and low categories. Religion-wise, 11.92 per cent, 23.14 per cent and 9.61 per cent of students were found under low, average and high mental health levels belonging to the Hindu religion, respectively. Senior secondary students belonging to Muslim community came out to be 6.59 per cent,

76.92 per cent and 16.48 per cent under low, average and high categories of mental health, respectively.

Similarly, the students belonging to the Christian community were 6.49 per cent, 60.17 per cent and 13.23 per cent in low, average and high categories of mental health, respectively. While comparing the mental health of the senior secondary school-going students, it was found that a large percentage (11.92 per cent) of students was found in the low category of mental health as compared to Muslim and Christian students. In the average category of mental health, the number of students from all the three religion was found almost equal. In this category, no significant variation has been marked. However, in the high category of mental health, again, the students from the Hindu community (9.61%) marked a low percentage than Muslim and Christian students. From this analysis, it is interpreted that the senior secondary school-going students in Ernakulam district of Kerala belonging to Hinduism were found slightly low in their mental health status as compared to Muslim and Christian students.

The diagrammatic representation of this data is presented in the bar chart no. 4.2.8. This bar chart further helps analyse the levels of social support of senior secondary school students as per their religions in the Ernakulam district of Kerala.

PART 4: LEVELS OF SPIRITUAL WELL-BEING, SOCIAL SUPPORT AND MENTAL HEALTH OF SENIOR SECONDARY SCHOOL GOING STUDENTS AS PER THEIR SETTLEMENT

To investigate the levels of spiritual well-being, social support and mental health of senior secondary school going students as per their settlement in Ernakulam district of Kerala, the researcher organised the collected data in table no. 4.2.9, table no. 4.2.10 and table no. 4.2.11.

Table 4.2.9 Levels of Spiritual Well-Being of the Students as per their Settlement

Settlement	Low	Average	High	Total
Rural	16 (7.62%)	159 (75.77%)	35 (16.67%)	210 (36.08%)
Urban	16 (11.19%)	107 (74.83%)	20 (13.98%)	143 (24.57%)
Semi Urban	20 (8.73%)	187 (81.66%)	22 (9.61%)	229 (39.35%)
Total	52 (8.94)	453 77.83%)	77 (13.23%)	582 (100%)

Figure 4.2.9 Levels of the Spiritual Well-Being of the Students as Per their Settlement

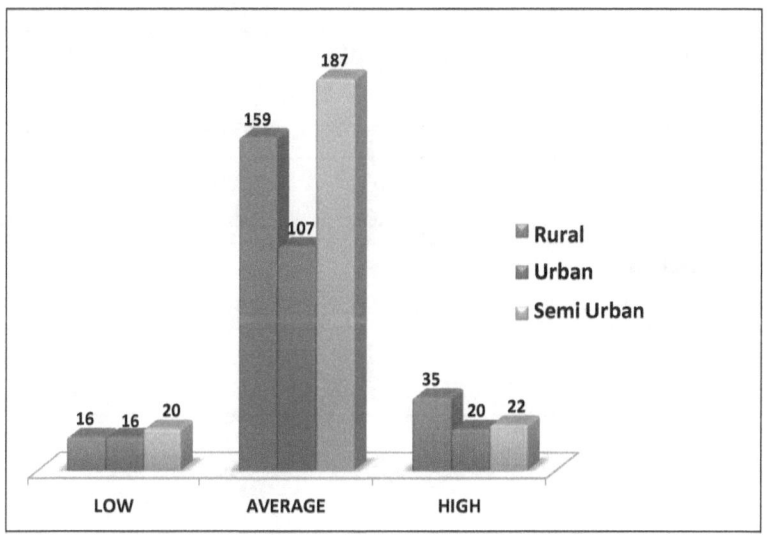

The cross-table no. 4.2.9 indicates the levels of the selected sample of 582 senior secondary school-going students in Ernakulam district of Kerala by taking into account the settlement. Spiritual well-being came out to be 36.08 per cent, 24.57 per cent and 39.35 per cent in rural, urban and semi-urban settlements respectively. Further, table no. 4.2.9 shows that the students coming from rural background have shown low spiritual well-being (7.62 per cent), average (75.77 per cent) and high level (16.67 per cent). The diagrammatic representation of this data is presented in the bar chart no. 4.2.9.

Table 4.2.10 Levels of Social Support of the Students as per their Settlement

Religion	Low	Average	High	Total
Rural	22 (10.48%)	144 (68.57%)	44 (20.95%)	210 (36.08%)
Urban	22 (15.38%)	103 (72.03%)	18 (12.59%)	143 (24.57%)
Semi-Urban	15 (6.55%)	181 (79.04%)	33 (14.41%)	229 (39.35%)
Total	59 (10.14%)	428 (73.54%)	95 (16.32%)	582 (100%)

Figure 4.2.10 Levels of Social Support of the Students as per their Settlement

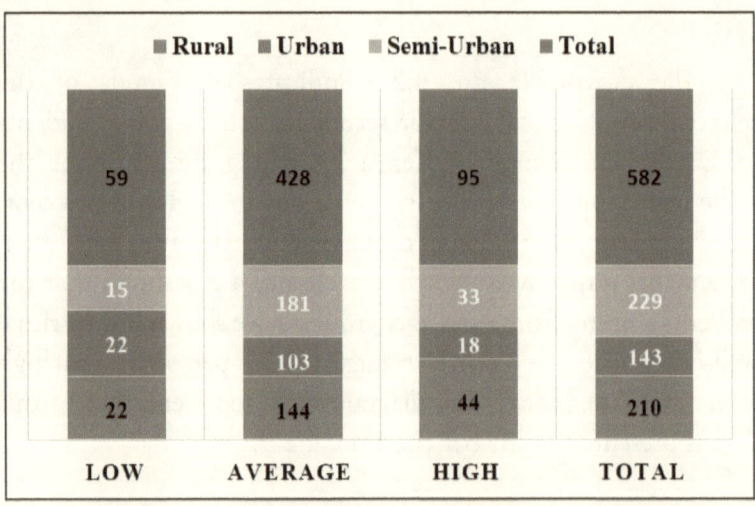

The above table no. 4.2.10 shows the levels of social support of the students as per their settlement. Students' levels in an average social support level came out to be 68.57 per cent, 72.03 per cent, 79.04 per cent for rural, urban and semi-urban localities, respectively. It shows that there is not much variation among the percentage of students. High-level social support is observed (20.95%) among the students of a rural background. Simultaneously, the students from the urban locality (12.59 per cent) have high-level social support. Similarly, 14.41 per cent of students are found with high social support from the semi-urban settlement. The general trend shows that many students have been found in a low social support level in an urban locality. All three levels of social support of the students were marked almost uniformly.

The diagrammatic representation of this data presented in the above figure no. 4.2.10 further helps analyse senior secondary school-going students' social support levels as per their settlement in the Ernakulam district of Kerala.

Table 4.2.11 Levels of Mental Health of the Students as per their Settlement

Religion	Low	Average	High	Total
Rural	11 (5.24%)	128 (60.95%)	71 (33.81%)	210 (36.08%)
Urban	22 (15.38%)	103 (72.03%)	18 (12.59%)	143 (24.57%)
Semi-Urban	15 (6.55%)	181 (79.04%)	33 (14.41%)	229 (39.35%)
Total	59 (10.14%)	428 (73.54%)	95 (16.32%)	582 (100%)

Figure 4.2.11 Levels of Mental Health of the Students as per their Settlement

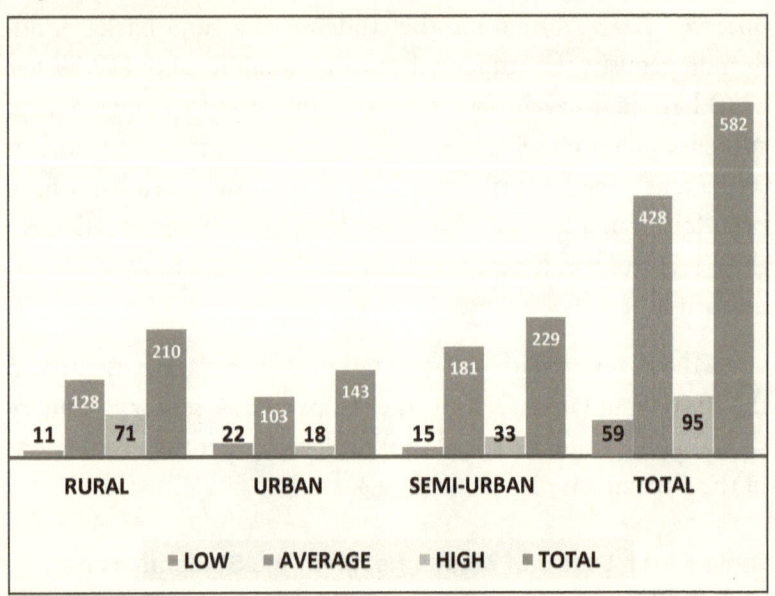

The above cross table 4.2.11 indicates the levels of the students' mental health scores such as high, average and low. The grades are computed in the P33 and P66 percentile values.

The rural background shows 5.24 per cent, 60.95 per cent, and 33.81 per cent under the categories of low, average and high mental health levels respectively.

It is observed that the students of urban and semi-urban areas are found 23.77 per cent and 22.71 per cent under a high level of mental health respectively, which is substantially lesser than the rural settlement. It indicates that rural background students are slightly better in their mental health in category high level.

The general trend indicates that most senior secondary school-going students are found in average and high levels of students' mental health. Only a nominal 5.24 per cent of students are with poor mental health coming from rural settlements.

The diagrammatic representation of this data presented in figure no. 4.2.11 further helps to analyse senior secondary school going students' mental health levels as per their settlement in the Ernakulam the students of the Ernakulam district of Kerala.

Figure. 4.2.12 THE COEFFICIENT OF CORRELATION VALUES AMONG SPIRITUAL WELL-BEING, SOCIAL SUPPORT AND MENTAL HEALTH OF THE STUDENTS

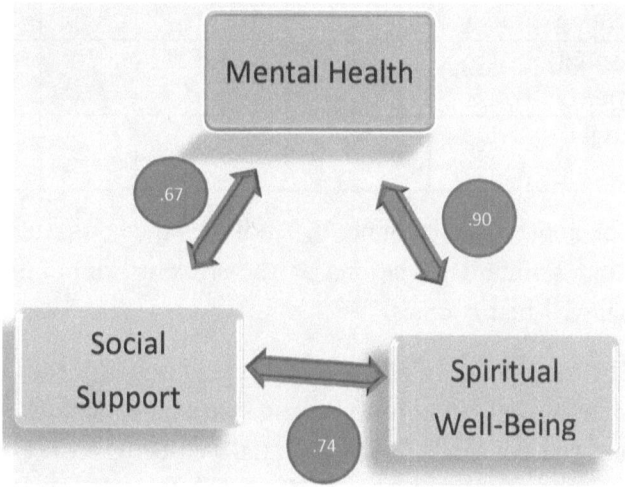

The above figure 4.2.12 indicates the coefficient of correlation values among the students' spiritual well-being, social support, and mental health.

To understand objective three better, the investigator used descriptive statistics to divide the scores of spiritual well-being and social support based on the number of senior secondary school-going respondents in the Ernakulam district of Kerala. Further, the investigator computed the mean, standard deviations of spiritual well-being and social support scores as summarised in table no. 4.3.0.

OBJECTIVE 3:
TO FIND OUT THE RELATIONSHIP BETWEEN SPIRITUAL WELL-BEING AND SOCIAL SUPPORT OF SENIOR SECONDARY SCHOOL STUDENTS IN KERALA

Table 4.3 Mean scores and Standard Deviations of the Components of Spiritual Well-Being of the Students

Variables	N	Minimum	Maximum	Mean	SDs
Religious Well-Being	582	10	60	46.33	9.678
Existential Well-being	582	10	60	43.90	8.193
Spiritual Well-Being	582	20	120	90.22	15.317

The above cross table no. 4.3 indicates the computed mean value and standard deviations of the students components of spiritual well-being scores.

The mean value of religious well-being is 46.33. Mean score of existential well-being is 43.90 and standard deviations for the religious well-being is 9.678. Existential well-being score is 8.193, which indicates there is no significant difference between the Ernakulam district students religious well-being and existential well-being.

For achieving a better clarity of the objective 4.3.2, the investigator used descriptive statistics to divide the scores of spiritual well-being and social support. Further, the investigator computed the means and SDs of spiritual well-being and social support scores as summarised in table no. 4.3.2

Table 4.3.1 Mean and Standard Deviation scores of the Spiritual Well-Being and Social Support of the Students

Variables	N	Minimum	Maximum	Mean	SDs
Religious Well-Being	582	20	120	90.22	15.317
Existential Well-being	582	10	60	43.91	8.137

The above table no. 4.3.1 points out the computed mean value and standard deviations of the students' spiritual well-being and social support scores. The mean value of spiritual well-being is 90.22, and social support is 8.137. The standard deviation of the spiritual well-being is 15.317 and social support is 8.137, which shows that there is a significant variance between the spiritual well-being and social support of the students of Ernakulam district in Kerala.

Table 4.3.2 The Coefficient of Correlation Values Between the Spiritual Well-Being and Social Support Scores of the Students

Variables	N	r-Value
Religious Well-Being	582	
Existential Well-being	582	0.74

The above table no. 4.3.2 indicates that the computed r-value between spiritual well-being and social support was found 0.74, which is greater than the criterion value 0.081 at .01 level for 1162 degree of freedom. Therefore, the computed r-value of 0.74 has been found significant. The formulated hypothesis (Ho): There is no significant relationship between the spiritual well-being and social support of senior secondary school students of Kerala is rejected. It is interpreted that there is a relationship between spiritual well-being and social support of class eleven students in Ernakulam district of Kerala.

OBJECTIVE 4:
TO FIND OUT THE RELATIONSHIP BETWEEN SPIRITUAL WELL BEING AND MENTAL HEALTH OF SENIOR SECONDARY SCHOOL STUDENTS IN KERALA

Table 4.4 Mean and Standard Deviations scores of the Components of Mental Health of the Students

Variables	N	Minimum	Maximum	Mean	SDs
Emotional Stability	582	3	15	9.41	2.04
Overall Adjustment	582	14	30	26.47	3.23
Autonomy	582	3	15	9.94	1.74
Security and Insecurity	582	4	15	9.10	2.54
Self-Confidence	582	3	15	8.85	2.83
Intelligence	582	10	30	22.57	4.09
Mental Health	582	29	105	85.02	12.3

Table no. 4.4 shows the means and standard deviations of components of mental health scores of senior secondary school-going students of Ernakulam district of Kerala. The means and standard deviations of emotional stability are 9.41 and 2.04 respectively, while the overall adjustment is 26.47 and 3.23. Then the scores of autonomy and security and insecurity are 9.94, 1.74, 9.10 and 2.54 respectively. According to the data, self-confidence and intelligence scores are 8.85, 2.83, 22.57 and 4.09. The mean score of the total mental health is 85.02 and SD is 12.3.

Table 4.4.1 Mean and Standard Deviations Scores of the Components of Spiritual Well-Being Mental Health of the Students

Components	N	Minimum	Maximum	Mean	SDs
Spiritual Well-Being	582	20	120	90.22	15.317
Religious Well-Being	582	10	60	46.3368	9.67528
Existential Well-Being	582	10	60	43.9072	8.19397
Mental Health	582	29	105	85.02	12.304
Emotional Stability	582	3	15	9.41	2.040
Overall Adjustment	582	14	30	26.47	3.234
Autonomy	582	3	15	9.94	1.744
Security-Insecurity	582	4	15	9.10	2.548
Self Confidence	582	3	15	8.85	2.838
Intelligence	582	10	30	22.57	4.092

From the above table no. 4.4.1, it is interpreted that the mean scores and standard deviation of spiritual well-being and mental health scores of the students do not differ significantly, and both variables are getting the equal spiritual well-being and mental health.

The components of mental health and their standard deviations indicate that the students' intelligence and overall adjustment are better connected than other variables.

Table 4.4.2 The Coefficient of Correlation Values Between the Spiritual Well-Being and Mental Health Scores of the Students

Variables	N	r-Value
Spiritual Well-Being	582	0.94
Mental Health	582	

The above table no. 4.4.2 indicates the computed r-value (0.90) between spiritual well-being and mental health was found 0.90, which is greater than the criterion value 0.081 at .01 level for 1162 degree of freedom. Therefore, the computed r-value of 0.90 has been found significant. Hence, the formulated hypothesis (Ho): there will be no significant relationship between the spiritual well-being and mental health of senior secondary school students in Kerala is rejected. From this, it is interpreted that there is a relationship between spiritual well-being and mental health of class XI CBSE school students in Ernakulam district of Kerala. The general trend is that an individual's spiritual well-being is directly related to their mental health status.

To achieve better clarity of objective 5, the researcher has used descriptive statistics to divide social support and mental health scores based on the number of senior secondary school-going students in the Ernakulam district of Kerala. Moreover, the investigator computed the means, standard deviations of social support and mental health summarised in tables 4.5.0 & 4.5.1.

OBJECTIVE 5:
TO FIND OUT THE RELATIONSHIP BETWEEN SOCIAL SUPPORT AND MENTAL HEALTH OF SENIOR SECONDARY SCHOOL STUDENTS IN KERALA

Table 4.5.0 Showing the Means Scores and Standard Deviations of the Components Social Support and mental health of the Students

COMPONENTS	N	MINIMUM	MAXIMUM	MEAN	SDs
Spiritual Well-Being	582	10	120	90.22	15.317
Religious Well-Being	582	3	60	46.3368	9.67528
Existential Well-Being	582	29	60	43.9072	8.19397
Mental Health	582	3	105	85.02	12.304
Emotional Stability	582	14	15	9.41	2.040
Overall Adjustment	582	3	30	26.47	3.234
Autonomy	582	4	15	9.94	1.744
Security-Insecurity	582	3	15	9.10	2.548
Self Confidence	582	10	15	8.85	2.838

The above cross table 4.5.0 indicates the computed mean value and standard deviations of the components of mental health scores of male and female students. The mean value of emotional stability is 9.41; overall adjustment is 26.47, autonomy is 9.94, security and insecurity are 9.10, self-confidence is 8.85 and intelligence 22.57 respectively. While the standard deviations of emotional stability are 2.04, overall adjustment is 3.23; autonomy is 1.74, security and insecurity are 2.51, self-confidence is 2.83, and the intelligence is 4.092.

For objective 5. the investigator further used the social support and mental health scores of senior secondary school-going students in Ernakulam district of Kerala and computed the coefficient of correlation by making use of Pearson's Product Moment Method, and computed results have been put in table 4.5.1

Table 4.5.1 The Co-Efficient of Correlation Values between the Social Support and Mental Health Scores of the Students

Variables	N	r-Value
Social Support	582	0.67
Mental Health	582	

The above table 4.5.1 shows the computed r-value (0.67) between social support and mental health is more significant than the criterion value 0.081 at .01 for 1162 degrees of freedom. Therefore, the computed r-value 0.67 has been found significant, and the formulated hypothesis Ho (3) there will be no significant connection between social support and mental health of senior secondary school students in Kerala is rejected. From this, it is interpreted that there is a relationship between social support and mental health of class XI CBSE school students in Ernakulam district of Kerala. The major trends of the correlation between social support and mental health indicate a significant relationship between the social support and mental health of class eleven school students in the Ernakulam district of Kerala.

To conclude, this chapter, the data analysis and the data after the statistical treatments are presented in the tables and then analysed to identify the general trends and findings. The statistical devices used for the data analysis are Percentage analysis, Karl Pearson's Coefficient of Correlation Test, t-test for equality of means and Two-Tailed Test. After the analysis, the general trends and findings are abstracted and presented after every table.

4.2 PART 1.B: NARRATIVE CASE STUDIES

After the quantitative analysis of the collected data, the researcher went ahead with narrative case studies which provided an opportunity to thoroughly investigate a phenomenon in a context connected to the phenomenon (Yin, 2009). A case study is a research procedure that is frequently used in social science. It is a research tactic and an empirical inquiry that investigates a phenomenon within its real-life context. The purpose of the case study was to look into the use of storytelling and narrative techniques in quantitative research fields.

Case study research focuses on narration of exciting stories which can be fitted into a theoretical framework (Neale & Thapa, 2006). Case studies collect data archives, interviews, questionnaires, and observations (Eisenhardt, 1989). Thus, the primary purpose of a case study approach is to find information from raw data available. This is one of the first types of research used in the field of qualitative methodology (Merriam, 1988). Thus, a narrative case study focuses on careful inspection of stories told by students. The researcher attempted to understand the students' experiences.

4.2. PART 1.B.1: REASONS FOR NARRATIVE CASE STUDY

Often case studies have been primarily used in the social sciences and it is really valuable in practice-oriented fields such as social work. According to Sturman (1997), a case study refers to a wide-ranging term for investigating an individual, group or phenomenon. Therefore, the narrative case study can be used to analyse an individual case in detail. It means that a mere description of the discovery process itself can be a process of research.

The methods may be qualitative, quantitative or mixed-method research. Crowe and colleagues argued that the data is collected in different ways assuming that it would give similar results. (Crowe, 2011). Eisenhardt (1989) combines quantitative data from questionnaires with qualitative evidence from interviews and observations.

The researcher has combined quantitative data from questionnaires with qualitative evidence from interviews and observations and selected five important cases to develop a holistic picture of the phenomenon. The researcher concluded that the students who have high mental health have average and above average spiritual well-being and social support from the quantitative data.

4.2. PART 1.B.2: OBJECTIVES OF THE NARRATIVE CASE STUDY

1. To obtain a better understanding of the students' mental health, spiritual well-being and social support, and how mental health is influenced by spiritual well-being and social support and vice versa.
2. The second objective is to understand the students' mental health experiences, spiritual well-being and social support and how those experiences enhance mental health and narrate the same.
3. The third objective is to explain how qualitative data agrees with quantitative data. The study examines how students' quantitative data on mental health is related to spiritual

well-being. Furthermore, how the students' mental health was maintained related to social support.

Narrative case studies of this research are related to the findings of this research in many ways. Firstly, the narrative case study evaluates the collected data of students' understanding and knowledge of their own mental health. It does not become part of the quantitative data such as mental health experiences; however, it affects the school and family.

Quantitative data on poor mental health pointed to low spiritual well-being and social support. Evidence from interviews and observations of the researcher also pointed out the same. Hence, the researcher decided to use the narrative case method to explain five important cases. In these cases, qualitative pieces of evidence helped the researcher to identify an explanation which is not previously explored in the studies. The researcher could match findings from his fieldwork with a previously conducted survey and adapt it for this purpose.

Many theorists contributed toward the development of the case study methodology. For instance, Stake's (1988) study highlights the definition of the case study approach to scientific research and praise case studies as important, instrumental and collective (Crowe, 2011). Thus, the case study of the researcher emphasises on either single or various cases and several levels of analysis. With due respect, confidentiality is maintained and the consent of the subject has been sought.

In-depth interviews were conducted with five students who had various experiences with mental health, spiritual well- being, and social support. It was also used as a source of data according to the researcher's concept. This study is quantitative and is guided by two theoretical methods: questionnaires and observation.

This study also trial to identify how storytelling can strengthen quantitative research and what values stories can offer to public research. Five thematic findings from the data were grouped under two headings. The first one includes the student's family, school and social background. Secondly the student's personal experiences with spiritual well-being, social support, and mental health care based on activities carried out at home, neighbourhood and school.

The themes were found to be dependable regarding four main theoretical functions of storytelling recognised in current studies: (a) sense-making; (b) meaning-making; (c) culture; and (d) communal function. The five themes that arose from this study include: (a) social context; (b) quantitative versus qualitative; (c) think and learn in terms of stories; (d) stories' tie involvements together; and (e) making logic and sense.

Reference is offered in the form of implications for various social contexts and other research topics are presented. The emerging use of storytelling in quantitative fields is one example of how the difference between quantitative and qualitative thinking may be reduced.

4.2. PART 1.B.3: METHOD APPLIED FOR NARRATIVE CASE STUDY

The researcher has chosen five different levels of correlations among spiritual well-being, social support and mental health after analysing data quantitatively. Accordingly, a Pilot project of the case study was carried out. From that Pilot project, the researcher is trying to put forward one example for each category of correlation levels, precisely in the student's words.

The researcher used a narrative case study approach to collect and analyse detailed narrations of clients' experiences. Narrative research began from curiosity, not knowing positions and focuses on questions that help the storyteller to detail the cultural context, feelings, thoughts, attitudes and ideas (Anderson, 2007).

The researcher categorised the cases into five levels of correlations to have an inquiry and an in-depth analysis. The levels are the following:

4.2. PART 1.B.4: LEVELS OF CORRELATION

1. High mental health, spiritual well-being and social support.
2. Low mental health, spiritual well-being and social support.
3. Average mental health, spiritual well-being and social support.
4. High spiritual well-being, average mental health and average social support.
5. High social support, average mental health and average spiritual well-being.

4.2. PART 1.B.5: CASE STUDY NO. 1: High mental health, spiritual well-being and social support. Student's name: Manisha (name is not original)

Manisha is 17 years of age and has two younger sisters aged 14 and 8 years, studying in ninth and third standards respectively. Manisha's father is an ITI (Industrial Training Institute) professional and her mother, a post-graduate in business. The parents got married 20 years back. Manisha spends sufficient time with her sisters and helps them in their studies whenever required.

The parents discuss most of the family's important events, including their subjects' selection. Manisha selected Science in Plus Two intending to pursue either medical studies or engineering. Both parents have deep faith in Jesus and encourage children to visit the church. Manisha is very regular in her catechism classes on Sundays and has many friends. From the parents, Manisha has also learned to respect others and understand others from their perspective.

Manisha's father has a well-furnished farmhouse which is 12 kilometres away from the house where all family members spend their weekend. The family has regular and routine activities such as waking up in the morning by 5.30, morning chores, visiting the church for morning Holy Mass, having breakfast and dinner together at a fixed time. In the evening, sufficient time is set aside for a family talk, discussion and information sharing.

Manisha has a grandmother, who is very sickly and aged, and stays with her uncle. Together with her mother, Manisha visits her grandmother and makes her happy by singing songs. The other family members also have a very good-natured relationship with one another. One of her uncles became sick and was admitted to the hospital.

During the day, Manisha's father spends most of his time on the farm. However, on weekends and holidays, he spends time in the panchayath office and with neighbours and it has helped him to have a good bond with the Panchayath and neighbourhood. Everyday evening, there is a joint family prayer lead by her mother. Children are encouraged to participate actively by reciting the prayers. From her mother, Manisha has learned to believe in a higher power and consider all children of God.

Manisha said, "My mother is very generous with her time and money for the poor and handicapped. Hence, it is easy for me to step into their shoes and understand their problems." She continues, "By supporting my mother and sisters, the little time that I get during Sundays and holidays helps me connect with all family members."

Manisha studies in a mixed school. According to her, school life is beautiful and memorable, which focuses not just on academics but also on behavioural and mental development.

Manisha said, "In my school, both boys' and girls' presence boosts self-esteem because I can interact with boys. There is no bar on discussions in our classroom, and it is important for personality development."

She also said that school education helps her to be a simple and straight-forward person with keen interest. She is confident and very empathetic towards family and friends. Manisha has the first rank in her class. Besides the academics, she participates in extra-curricular activities such as sports. Last Sports Day, she participated in many events but got a prize only for long jump. However, she said that she is not upset because she believes that one cannot be excellent in everything. One needs to accept one's limitations as well.

According to Manisha, school life and family relationship give many stressful moments. There are occasions when friends misunderstand each other and pick up quarrels. However, Manisha manages to overcome these challenging moments being aware of breath meditation and appreciation of oneself and others. Manisha believes that she is loved and cared for, esteemed and valued and part of a social network, such as a family and teachers.

Manisha's mental health was tested during the Kerala floods. She narrated how she responded to the disaster. In her opinion, people think that adolescents are wasting their time on social media without any purpose. However, during the flood, she proved it wrong by using social media, especially the WhatsApp, to help the flood victims, using the social support she had within her limit. Manisha formed a small WhatsApp group in which she shared information for the victims to move to a safe location. Manisha's family members were reluctant to move to safe places. However, she encouraged everyone and used a country boat to take the family members to a safer place, such as a relative's house.

During the interview session, Manisha acknowledged that teachers and friends in the school helped her a lot to have a purpose and meaning in life. Since younger days, she could experience a connection with a power greater than herself, realise her abilities and manage everyday stresses of life. It got reflected in her academic success and the contribution made on the day of flood remains in her memory deeply.

4.2. PART 1.B.5: CASE STUDY NO. 2: Low mental health, spiritual well-being and social support. Student's name: Pranab (name is not original)

Pranab, 17-years-old, is a quiet child in the family and a silent student in the classroom with below-average academic performance. He wakes up late in the morning, and parents have a tough time making him reach school on time. His father (51), C.A. professional and mother (43), homemaker, make every effort to keep Pranab motivated. Pranab has a younger sister studying in VI Standard.

Pranab said, "My family has no regular prayer at home and minimal contact with neighbours." Though Pranab's mother is a very spiritual person, he is not attracted to the higher power and rarely goes to the place of worship. Hence, Pranab has very little knowledge about spirituality and spiritual experiences.

Pranab is interested in playing with children in his neighbourhood. Often, his father controls him, preventing the interactions with neighbours telling, "You will develop a friendship with bad people." Pranab's grandparents love to spend some time with him, and they often invite him to come to their house. Unfortunately, only Pranab's parents go to their house. However, he has the possibility of talking with them.

Pranab always keeps an account of all the support that his parents give to his younger sister. He feels that his sister gets more attention from parents than him. Pranab said, "My parents do not go to any place of worship and speak about positive things. I do not have an opportunity to interact with my relatives and neighbours. They only insist that I study well."

Pranab was born after a long labour. His health was okay after the birth but did have difficulty feeding and was restless. His mother was delighted with her new baby. Still, she suffered from postnatal depression for several months due to the feeding problem the baby faced.

According to Pranab, before he starts his studies, his mother helps him spend some time meditating together with his father. Still, Pranab finds it very difficult to concentrate while studying. The main difficulty is the lack of trust in oneself and others. He is close to his affectionate mother than to his strict father.

He becomes stubborn at times; mainly when something is done without his permission. For example, buying any gadget in the family and his friends doing something without informing him. Pranab suffers from stammering and it becomes severe when he is asked to do something in a group. His mother is at a loss as to know how to reassure him and manage him when he is at home, especially in Pranab's father's absence. His outbursts in the family against his parents can go on for a long time. Sometimes he is better when his mother sits with him to teach him, but not always.

At the school, teachers are happy with Pranab as he is a reticent but pleasant student. In Pranab's opinion, only two teachers listen to him. He tells that even if he gets upset, eventually he calms down within ten minutes. In the classroom, Pranab sits quietly and does not have much contact with his classmates.

Pranab's relationship with his family members is not very strong and lively. Pranab's external behaviour appears to be very orderly; however, he is a disturbed student seeking attention and appreciation. Lately, he has started doubting people without any evidence. He even suspects his mother and younger sister. According to Pranab, recently, his intensity of stammering has increased due to exam fear.

Pranab feels insecure in his family as he finds none so comforting. He has grown jealous of his sister. The only person whom he finds close, sometimes, is his mother. His relation at home, he says, has brought a change in his behaviour which is gradually taking a toll in his nature.

Therefore, Pranab finds that his friends are also ignoring him after several incidents where he mistrusted them. He says regretfully, "I am losing the support of my family, friends and others. It is making me nervous, stressed and also not allowing me to concentrate on my studies."

He is aware that most of his friends have some relatives or family member to support during difficulties. According to him, visiting places of worship also would have increased his happiness and trust. Finally, he also acknowledged that he would have had very little stress if he had more opportunity to interact with his family and relatives. He confessed that he could have had cordial relations in society if his father had not been so strict.

4.2. PART 1.B.5: CASE STUDY NO. 3: Average Mental Health, Spiritual Well-Being and Social Support. Student's Name: Aisha (name is not original)

Aisha is an 18-year-old girl living in a poor house with her parents, Muhamad and Afsana. Aisha's younger sister is Amna, 13-year-old, studying in 6th standard. Aisha's father is a farmer and mother, a homemaker. Aisha says her father talks very rarely to her. She is afraid to talk to others, in the presence of her father, either at home or even outside. Aisha looks up to her mother for inspiration and encouragement.

According to Aisha, though her mother has only school-level education, she still encourages and supports the daughters. However, the whole family atmosphere is not as lively, as they are living in a house without many facilities. Her father is the only earning person in the household. Aisha also pointed out that since they are economically poor, even the neighbours do not pay attention to them. Aisha's mother is a religious person and helps her to pray. She speaks about God and superior power. However, Aisha enjoys very little freedom at home due to the neighbourhood and society's restrictions at large. Aisha's father encourages her to study well and to be active in the school. Aisha recalls her childhood days when her father was working abroad. It was her mother who took care of her and her younger sister. Because of this, she developed a fear of talking with men which continued to be with her and did not permit her to mix well.

Aisha is a pious girl who has acquired simplicity from her mother. She acknowledges that there is a superpower beyond human beings that helps her to have a sympathetic attitude towards her companions and neighbours. However, she mostly keeps quiet due to her fears. The teachers and her friends appreciate Aisha's empathetic attitude towards other people. Aisha loves her school, teachers and friends. She is talented and gets B+ grade in most subjects and has a couple of friends with whom she talks and plays. Aisha admits she always suffers glossophobia. She always suffer from an insecurity feeling and fear of social humiliation. Aisha makes an effort to participate in cultural programmes in the school. She loves to dance. Even though she tries hard to be with her classmates during extra-curricular activities, there is always a block within her as she faces the public. Moreover, it is connected to her upbringing.

According to Aisha, she has only a couple of friends in the neighbourhood. The elders are very friendly and encourage youngsters to participate in all activities. During the flood disaster, Aisha joined a team to help the flood victims. Aisha was hesitant to take the lead, but gradually with her friends' support, she was able to help, especially the poor, by providing them food and clothing. Aisha does not go for picnics with her friends, due to her nature and monetary issues, which played a significant role in her personality development.

Aisha has a big age-gap with her younger sister, so she is more compatible with her mother. She tries to help her sister in her studies. However, she finds herself to be a lousy teacher, according to her, may be due to a vocabulary crisis. Aisha is always told to behave like a grown-up since her childhood, by her father. Often, she feels that she lost her childhood and has become an introvert.

Poverty restricted her ability to "hand in charity". Nevertheless, she would inform her mother and take her and her sister's old clothes to donate to the poor outside the mosque. That would give her inner peace and happiness. Aisha's personality indicates only average mental health, spiritual well-being and social support.

4.2. PART 1.B.5: CASE STUDY NO. 4: High Spiritual Well-Being, Average Mental Health and Average Social Support.
Student's Name: Michael (name is not original)

Michael is a 17-year-old boy whose family consists of his parents and two younger brothers. His father is a 46-year-old railway employee and mother, a 42-year-old teacher, teaching in the same school where Michael studies. His younger brothers are studying in the same school, in class 5 and class 8 respectively.

Michael loves his mother as he gets all the pieces of advice needed for his life from her. According to Michael, he gets up together with his parents at 5.30 am and goes to church every day to pray. This experience motivates him to study and build up a good relationship with his teachers and friends.

Michael's father does not insist on praying too long with his children but encourages them to read the biography of great spiritual leaders such as Pope Francis, Dalai Lama and Mother Teresa. At home, there is also an audio collection of great spiritual leaders to motivate the family members.

The family has a small bookshelf which contains many spiritual books. His parents always encourage the children to read. Michael is always inclined to spiritual books that he feels gives him peace and happiness. Every day together with his mother, he spends some time reading the holy book and other spiritual books. Michael's mother is a very well-appreciated teacher in the school both by the management and students. Her simplicity and dedication always attract students and Michael feels happy about it and loves his mother.

Michael says, "Our family members gather to have a time of family prayers every night. We talk about correct behaviour, how things should be handled and pray together about life issues and for the blessings for our family. He also recalls his mother's statement that, "I hope that my children would understand why we pray and why we are committed to God and they would choose to build their relationship with God at some point in their life." In school, Michael leads the prayers as he is a leader in the assembly group. Michael was feeling very low when he got less marks in the last exams. For a couple of days, Micheal could not sleep well due to shame and stress. However, as the days went by, he continued with his daily spiritual practices. He could experience much positive spiritual well-being which helped him cope with the physical difficulties.

Michael has accepted his academic discomfort and has come to terms with it. He continued his affection for spiritual practices. Many teachers do not like Micheal's attitude towards spiritual practices. They complain about it to his mother, which he does not like. Nevertheless, he has no option. Michael is a good musician, and he finds solace in playing the guitar. Sometimes he gets chosen for the school orchestra, but mostly he backs out due to bullying.

Michael feels that his neighbours are reasonable people, and he helps them only when they request him. Michael is aware that his personality is Similar to that of his father. Helping attitude does not come naturally to him. He is happy to help people and happier in helping his classmates in connection with spiritual assistance. His teachers are happy to entrust him any work related to spiritual activity. Michael said that he finds them easy to do.

Michael does not have many friends as his fellow mates of school keep themselves away. The reason is that he is a teacher's ward and his schoolmates assume that he is privileged. This social distance has not made him a socially friendly person. Therefore, he avoids trips with his friends. To calm himself down from these problems, he would meditate and read spiritual books.

According to Michael, he can keep and maintain a balance and control of life, feels the purpose and meaning of life despite his average academic skills and social relationship due to self-awareness and meditation.

4.2. PART 1.B.5 CASE STUDY NO. 5: High Social Support Average Mental Health and Average Spiritual well-being.
Student's name: Arun (name is not original)

Arun, a seventeen-year-old boy, hails from a middle-class family. Arun's family consists of six members. His father's name is Prakash, a 47-year-old lawyer in the city. His mother's name is Lakshmi, a 44-year-old bank employee in SBI. Arun has an elder sister who is 20 years old, pursuing her B.Com. Arun's grandparents are Krishnan, 75 years old and Karthiyani, 70 years old. Since a young age, Arun was a self-assured child who moved around in the family and relations. According to Arun, his father taught him cycling at eight, and his mother taught him music. He learned many songs and used to be a star during the family get-together. Arun's sister is a dancer who is always ready to support him in his studies.

Arun's father is a Yoga teacher besides being a lawyer. Arun learned Yoga from his father, and he practices daily along with his father. Arun gets much encouragement from his grandparents to participate in many events in the school and neighbourhood. Their encouragement motivates him to be active in his school, especially to take part in extra-curricular activities. His enthusiastic nature makes him essential in school, as he is also the school leader. In academics, he is an average student. His parents feel that communication skills are more important than being a book worm. So, he too takes life lightly and studies only during exams. He is always in the good books of most teachers except his physics teacher who feels that he invests more time in self-importance than studies. Arun does not visit temples or prayer places regularly but is interested in helping people. According to Arun, during the flood in Kerala, he joined the school team students to help the flood victims reach a safe place and made arrangements to prepare food in a private home. Arun says, "I believe in helping humanity rather than visiting places of worship as God resides in everyone."

According to Arun, last year during Onam celebration (Harvest festival in the state of Kerala) he participated in many programmes and won many prizes. Even though the celebration was dampened by consecutive floods, together with his friends, Arun took the initiative to celebrate the festival with lots of games and songs. Arun's family also prepared 'Sadya' (feast) at the relief camps.

In school, Arun is an active student who is ready to help his friends and teachers. Hence, teachers often find in him a student who is responsible and helpful. Arun considers himself a person who can adapt to any situation and feels happy when helping someone. He says, "I got this personality from my parents" Arun is only an above-average student in his studies; however, he feels confident in public and often becomes a group leader. Arun believes that family support helps him to overcome the problems he faces in his daily life. Besides teachers and companions, he has good relatives in whom he can confide and get guidance.

4.2 PART I.B.6 INFERENCE

From the above discussion, it may be concluded that the quantitative and qualitative data show that the majority of the senior secondary school-going students in Ernakulam district have been found with average and above-average mental health. A good majority of students enjoyed average and above average social support. Hence, the study is warranted to confirm that taking care of spiritual well-being and social support are critical. The mental health of male and female students is equally good. The qualitative analysis based on case studies also supports this quantitative data.

4.3 PART 2: THE STRENGTH OF THE HYPOTHESES

In this study, the researcher intends to verify a few research hypotheses. The research hypotheses are represented by the alternative hypothesis (Ha), and the null hypotheses (Ho). These hypotheses are further tested based on the results got from suitable statistical treatment.

HYPOTHESES NO. 1

Ha (a): There is a significant relationship between spiritual well-being and social support of senior secondary school students in Kerala

Ho (a): There is no significant relationship between spiritual well-being and social support of senior secondary school students in Kerala

The sub variable of spiritual well-being is religious well-being, and it's mean value is 46.33. The second sub variable of spiritual well-being is existential well-being. It's mean value is 43.90. This indicates that no significant difference between the components of spiritual well-being.

Moreover, the computed r-value (0.74) between spiritual well-being and social support was found more significant than the criterion value 0.081 at .01 for 1162 degrees of freedom. Therefore, the computed r-value 0.74 has been found significant. Therefore, the alternative hypothesis (Ha): "There will be a significant relationship between spiritual well-being and social support scores of senior secondary school-going students in Kerala" is accepted. The null hypothesis (Ho): "There is no significant relationship between spiritual well-being and social support of senior secondary school students in Kerala" is rejected.

HYPOTHESIS NO. 2

Ha (b): There is a significant relationship between spiritual well-being and mental health of senior secondary school students in Kerala

Ho (b): There is no significant relationship between spiritual well-being and mental health of senior secondary school students in Kerala

Table no. 4.4 shows the means and standard deviations of components of mental health scores of senior secondary school-going students of Ernakulam district of Kerala. The means and standard deviations of emotional stability are 9.41 and 2.04 respectively. The overall adjustment is 26.47 and 3.23. The r-value of spiritual well-being and mental health is 0.903, which is positively correlated. Hence the hypothesis (Ha): "There is a significant relationship between the spiritual well-being and mental health scores of senior secondary school-going students in Kerala" is accepted. The hypothesis (Ho): "There is no significant relationship between the spiritual well-being and mental health of senior secondary school students in Kerala" is rejected.

HYPOTHESIS NO. 3

Ha (c): There is a significant relationship between social support and mental health of senior secondary school students in Kerala

Ho (c): There is no significant relationship between social support and mental health of senior secondary school students in Kerala

The table 4.5 indicates the computed mean value and standard deviations of the components of mental health scores of male and female students. The computed mean value of autonomy is 9.94, security and insecurity are 9.10. The SDs of emotional stability is 2.04 and overall adjustment is 3.23. It indicates better relationships between mental health components. The r-value of mental health and social support score is 0.676, which is positively correlated. Hence, the hypothesis: (Ha) "There is a significant relationship between social support and mental health of senior secondary school students in Kerala" is accepted. The null hypothesis (Ho): "There is no significant relationship between social support and mental health of senior secondary school students in Kerala" is rejected.

4.3 PART 2.1: INFERENCE

The null hypothesis in this investigation got rejected. The researcher accepted the three alternative hypotheses because the calculated values are higher than the table values. There is a significant relationship between the levels of spiritual well-being, social support and mental health of senior secondary school students in Ernakulam district of Kerala.

4.3 PART 3: DATA INTERPRETATION

In this portion of the chapter, the analysed data and the identified trends are explained in the light of the available theories, essential documents, and established research findings. These scientific interpretations are further used in the process of verifying the strength of the hypotheses. The arguments are organised in the order of the following specific objectives.

1) **To analyse the socio-demographic profile of senior secondary school students in Kerala with their gender, religion, and settlement**

The study's first objective is to analyse the students' socio-demographic profile with their gender, religion and settlement. The data collected through the questionnaire were treated with percentage analyses to identify the results. Besides, the case studies also support the quantitative data.

According to the general trends identified (Table no. 4) among the senior secondary school students in Kerala, 53.1 per cent are females, while 46.9 per cent are males. Among them, 44.7 % are Hindus, while 39.7% are Christians, and 15.9% are Muslims.

Regarding students' settlement, 39.3 per cent live in semi-urban settlement.

36.1 per cent of the students reside in a rural settlement, while 24.6 per cent of the students come from the urban settlement.

The trends say that there is gender equality in senior secondary education in the State. There is a slight increase in the number of girl students in senior secondary CBSE schools in Kerala than boys. In the case of the students' religious background, most of the students are Hindus or Christians compared to the representation of the Muslim students. Furthermore, under the students' settlement, the percentage analysis indicates that a vast majority of the students come from the semi-urban and rural settlements. Less than one-fourth of the students were settled in urban settlement.

This situation is significant as literacy rate in the Ernakulam district rural areas is 95.18 per cent as per census data 2011. Gender-wise, male and female literacy stood at 96.86 and 93.54 per cent. Religion-wise, in Ernakulam district, Hinduism constitutes 45.99 per cent, Christians 38.03 per cent and Muslims are a minority, forming 15.67 per cent of the total population.

The above socio-demographic profile of the students shows the importance of the research. In Kerala children and adolescents, both boys and girls get adequate training in their faith and almost equal chance for studies. State of Kerala proved to be an exception for the gender differences which is common all over India despite many enterprises by various States. According to the 2010 Economic Review, Kerala's female literacy is 92 per cent, while the equivalent figure at the national level is only 65 per cent (Sivaraman, 2017).

Similarly, in Kerala, Hindus, Christians and Muslims impart their faith to adolescents by various means such as bhajan singing, Archana or Murti worship, reading of Holy Books, catechism classes, memorizing major surahs of the Quran and so on. Scholars put forward that females are more religious than males because females face more existential insecurity such as lack of income on their own and concerns regarding physical safety, urging them to seek support in religion (Fahmy, 2018). Likewise, children raised in rural surroundings grow up to have stronger immune systems. They might be at lower risk of mental illness (Best, 2018).

2) To assess the levels of spiritual well-being, social support and mental health of senior secondary school students in Kerala

The second purpose of the investigation is to assess the levels of spiritual well-being, social support and mental health of senior secondary school children in Kerala. The data collected through the standardised scales were treated with percentage analyses to identify the results.

2. a) General trends of spiritual well-being identified (Table No. 4.1)

The general trend of spiritual well-being identified (Table No. 4.1) indicated that 13.23 per cent of students are found to be in the category of high level. Moreover, 8.93 per cent are found to be in a low level of spiritual well-being. However, out of the total adolescents (Table No. 4.1), the majority of the students, 77.84 per cent came out to be at the average spiritual well-being level. Around 91 per cent of students were observed to be average and above average. The case study revealed that students with average and above- average spiritual well-being did manage their stressful events and relationships better than students who had very poor spiritual well-being.

The trends (Table No. 4.1) say that most students have average and above average spiritual well-being. This trend is present in the case of female adolescents. At the same time, the total majority scored average.

Musa's (2015) research studies substantiate this trend identified while investigating the relatively high means of spiritual well-being among males and females. Additionally, the present research results point out that female students (91.30 mean score) have slightly higher spiritual well-being than male students (89.00 mean score). This result is supported by Rich (2012) who conducted a similar study on "Gender and spirituality: Are women more spiritual?".

According to Anye et al. (2013), 64 per cent of the American university students have high spiritual well-being levels. Moreover, the study conducted by Kneipp et al. (2009) indicated that 97.9 per cent of the university students of Jordan prove the fact that spirituality, religiosity, faith and meaning of life are important to students' lives.

Thus, according to these authors, students' high spiritual well-being levels are linked with religious beliefs and practices (Musa, 2015). Similarly, the present investigation also reveals the trend that there is a positive link in the spiritual well-being between the males and females students of senior secondary schools in Ernakulam district, Kerala. Henceforth, it may be concluded that students with spirituality, religiosity, faith and meaning of life have better spiritual well-being.

Social scientists David Voas, Siobhan Mac Andrew and Ingrid Storm, from the University College, London and the University of Bristol and University of Manchester respectively, argued that in Europe, the difference between the genders reduces with modernization. This is because women gain more security through economic development. But this interest towards religious commitment fades as women's values align with men's security and rationality (De Vaus & Ian McAllister, 1987). However, these results need not be the case in Kerala or India as the study is conducted in Europe. Studies show that the situation here is different. For example, a study directed by Sonawat on "Understanding families in India: a reflection of societal changes" points out that regardless of the urbanization and industrialization in the modern Indian society, the family remains a focal point to play a central role in the lives of people (Sonawat, 2001).

Thus, the study on the general trends of spiritual well-being identified in this study helps the researcher to evaluate various studies on spiritual well-being. Moreover, the findings of this study points to the greater need to include spiritual well-being in students' lives by changing educational programs. This will help the students to enhance a sense of peace, hope, faith and comfort which can lead to an increase in happiness and life satisfaction.

2. b) General trends of social support identified (Table No. 4.2)

The general trends of social support identified (Table No. 4.2) show that 16.32 per cent students are found in the category of a high level of social support and 10.14 per cent students in the low level of social support. However, 73.54 per cent of students are found with the average level of social support.

Demir & Leyendecker (2018) in their study point out that high levels of social support in the school can make the students more confident and positive with an ability to adjust and internalise self-concept. Similarly, the case study (No.1) conducted in the research also points out that a student who has excellent social support also has excellent spiritual well-being, ultimately leading to excellent mental health.

The research studies of Aydin et al., (2016) substantiate the trend identified in this investigation by stating that adolescents' perceived social support is an important resource in their lives and linked with a wide range of psychological outcomes. Similarly, it has found that school-related social support directly affects school-related stress. This has an indirect effect on global health, as higher perceived support predicts lower levels of stress (García-Moya et al., 2013). These results validate the findings of this investigation.

Therefore, the discussion on the general trends of social support helps the researcher to understand protective factors for senior secondary school students. It also helps to understand the most critical places where social support contacts happen which is a definite link with overall good health without gender difference.

This study's findings also indicate that perceived social support from teachers and companions impact a large part of students' well-being and academic excellence.

2. c) General trends of mental health identified (Table No. 4.2.2, 4.2.5 & Case No.1-3)

The overall mental health patterns identified (Table No. 4.2.2) indicate that 67.5 per cent of students scored the average level of mental health and 27 per cent of students scored a high level of mental health. In comparison, 5.5 per cent of students scored a low level of mental health.

This preliminary analysis major trends that most senior secondary school-going students in the Ernakulam district have average mental health. Furthermore, many students have a high level of mental health. There is no significant difference between the mental health scores of male and female students.

Sagone & Indiana (2017) in their study on "The relationship of positive affect with resilience and self-efficacy in life skills in Italian adolescents" point out that the level of perceived self-efficacy in a life skill, high level of adaptability and resilience are noticed among the adolescents with high positive affect. Likewise, adolescents with low positive affect demonstrate a low level of adaptability and life skills and low resilience capacity. Thus, this study supports the present investigation with the knowledge of levels of mental health.

In the study of Kessler et al. (2005) no significant differences in men and women's psychopathological rates were found. These findings support the present investigation trend with senior secondary school students by stating that male and female students' mental health is almost equal.

However, Patel & Flisher (2007) specified that the causes of gender differences in mental health problems among adolescents are not fully understood. Besides, the research study of Van Droogenbroeck & Spruyt (2018) showed that girls score significantly higher on psychological distress, depression and anxiety than boys, which does not agree with the result of the present investigation. Here, the researcher would argue Van Droogenbroeck & Spruyt (2018) conducted the study on Belgian adolescent girls who are emotionally very sensitive and suffer more from stressors such as, the death of friends or relatives, family violence, abuse and school performance pressures. Situation in Kerala is different because of the significant literacy rate of male (96.11%) and female (92.07 %) as per census data 2011.

Similarly, in Kerala, the achievement of health targets for all and the presence of strong family institutions are the keys to improving adolescents' mental health (Praveenlal, 2000 & Sonawat, 2001).

However, earlier research has shown that boys may have more difficulties in admitting their mental health problems. Instead of seeking help, they engage in activities which result in antisocial personality disorders and substance abuse. (Patel & Flisher, 2007).

Thus, the objective on the levels of mental health of the students indicates that differences in the levels of mental health point out lower educational achievements, substance abuse, violence and shortage of mental health professionals.

3. To find out the relationship between the spiritual well-being and social support of senior secondary school students in Kerala

The third objective of the investigation is to assess the relationship between spiritual well-being and social support of senior secondary school students in Kerala. For this purpose, the investigator used the spiritual well-being and social support scores of students and computed the correlation coefficient using the Pearson's Product Moment method.

Table No. 4.3 indicates the computed mean value and standard deviation of the students' components of spiritual well-being scores.

The mean value of religious well-being is 46.33; existential well-being is 43.90; standard deviation for the religious well-being is 9.678, and existential well-being, 8.193. This indicates that no significant difference were found between students' religious well-being and existential well-being.

Similarly, Table No. 4.3 points out the computed mean value and standard deviation of the students' spiritual well-being and social support scores. The standard deviation of spiritual well-being is 15.317 and social support is 8.137, which directs a significant difference between the spiritual well-being and social support of the Ernakulam district's senior secondary school students in Kerala.

Table No. 4.3 points out the computed mean value and standard deviation of the students' spiritual well-being and social support scores. The computed r-value between spiritual well-being and social support was found to be 0.74, which has been significant. Moreover, the case study (Case No. 4) results indicate that a high spiritual well-being student had at least average social support. Moreover, the general trend shows a significant relationship between the spiritual well-being and social support scores of senior secondary school-going students in Ernakulam district of Kerala.

Spiritual well-being among school students and adolescents was investigated in different research studies indicating that adolescents reported comparatively high spiritual well-being among both males and females (Musa, 2015). Spiritual well-being was related with better adjustment (Kneipp, Kelly & Cyphers, 2009), health-promoting behaviours, quality of life, a higher level of happiness and better social support (Hsiao & Huang, 2010).

The research studies of Musa (2015) and others support the trend identified in this investigation about the relatively high means of spiritual well-being among males and females. Additionally, the results showed that female students had slightly higher spiritual well-being than male students (Rich, 2012).

According to Anye et al. (2013), 64 per cent of university students had high spiritual well-being levels. Moreover, the study conducted by Kneipp et al. (2009) indicated that 97.9 per cent of university students thought that spirituality, religiosity, faith, and meaning of life are important to students' lives. Thus, these authors point to the high spiritual well-being levels among students linked with more religious beliefs and practices (Musa, 2015).

Hence, it may be concluded that the current study revealed a significant positive relationship between the sub-variables of spiritual well-being (existential well-being and religious well-being) with social support. These results are similar to the findings of other studies that disclose spiritual beliefs and religious attitudes, which encourage engagement in social support (Sawatzky, 2009). Furthermore, this indicates that students with high levels of meaning and purpose in their lives had high levels of life satisfaction and social involvement, giving them a more positive vision of life.

In their study, John et al. (2011) indicate that adolescents' overall satisfaction includes the house's basic needs, finance, and health along with religious practices and social support. Similarly, the findings of this study exposed a substantial positive connection between spiritual well-being and social support. Thus, the results of this investigation suggest integrating dimensions of spiritual well-being in students' lives. It is achieved by developing educational programs with high levels of sense and purpose in adolescents' lives.

All these studies substantiate the present investigation findings and show how to explore the students' spiritual resources and explain how spiritual well-being is related to social support.

Better spiritual well-being and social support could be achieved through an academic course, such as meditation, yoga or sharing experiences. For students, this can be achieved through debate which can help them explore the meaning of life, faith, religious beliefs, and practices. These courses could be made available for all school students. It would encourage students to develop social support among young people which protects them against mental health problems.

Thus, the interpretation on the relationship between the spiritual well-being and social support helps the social worker to attain new knowledge. Moreover, it enables the social worker to offer extra-curricular activities focusing on community services such as offering compassion and caring for weak people. Furthermore, this progress must be assessed continuously to plan, develop, and promote students' sense of self-esteem, emotional stability, intelligence and self-confidence. Better adjustment, high level of happiness and health-promoting behaviours of the adolescents can lead to better mental health.

4. To find out the relationship between spiritual well-being and mental health of senior secondary school students in Kerala

The fourth objective of the investigation is to assess the relationship between spiritual well-being and mental health of senior secondary school students in Kerala. To this end, the investigator used the spiritual well-being and mental health scores of senior secondary students and computed the correlation coefficient using the Pearson's Product Moment method.

Table No. 4.4 shows the mean and standard deviation of components of mental health. The mean score of the total mental health is 85.02, and the standard deviation is 12.3. Table No .4.4.1 points out that the mean scores and standard deviation of the students' spiritual well-being and mental health scores do not differ significantly. Table No. 4.4.2 indicates the computed r-value (0.90) between spiritual well-being and mental health was found 0.90, which is greater than the criterion value 0.081 at .01

level for 1162 degree of freedom. This points out that spiritual well-being, has influenced the students' mental health.

Case no. 4 supports the above data and points out that spiritual well-being and mental health are correlated. The case also points out that students with high spiritual well-being will have at least an average mental health.

The trends (Table No. 4.4 & Table No. 4.4.1) indicate the link between sub-variables of the students' spiritual well-being and mental health scores.

Table No.4.4.1 interprets that the mean scores and stand deviation of the students' spiritual well-being and mental health scores do not differ significantly.

Table No. 4.4.2 indicates that the computed r-value 0.90 between the spiritual well-being and mental health scores of senior secondary school-going students in Ernakulam district of Kerala.

The study of Jafari & Dehshiri (2010) supports the trend identified in this study, confirming a relationship between spiritual well-being and mental health. In their study, the regression analysis results showed that religious and existential well-being was important in mental health. The study also states that spiritual and existential well-being in females was significantly higher than males. This relationship's study points out that spirituality contributes to promoting mental health by providing a sense of integrity and existential connection.

Hence, it may be argued that individuals with spiritual experience and religious beliefs can manage their stress and psychological problems. Studies also reveal that spirituality generates a power which influences the physical postures, feelings, thoughts and communications. Thus, spiritual well-being leads adolescents to a physically and psychologically healthy life. It develops supportive behaviours such as less substance use and more physical activity, possessing goals and meaning in life. The study proves that spiritual well-being can increase hopefulness and optimism and improve adolescents' status.

Significant correlations have been reported between spiritual well-being and religious deeds (Bassett et al. 1991). It includes self-esteem and internal religious orientation (Genia, 2001). Thus, the study shows that spiritual well-being positively affects individual mental health and decreases mental disorders and intimidating factors of the different mental health fields.

The study of Bassett et al. (1991), "Measuring Christian maturity: A comparison of several scales", support the trend identified in this investigation about the relatively high means of spiritual well-being among males and females. Additionally, the results showed that girls had slightly higher spiritual well-being than boys (Rich, 2012).

It is to be noted that there have been no studies, and no reviews conducted to my knowledge to identify the relationship between spiritual well-being and mental health of senior secondary school students in Ernakulam district, Kerala. Hence, carrying out such an investigation is of high importance as students constitute a relatively large class of people in society. It is a step towards identifying the influential factors on mental health.

Therefore, it may be determined that the present study indicates a significant positive relationship between the sub-variables of spiritual well-being and the sub-variables of mental health.

5. To find out the relationship between social support and mental health of senior secondary school students in Kerala

The study's fifth objective is to assess the relationship between social support and mental health of senior secondary school students in Ernakulam district in Kerala. For this purpose, the investigator used the social support and mental health scores the students and computed the correlation coefficient using the Pearson's Product Moment method. Table no. 4.5.1 shows the r-value 0.67, which is greater than the criterion value 0.081 at .01 level for 1162 degree of freedom.

It is essential to pay attention to the social factors that influence mental health. Social support provides physical and psychological advantages for adolescents, reducing psychological distress when faced with stressful events. Many studies point out the effect of social support on mental health in recent decades. Lester (2013) pointed out the relationship between school connectedness and mental health. The findings show reciprocal relationships between contacts with people and mental health. Increased connectedness to the school was associated with decreased depression and anxiety. Hence, it is essential to hold seminars for the families of the students and offer training brochures to them to make them aware of their irreplaceable support in the family, school and society and provide them with practical strategies for improving relationships.

School children undergo rapid mental, emotional, and social changes and are susceptible to psychiatric disorders (Dhuria et al., 2009). Hence, school counselling should include practical strategies for parents and teachers as well.

Students must improve the family relationship in its volume and quality to reduce mental stress. It is crucial to identify adolescents with difficulties and encourage them to seek help.

Case No. 5 also specified that high social support would lead to average mental health. From the case study, it was clear that social support is correlated with mental health. Social support can act as a buffer and eventually lead to better mental health.

Social support is exceptionally essential for keeping good physical and mental health. The general trends (Table No. 4.5.1) point out that there is a significant relationship between the social support and mental health scores of senior secondary school-going students in Ernakulam district of Kerala.

The research findings of Hussong (2000) support the trend found in the present study. The correlation between social support and mental health scores of the present study suggest that social support may help youth against the adverse effects of stressors and promote more positive mental health outcomes.

According to Bierman & Aneshensel (1999), many works which concentrate on the positive effects of social support on psychological health have emphasised the role of perceived support with a specific source. However, there is an urgent need for research about how social support from multiple sources (i.e., parents, peers and community) affect adolescents' mental health conditions.

Researchers and practitioners must make more up-to-date decisions regarding where to focus on prevention and intervention efforts. Moreover, little care has been given to how social support is related to positive mental health indicators, such as hope for the future. Such research might clarify ways to encourage optimism and self-esteem among school-going students.

4.4 SUMMARY OF THE CHAPTER

From the above discussions and findings, the researcher could establish an intricate maze of connection between spiritual well-being, social support, and mental health. Every student is a part of a social group, the smallest unit being the family that may or may not offer support and teach values. Finally, every student is partially responsible for what he or she makes of his or her life.

Maintaining overall health is a person's responsibility which includes accepting help from others and the Supreme Power. But there is no strict rule about the importance or precedence of any of these factors. We cannot say that the students are a product of the society or the family. People may deviate from values taught in a family due to the impact of society. Conversely, the society's point of view may influence one's family too. Spiritual health gives confidence to a person, giving the necessary support to face life's harsh realities. However, a person already in distressing experience may never seek the help from religion or a spiritual experience.

There is no way to explain how sometimes a particular factor is a cause and sometimes the effect. Besides, some factors make a person weak. The family is where one first learns about the negative side of life, such as, neglect, carnal fears and desires, indifference and injustice, unhealthy competition and selfishness, making compromises and so on. The family is also the first place of support for a person where positive attitudes are built. Similarly, society is a place where one feels integrated and confident. It is also the scene where one gets scared and insulted. Spiritual well-being and social support also have its ups and downs. It reassures and encourages one with a healthy mind while fills guilt and fear into an unhealthy mind.

The five case studies conducted among senior secondary school students of CBSE schools in Ernakulam district, Kerala have proved that the underlying factors can never be fully explored or understood, much less experienced. Academically life can be classified into many divisions. But in reality, when these parts are joined together, they never equal whole. The social intervention in each of the five students was minimal and with no significance. There was also unhealthy repression and justification among the adolescents which are simply plans without any therapeutic value. Blaming others or oneself or life's situations is not the solution. Building a sound system of social support and spiritual well-being is important for mental health. To sum up, the right balance of spiritual well-being and perceived social support can enhance mental health among adolescents.

The purpose of the study is fulfilled when the findings and conclusions interpreted from the data analysis is explained properly. The next chapter elaborates on this and also provides academic and practical recommendations for the improvement of the social scenario regarding spiritual well-being, social support and mental health.

Chapter 5

FINDINGS, CONCLUSIONS AND RECOMMENDATIONS

This chapter provides important findings, conclusions and meaningful recommendations. The findings from the analysis are used to arrive at conclusions for further research. Finally, after the findings and conclusions, academic and practical recommendations have been provided.

5.1 FINDINGS

The findings of this research study are presented in the order of specific objectives.

To study the socio-demographic profile of senior secondary school students in Kerala as per their gender, religion and settlement

The percentage of female students who took part in the research is slightly higher than the male students. Community-wise, most of the students are from Hindu community, the second-largest group being Christian students, followed by those students of

Muslim faith. Most of the students come from semi-urban and rural settlements rather than urban settlement.

The socio-demographic profile showed a good representation of gender, religion and settlement among the students, which would in take the research result more accurate and reliable.

To assess the levels of (i) spiritual well-being, (ii) social support and (iii) mental health of senior secondary school students in Kerala

The primary trend showed that the majority of the students came under the average level of spiritual well-being. This indicates adequate social support among most of the senior secondary school students in Kerala.

The majority of the senior secondary school-going students have been found to be average and above average in their mental health. This points out that only a few students have been found inadequate in their mental health.

The male and female students do not vary broadly in their performance or spiritual well- being scale as the computed t-value came out to be 1.812, which is less than the table-value (1.96) at 0.05 level significance for 582 df. Students have equal status in their spiritual well-being irrespective of their gender. The primary trend identified from the sample is that, the high level is less than the average level and low-level of spiritual well-being.

The computed t–value for social support came out to be 0.031, which has been found lesser than the table t- value (1.96) at 0.5 level of significance for 582 df. This means there is no discrimination between male and female senior secondary school students in the family regarding social support.

A significant number of students had the percentile of P33 and above regarding social support. This shows the status of adequate social support.

Regarding mental health, no significant difference was found between male and female students. Majority of the senior secondary school-going students have an average and above-average level of mental health. The primary trend indicated that male and female students' mental health is equally good in the Ernakulam district of Kerala and good mental health helps the students in their academic and affective behaviour.

In the average category of spiritual well-being, the number of students belonging to Hindu and Christian religions were almost equal, and the islam religion had a lower average. Nevertheless, in the high category of spiritual well-being, the students from the Muslim community marked a high percentage compared to the Hindu and the Christian students.

In the case of a high social support level, the primary trend shows that the students belonging to Hindu communities need more social support than Muslim and Christian communities.

No significant variation was found among students in their mental health regarding religion. The primary trend showed that students belonging to Hinduism were found slightly low in their mental health status compared to Muslim and Christian students.

No significant variation in the mental health distribution was observed among the students coming from various settlements. The primary trend showed that students from rural and semi-urban settlements showed average and high mental health in the Ernakulam district of Kerala.

High-level of social support was observed more (20.95 per cent) among the students coming from the rural background. The primary trend indicated that the students' social support from the three levels of settlement is almost consistent. The trend indicated that most senior secondary school-going students are found in average and high levels of social support.

The relationship between spiritual well-being and social support of senior secondary school students in Ernakulam district of Kerala

The primary trend showed a significant relationship between students' spiritual well-being and social support scores in Kerala.

The relationship between spiritual well-being and mental health of senior secondary school students in Ernakulam district of Kerala

The mean and standard deviation scores of general adjustment (26.47, 3.23) and intelligence mean and standard deviation score (22.57, 4.09) agree with other sub-variables of mental health among the students. The students' autonomy, security-insecurity, and self-confidence scores have less correlation between the variables and mental health.

The trend points out that spiritual well-being has influenced the students' mental health. The general trend shows that an individual's spiritual well-being is directly related to mental health.

The relationship between social support and mental health of senior secondary school students in Kerala

The mean scores and standard deviation of sub-variables of social support and the students' mental health scores do not differ significantly, and both variables are getting equal scores.

The computed r-value has been found significant and this shows a significant relationship between senior secondary school-going students' social support and mental health.

5.2 CONCLUSIONS

Based on the following studies, it may be concluded that spiritual well-being, social support and mental health are correlated. The sub-variables of spiritual well-being and social support are correlated. At the same time, some sub-variables of mental health do not mix well with each other. This points out the importance of this research which analyses how the sub-variables of spiritual well-being, social support and mental health are essential to enhance the mental health of the students.

This study was taken up by the researcher because an external scientific intervention might be necessary for many young people whose lives are spent aimlessly. This study is necessary for a generation caught up in the web of false information and duplicity of individuals and the society. A generation that exists in an atmosphere of doubt and despair cannot contribute much. They will remain as miserable viewers.

The deterioration that set in long ago is now disturbing the roots. The society, who is supposed to help, turns a deaf ear to the silent screams of those in need. Scientific approaches and greater involvement and participation of the students are needed. Many families have broken apart, and children have lost their childhood as they try to face the realities of life. In such situations the students are slowly accepting false values, thinking that would help them in their fight against a corrupt society.

The institutions like religion, family and neighbourhood relationships used to give social support to young people. However, they are already being torn to shreds and replaced by merely nothing. A student, born and brought up in this situation cannot be mentally healthy as the spiritual and social vacuum continue to exist.

This investigation's main goal was to explore the senior secondary school students' mental health status with spiritual well-being and social support and to understand what was going on with the present education system. Even though great progress has taken place in education, mental illness and physical disorders have increased. Schools have been producing a large number of students who have become misfits in the society. Schooling is becoming meaningless to many. Those who find it meaningful are some and they struggle to gain something out of it. The education system is not transforming, but to a great extent, deforming students. Students are becoming puppets in the hand of manipulators, thus indulging in crime and abuse. They cannot be expected to produce good quality thoughts from their mental factory.

At the very beginning of the research itself, it was clear that students are not aware of the importance of spirituality and social support. The concepts of God or the role of a Supreme Power was given up in the name of pseudo-secularism and Value Education. Without spiritual wholeness and social support, students started to look elsewhere for satisfaction. Society had ready-made solutions for all the ills even though it is immoral, illicit or criminal. Furthermore, students without support from family or society were falling quickly into this trap. Education must be all-encompassing and universally available. More research need to be conducted to bring about ground-breaking policy changes, integrate various strategies to make a comprehensive educational plan.

5.3 RECOMMENDATIONS

To make the research findings and conclusions purposeful, the research puts forward the following recommendations for future research and the practical purposes of social work. It is also recommended for other related practices like education, psychology, and other service professions.

5.3.1 ACADEMIC RECOMMENDATIONS

The research results show that the connection between spiritual well-being, social support and mental health are high. Hence, the researcher suggests studying the various mental health components such as spiritual well-being, social support and their sub-variables. Once the study of various sub-variables is over, the knowledge will enhance the mental health of the adolescents.

The results of similar studies indicate that spirituality can improve one's ability to manage problems and bring about physical and mental well-being. Many factors contribute to spiritual well-being, like adequate sleep and healthy eating, mindfulness, reflection, prayer or taking time to be quiet to focus on inner examination.

Educational activities such as curricular programs with spiritual well-being as the central part, elective subjects and programs will help to develop a sense of trust, peace, hope and faith. This will lead to increase in happiness and life satisfaction.

The environments in school, family and society affect the functioning of the spiritual well-being and social support of adolescents. Hence, future research must focus on these factors.

Another suggestion is to conduct detailed case studies to identify the impact of these variables and their relation with the sub-variables of the spiritual well-being, social support and mental health, to discover the real variations between variables. This process will be a motivation booster in any research work.

Presently, schooling is mostly about gaining knowledge, ignorant of the importance of mental health and its sub-variables.

However, this study led the researcher to believe that the school is the uniting factor. The students find the school as an extension of their own homes. There are mentors and guides in the school, just like the members of one's family. Mentors with value-based education in school are much better than in any other part of society. The school must now attempt to become the hope for this generation. The school is still the guide for many students even after being neglected by the family and saddened by society.

The school should go beyond the limits of academics and trivial activities. The school must transform itself into the new family and the new society. The school must start nurturing and guiding young minds, teaching positive ideas and helping build new trends, thereby achieving the benchmarks of progress. Comprehensive health of the student must be the basis of any educational policy. The school should produce young people who can learn to live realistically, achieve gracefully and co-exist peacefully. The researcher found that the awareness about these three aspects - mental health, spiritual growth and social support - can bring a great change in today's society with the school acting as a catalyst. These factors need to be considered when designing the curriculum and adopting new educational policies. Similarly, the findings are cross-sectional; longitudinal studies are needed in future to understand better how spiritual well-being, social support are related to the students' mental health.

5.3.2 PRACTICAL RECOMMENDATIONS

Overall, all students in the research proved to have high levels of spirituality in their lives. The research also proved that spiritual well-being is comprised of two distinct domains namely how a student perceives the well-being of his/her spiritual life connected with God or Higher Power (religious well- being) and how well a student is adjusted to self, family and school surroundings together with the life purpose, satisfaction and positive or negative life experiences (existential well- being).

The role of social workers and counsellors in the school should be increased through continuous assessment of plans to promote students' spiritual well-being.

Teachers, social workers and other significant team members should develop interpersonal relationships and help-seeking behaviour among adolescents to improve social support. The gifted but troubled adolescents must be specially guided and provided with responsibilities to become dynamic and creative members in society. Adolescents' problems should be treated accordingly through useful programmes, strategies and interventions rather than announcing it in public and embarrassing them. The knowledge of social support in adolescents' lives helps the school management and teachers view adolescents in a new light. This knowledge should be utilised in the diagnosis, treatment, problem-solving practices and mental health enhancement of the adolescents.

The professional social workers and other school and community-based working professionals should try to make the parents conscious of how well the components of social support are related with spiritual well-being and ultimately, mental health of the adolescents. Parents and family members should be oriented to help their adolescent children utilise their creative capabilities by motivating them to take up a variety of career options and learn to accept and be compassionate towards the differences.

The school management, teachers, parents and other significant people should be aware of the social media trends and their influence on adolescents. Those adolescents who are highly creative should be identified and appropriate help should be given to them according to their interests and capacities. It will also help them to discover creative and natural expressions and achieve their original potentials.

Professional social workers, teachers and policy-makers and its implementors should develop training programmes and intervention schemes to increase the social support for adolescents and to use their talents for a better result. Such training programmes will ultimately improve the adolescents' social support, which in turn enhance mental health.

The ambiguities and uncertainties will lead to further divisions and anxiety. They will only destroy the social support and mental health of the adolescents.

The research findings also indicate that the adolescents are viewed as persons with compassion, energy, creativity, actions and interactions, rather than as old-fashioned rule-breakers. Hence, adolescents should be given freedom and independence to make their own choices. They should be given support to follow a spirituality suitable to their well-being and the knowledge of social support to enhance their mental health.

Furthermore, it would expand their natural capabilities and capacities which would lead to a better future for themselves and society The conflicts and frustrations in adolescents should be overcome to enhance mental health. Thus, they are to understand their abilities, potentialities, aptitudes and interest to work along with others.

REFERENCES

Adams, T.B, Bezner, J.R., Drabbs, M.E., Zambarano, R.J., & Steinhardt, M.A. (2000) Conceptualization and measurement of the spiritual and psychological dimensions of wellness in a college population. *Journal of American College Health*, 48(4), 165-173. https://doi.org/10.1080/07448480009595692

Adewuya, A. O., Ola, B. A., & Adewumi, T. A. (2007). The 12-month prevalence of DSM-IV anxiety disorders among Nigerian secondary school adolescents aged 13-18 years. *Journal of adolescence*, 30(6), 1071–1076. https://doi.org/10.1016/j.adolescence.2007.08.002

Adler, R. B., & Towne, N. (1981). *Looking out/looking in: Interpersonal communication*. Holt, Rinehart and Winston.

Afrooz Q, Taghizadeh H. (2014). Comparison of Perceived Social Support and Mental health of Mothers of Children with and without Hearing. *Exceptional Education*, 2 (124), 7–17.

Agarwal, S. P. (2004). Child and adolescent mental health: A pragmatic perspective. In D. S.S. P. Agarwal, *R. N. Salhan, & S. Shrivastava (Eds.), Mental health: An Indian perspective (1946–2003)* (pp. 290–292). New Delhi: Directorate General of Health Services, Ministry of Health & Family Welfare, India.

Agarwal, S.P. et al. (2004). *Mental Health: An Indian Perspective, 1946–2003*. New Delhi, Directorate General of Health Services / Ministry of Health and Family Welfare.

Allinson, R.E. (1992). The golden rule as the core value in Confucianism & Christianity: Ethical similarities and differences. *Asian Philosophy: An International Journal of the Philosophical Traditions of the East*, 173-185. https://doi.org/10.1080/09552369208575363

Alorani, O. I. & Alradaydeh, M., F. (2017). Spiritual well-being, perceived social support, and life satisfaction among university students. *International Journal of Adolescence and Youth*, 1-8. https://doi.org/10.1080/02673843.2017.1352522

Altimus, C., Ford, W., Chapman, W. B., & Tillery, C. (2011). The importance of a holistic safety, health, and wellness research program. *NIJ Journal*, 278, 1-3.

Amy, L. A. (2000). Spiritual well-being, spiritual growth, and spiritual care for the aged: A cross faith and interdisciplinary effort. *Journal of Religious Gerontology*, 11(2), 3-28. https://doi.org/10.1300/J078v11n02_02

Anand, S. P. (1988). RCE Mental Health Scale. *Indian Educational Review*, 23 (1), 41-47.

Anderson, H., & Gehart, D., (Eds) (2007). *Collaborative Therapy: Relationships and Conversations that Make a Difference*. Routledge.

Ant, A. (n.d.). *Adam Ant Quotes*. AZQuotes.com. Retrieved October 27, 2020, from https://www.azquotes.com/quote/9157.

Anye, E. T., Gallien, T. L., Bian, H., & Moulton, M. (2013). The relationship between spiritual well-being and health-related quality of life in college students. *Journal of American college health: J of ACH*, 61(7), 414–421. https://doi.org/10.1080/07448481.2013.824454

Armbruster, P., Gerstein, S. H., & Fallon, T. (1997). Bridging the gap between service need and service utilization: a school-based mental health program. *Community mental health journal*, 33(3), 199–211. https://doi.org/10.1023/a:1025033326743

Arora, R. & Kaur, J. (2010). Effect of self-concept and mental health on academic achievement of secondary school students. *Indian Journal of community psychology*, CPAI, 6(2). 275-281.

Asanbe, C., Gaba, A., & Yang, J. (n.d.). *Mental Health is a Human Right*. APA.org. https://www.apa.org/international/pi/2018/12/mental-health-rights

Assagioli, R. (1973). *Principi e metodi della psicosintesi terapeutica (Psychosynthesis: A manual of principles and techniques)*. Astrolabe Ubaldini.

Aurobindo, S. (1997). *The Foundations of Indian Culture*. Sri Aurobindo Ashram Publications Department.

Aydin, B., Akbas, S., Turla, A., & Dundar, C. (2016). Depression and post-traumatic stress disorder in child victims of sexual abuse: perceived social support as a protection factor. *Nordic journal of psychiatry*, 70(6), 418–423. https://doi.org/10.3109/08039488.2016.1143028

Azarsa, T., Davoodi, A., Khorami Markani, A., Gahramanian, A., & Vargaeei, A. (2015). Spiritual wellbeing, Attitude toward Spiritual Care and its Relationship with Spiritual Care Competence among Critical Care Nurses. *Journal of caring sciences, 4*(4), 309–320. https://doi.org/10.15171/jcs.2015.031

Azmitia, M. S. (2013). Finding your niche: Identity and emotional support in emerging adults' adjustment to the transition to college. *Journal of Research on Adolescence, 23*(4), 744–761. https://doi.org/10.1111/jora.12037

Barker, G. (1996). *Integrated service models for youth: An analysis of selected international experiences.* World Bank (unpublished working paper). Washington.

Barker, Gary. (2007). Adolescents, social support and help-seeking behaviour : an international literature review and programme consultation with recommendations for action / Gary Barker. World Health Organization. https://apps.who.int/iris/handle/10665/43778

Bashir, H. & Liyaqat, B. (2016). Investigating the relationship between self-regulation and the spiritual intelligence of higher secondary school students. *Indian Journal of Health and Wellbeing,* 7(3), 327-329. http://www.iahrw.com/index.php/home/journal_detail/19#list

Bassett, R. L., Camplin, W., Humphrey, D., Dorr, C., Biggs, S., Distaffen, R., Doxtator, I., Flaherty, M., Hunsberger, P. J., Poage, R., & Thompson, H. (1991). Measuring Christian maturity: A comparison of several scales. *Journal of Psychology and Theology, 19*(1), 84-93. https://doi.org/10.1177/009164719101900108

Basu, S. (1995). *How the spiritual dimension of health was acknowledged by the World Health Assembly-a report.* NAMAH: NAMAH.

Batson, C. (2011). *Altruism in Humans.* Oxford University Press.

Baumeister, R. F., & Leary, M. R. (1995). The need to belong: desire for interpersonal attachments as a fundamental human motivation. *Psychological bulletin, 117*(3), 497–529.

Beers, C. (1937). *A mind that found itself.* Doubleday, Draw & Co. Belmont, CA: Wadsworth.

Berger, C. R., & Calabrese, R. J. (1975). Some explorations in initial interaction and beyond: Toward a developmental theory of interpersonal communication. *Human Communication Research,*

1(2), 99-112. https://doi.org/10.1111/j.1468-2958.1975.tb00258.x

Berger, P. L. & Luckmann, T. (1991). *The Social Construction of Reality A Treatise in the Sociology of Knowledge.* Penguin Books.

Berkman, L. F., Glass, T., Brissette, I., & Seeman, T. E. (2000). From social integration to health: Durkheim in the new millennium. *Social science & medicine (1982), 51*(6), 843–857. https://doi.org/10.1016/s0277-9536(00)00065-4

Bertolote, J. (2008). The roots of the concept of mental health. *World Psychiatry,* 72(2), 113-116. https://doi.org/10.1002/j.2051-5545.2008.tb00172.x

Best, S. (2018). *Children raised in cities are more likely to have mental health problems than those in the countryside.* Retrieved November 23, 2020, from https://www.mirror.co.uk/science/children-raised-cities-more-likely-12467722

Bierman, A., Phelan, J. C., & Aneshensel, C. S., (Eds) (1999). *Handbook of the Sociology of Mental Health.* Springer.

Birla, N. (2019, October 10). Mental health in India: 7.5% of the country affected; less than 4,000 experts available. *The Economic Times.* https://economictimes.indiatimes.com/magazines/panache/mental-health-in-india-7-5-of-country-affected-less-than-4000-experts-available/articleshow/71500130.cms

Bisht, D. B. (1985). *The Spiritual Dimension of Health.* New Delhi: Directorate General of Health Services.

Bizumic, B., Katherine, J., Reynolds, K., Turner, J., Bromhead, D., & Subasic, E. (2009). The role of the group in individual functioning:School identification and the psychological well-being of staff and students. *Applied Psychology. An International Review, 58*(1), 171–192. https://doi.org/10.1111/j.1464-0597.2008.00387.x

Bloom, B. L. (1965). The medical model, miasma theory, and community mental health. *Community Mental Health Journal, 1*(4), 333–338. https://doi.org/10.1007/BF01434389

Böckler, A., Herrmann, L., Trautwein, F., & Singer, T. (2021). Know Thy Selves: Learning to Understand Oneself Increases the Ability to Understand Others. *Journal of Cognitive Enhancement, 1,* 197-209. https://doi.org/10.1007/s41465-017-0023-6

Bordages, J. W. (1985). Self-Actualization and Personal Autonomy. *Psychological Reports, 64*(3), 1263-1266. https://doi.org/10.2466/pr0.1989.64.3c.1263

Boulton, M. (2005). School peer counselling for bullying services as a source of social support: a study with secondary school pupils. *British Journal of Guidance & Counselling, 33*(4), 485-494. https://doi.org/10.1080/03069880500327546

Bouteyre, E., Maurel, M., & Bernaud, J. (2007). Daily hassles and depressive symptoms among first-year psychology students in France: The role of coping and social support. *Wiley InterScience, 23*(2), 93-97. https://doi.org/10.1002/smi.1125

Bowlby, J. (1969). *Attachment and loss:* Vol. 1. Attachment. Hogarth Press.

Bowlby, J. (1973). *Attachment and loss:* Vol. 2. Separation: Anxiety and Anger, Attachment and loss: Vol. 2. Separation: Anxiety and anger. London: Hogarth Press.

Bowlby, J. (1980). *Attachment and loss:* Vol. 3. Loss. New York: Basic Books.

Brännlund, A., Strandh, M. & Nilsson, K. (2017). Mental-health and educational achievement: the link between poor mental-health and upper secondary school completion and grades. *Journal of Mental Health.* 26(4), 318-325. https://doi.org/10.1080/09638237.2017.1294739

Briggs, M. K., Akos, P., Czyszczon, G., & Eldridge, A. (2011). Assessing and promoting spiritual wellness as a protective factor in secondary schools. *Counseling and Values, 55*(2), 171-184. https://doi.org/10.1002/j.2161-007X.2011.tb00030.x

Brummett, B. H., Mark, D. B., Siegler, I. C., Williams, R. B., Babyak, M. A., Clapp-Channing, N. E., & Barefoot, J. C. (2005). Perceived social support as a predictor of mortality in coronary patients: effects of smoking, sedentary behaviour, and depressive symptoms. *Psychosomatic medicine, 67*(1), 40–45. https://doi.org/10.1097/01.psy.0000149257.74854.b7

Bufford, R.K., Paloutzian, R.F., & Ellison, C.W. (1991). Norms for the Spiritual Well-Being Scale. *Journal of Psychology and Theology,* 19 (1), 56-70. https://doi.org/10.1177/009164719101900106

Bühler, C. (1971). Basic theoretical concepts of humanistic psychology. *American Psychologist,* 26, 378–386. https://doi.org/10.1037/h0032049.

Burke, S., Kerr, R., & McKeon, P. (2008). Male secondary school student's attitudes towards using mental health services. *Irish Journal of Psychological Medicine*, 25(2), 52-56. https://doi.org/10.1017/S0790966700010946

Burkhardt, M. A., & Nagai-Jacobson, M. G. (2002). *Spirituality: Living our connectedness*. Delmar Thompson Learning.

Burt, M. R., Resnick, G., & Novick, E. R. (1998). *Building supportive communities for at risk adolescents: It takes more than services*. American Psychological Association. https://doi.org/10.1037/10255-000

Byrne, D. G., Davenport, S. C., & Mazanov, J. (2007). Profiles of adolescent stress: the development of the adolescent stress questionnaire (ASQ). *Journal of adolescence*, 30(3), 393–416. https://doi.org/10.1016/j.adolescence.2006.04.004

Camara, M., Bacigalupe, G., & Padilla, P. (2017). The role of social support in adolescents: Are you helping me or stressing me out? *International Journal of Adolescence and Youth*, 22(2), 123–136. https://doi.org/10.1080/02673843.2013.875480

Cameron, W. B. & McCormick, T. C. (1954). Concepts of Security and Insecurity. *American Journal of Sociology*, 59(6), 556-564. https://doi.org/10.1086/221442

Canty-Mitchell, J., & Zimet, G. D. (2000). Psychometric properties of the Multidimensional Scale of Perceived Social Support in urban adolescents. *American journal of community psychology*, 28(3), 391–400. https://doi.org/10.1023/A:1005109522457

CBSE & NPSC (2019). *Transformation and engagement Practicorner's perspective*. (Wattal, A.M. Ed.) New Delhi: CBSE Publication. http://cbseacademic.nic.in/ web_material/Manuals/Transformation_Engament.pdf

CBSE (2008). *Counselling in Schools, Circular no. 08 of 2008*. Circular no. 08. www.cbse.nic.in/welcome/htm

Census, I. (2011). *Census of India 2011*. New Delhi: Government of India. http://www.censusindia.gov.in/2011provlts/data_files/india/Rural_Urban_2011.pdf.

Centre for Mental Health. (2019, January 3). How mental health can be affected at various stages of development. *Centre for Mental Health*, p.3. Retrieved from https://www.centreformentalhealth.org.uk/how-mental-health-can-be-affected-various-stages-development

Charlier, P., Coppens, Y., Malaurie, J., Brun, L., Kepanga, M., Hoang-Opermann, V., Correa Calfin, J. A., Nuku, G., Ushiga, M., Schor,

X. E., Deo, S., Hassin, J., & Hervé, C. (2017). A new definition of health? An open letter of autochthonous peoples and medical anthropologists to the WHO. *European journal of internal medicine, 37*, 33–37. https://doi.org/10.1016/j.ejim.2016.06.027

Cheng, Y., Li, X., Lou, C., Sonenstein, F. L., Kalamar, A., Jejeebhoy, S., Delany-Moretlwe, S., Brahmbhatt, H., Olumide, A. O., & Ojengbede, O. (2014). The association between social support and mental health among vulnerable adolescents in five cities: findings from the study of the well-being of adolescents in vulnerable environments. *The Journal of adolescent health : official publication of the Society for Adolescent Medicine, 55*(6 Suppl), S31–S38. https://doi.org/10.1016/j.jadohealth.2014.08.020

Clair-Thompson, H. (2014). Mental toughness in secondary schools. In Strycharczyk, D., & Clough, P. (Eds.), *Developing mental toughness in young people: Approaches to achievement, well-being, employability, and positive behaviour; severe, developing mental toughness in Young people: Approaches to achievement, well-being, employability, and positive behaviour* (pp. 149-156). Karnac Books.

Cobb S. (1976). Presidential Address-1976. Social support as a moderator of life stress. *Psychosomatic medicine, 38*(5), 300–314. https://doi.org/10.1097/00006842-197609000-00003

Cohen, S. (1988). Psychosocial models of the role of social support in the aetiology of physical disease. *Health Psychology, 7*(3), 269-297. https://doi.org/10.1037/0278-6133.7.3.269

Cohen, S. (2008). Social Support. In Rick E. Ingram (Eds.), *The International Encyclopedia of Depression* (pp. 514-517). Springer Publishing Company.

Cohen, S., & Hoberman, H. M. (1983). Positive events and social supports as buffers of life change stress. *Journal of Applied Social Psychology, 13*(2), 99–125. https://doi.org/10.1111/j.1559-1816.1983.tb02325.x

Cohen, S., & Wills, T. A. (1985). Stress, social support, and the buffering hypothesis. *Psychological Bulletin, 98*(2), 310–357. https://doi.org/10.1037/0033-2909.98.2.310

Cokrin, R. (1997). *Social Basics of Mental Diseases*. Roshd publication.

Cole, D. (1991). Preliminary support for a competency-based model of depression in children. *Journal of Abnormal Psychology, 100*(2), 181-190. https://doi.org/10.1037/0021-843X.100.2.181

Cooper. C. L., & Marshall, J. (1976). Occupational sources of stress: a review of the literature relating to coronary heart disease and mental ill-health. *Journal of Occupational Psychology*, 49, 11-28. https://doi.org/10.1057/9781137310651_1

Cornah, D. (2006). *The Impact of Spirituality on Mental Health: A Review of the Literature*. London: The Mental Health Foundation.

Costello, J. P. (2001). *Social supports for children and families: A matter of connections*. Chicago: Chapin Hall Centre for Children at the University of Chicago (Draft manuscript).

Cotton, S., Larkin, E., Hoopes, A., Cromer, B. A., & Rosenthal, S. L. (2005). The impact of adolescent spirituality on depressive symptoms and health risk behaviors. *The Journal of adolescent health: official publication of the Society for Adolescent Medicine*, 36(6), 529. https://doi.org/10.1016/j.jadohealth.2004.07.017

Cotton, S., Zebracki, K., Rosenthal, S. L., Tsevat, J., & Drotar, D. (2006). Religion/spirituality and adolescent health outcomes: a review. *The Journal of adolescent health : official publication of the Society for Adolescent Medicine*, 38(4), 472–480. https://doi.org/10.1016/j.jadohealth.2005.10.005

Crisp, J. T. (2005). *Potter and Perry's fundamental of nursing*. 1st ed. Philadelphia: St Louis.

Crowe, S., Cresswell, K., Robertson, A., Huby, G., Avery, A., & Sheikh, A. (2011). The Case Study Approach. *BMC Medical Research Methodology*, 11(1), 1-9. https://doi.org/http://dx.doi.org/10.1186/1471-2288-11-100

Cutrona, C. E., Hessling, R. M., & Suhr, J. A. (2005). The influence of husband and wife personality on marital, social support interactions. *Personal Relationships*, 4(4), 379-393. https://doi.org/10.1111/j.1475-6811.1997.tb00152.x

Danielsen, A. G., Samdal, O., Hetland, J., & Wold, B. (2009). School-related social support and students' perceived life satisfaction. *The Journal of Educational Research*, 102(4), 303–318. https://doi.org/10.3200/JOER.102.4.303-320

Darvyri, P., Galanakis, M., Avgoustidis, A.G., Vasdekis, A.A., Artemiadis, A.K., Tigani, X., Chrousos, G.P., & Darviri, C. (2014). *The Spiritual Well-Being Scale (SWBS) in Greek Population of Attica. Scientific Research*, 5(13), 1575-1582. https://doi.org/10.4236/psych.2014.513168

De Souza, M. (2009) Spirituality and well-being, *International Journal of Children's Spirituality*, 14(3), 181-184, https://doi.org/10.1080/13644360903086430

Deb, S., McGirr, K., & Sun, J., (2016). Spirituality in Indian University Students and its Associations with Socioeconomic Status, Religious Background, Social Support and Mental Health. *Journal of religion and health*, 55(5), 1623–1641. https://doi.org/10.1007/s10943-016-0207-x

Demir, M., & Leyendecker, B. (2018). School-Related Social Support Is Associated with School Engagement, Self-Competence and Health-Related Quality of Life (HRQoL) in Turkish Immigrant Students. *Frontiers in Education*. 3, 83. https://doi.org/10.3389/feduc.2018.00083

Deniz, L. (2010). Excessive Internet Use and Loneliness Among Secondary School Students. *Journal of Instructional Psychology*, 37(1), 20-23.

Desjarlais, R. (1995). *World mental health: problems and priorities in low-income countries*. Oxford University Press.

Dhar, A. (2011, February 26). Many challenges remain for India's youthful population. *The Hindu*. https://www.thehindu.com/news/national/lsquoMany-challenges-remain-for-Indias-youthful-populationrsquo/article15458506.ece

Dhar, N., Chaturvedi, S. K., & Nandan, D. (2013). Spiritual health, the fourth dimension: a public health perspective. *WHO South-East Asia journal of public health*, 2(1), 3–5. https://doi.org/10.4103/2224-3151.115826

Dhar, N., Chaturvedi, S.K., & Nandan, D. (2011). Spiritual health scale 2011: defining and measuring four dimensions of health. *Indian journal of community medicine: official publication of Indian Association of Preventive & Social Medicine*, 36(4), 275–282. https://doi.org/10.4103/0970-0218.91329

Dhuria, M. S. N., Taneja, D. K., Kumar, R. & Ingle, G.K. (2009). Assessment of mental health status of senior secondary school children in Delhi. *Asia-Pacific Journal of Public Health*, 21(1), 19-25. https://doi.org/10.1177/1010539508327031

Diener, E., & Fujita, F. (1995). Resources, personal strivings, and subjective well-being: A nomothetic and idiographic approach. *Journal of Personality and Social Psychology*, 68(5), 926–935. https://doi.org/10.1037/0022-3514.68.5.926

Dogra, N. O. (2012). Nigerian secondary school children's knowledge of and attitudes to mental health and illness. *Clinical Child Psychology and Psychiatry*, 17(3), 336-353. https://doi.org/10.1097/YCO.0b013e3283543976

Donald, M. D. (2000). *The Queensland young peoples' mental health survey report.* The University of Queensland. Brisbane, Australia: Centre for Primary Health Care, School of Populations Health and Department of Psychiatry.

Dossey, L. (1999). Do religion and spirituality matter in health? A response to the recent article in the Lancet. *Alternative Therapies*, 5(3), 16–18.

Dowdy, E., Furlong, M., Raines, T. C., Bovery, B., Kauffman, B., Kamphaus, R. W. & Murdock, J. (2015). Enhancing School-Based Mental Health Services With a Preventive and Promotive Approach to Universal Screening for Complete Mental Health. *Journal of Educational & Psychological Consultation*, 25(2/3), 178-197. https://doi.org/10.1080/1047441 2.2014.929951

Duffy, R.M., & Kelly, B.D. (2017). Rights, laws and tensions: A comparative analysis of the Convention on the Rights of Persons with Disabilities and the WHO Resource Book on Mental Health, Human Rights and Legislation. *Int J Law Psychiatry*, 54, 26-35. https://doi.org/10.1016/j.ijlp.2017.07.003

Dumbili, E. W. (2015). A review of substance use among secondary school students in Nigeria: Implications for policies. *Drugs Education, Prevention & Policy.* 22(5), 387- 399. https://doi.org/10.3109/09687637.2015.1041455

Durkheim, E. (1915). *The Elementary Forms of the Religious Life: A Study in Religious Sociology.* Allen & Unwin.

Eckersley, R. (2007). Culture, spirituality, religion and health: looking at the big picture. *Medical Journal of Australia*, 186(10), 54. https://doi.org/10.5694/j.1326-5377.2007.tb01042.x

Eisenhardt, K. M. (1989). Building theories from case study research. *The Academy of Management Review*, 14(4), 532-550. https://doi.org/10.2307/258557

Ek⊠i, H., & Karda⊠, S. (2017). Spiritual Well-Being: Scale Development and Validation. *Spiritual Psychology and Counseling*, 2(1),73-88. https://doi.org/10.12738/spc.2017.1.0022

Ellen, M. (2015). Schools need mental health education. *Therapy Today*, 26(9), 5.

Elliott, A. (1999). *Contemporary Social Theory*. Oxford: Blackwell.

Ellison, C, D., & Levin, J. S. (1991). The religion-health connection: Evidence, theory, and future directions. *Health Education and Behaviour*, 25(6), 700-720. https://doi.org/10.1177/109019819802500603

Ellison, C. W. (1983). Spiritual well-being: Conceptualization and measurement. *Journal of Psychology & Theology*, 11(4), 330-340. https://doi.org/10.1177/009164718301100406

Ellison, C. W., & Smith, J. (1991). Toward an integrative measure of health and well-being. *Journal of Psychology and Theology*, 19(1), 35–48. https://doi.org/10.1177/009164719101900104

Erikson, E. (1963). *Childhood and Society* (2nd ed.). W.W. Norton.

Erikson, E. (1994). *Identity and the Life Cycle*. W. W. Norton.

Esfahani, M. (2010). Spiritual health and comments. *Q J Med Ethics*, 14, 41-49.

Fahmy, D. (n.d.). *Christian women in the U.S. Are more religious than their male counterparts*. Pew Research Center. Retrieved November 24, 2020, from https://www.pewresearch.org/fact-tank/2018/04/06/christian-women-in-the-u-s-are-more-religious-than-their-male-counterparts/#:~:text=More%20than%20seven-in-ten%20U.S.%20Christian%20women%20%2872%25%29%20say,Pew%20Research%20Center%E2%80%99s%202014%20U.S.%20Religious%20Landscape%20Study.

Fairbrother, N. (2011). Social support. *Visions Journal*, 6 (4), 7. https://www.heretohelp.bc.ca/visions/social-support-vol6/social-support

Fehring, R. J., Miller, J. F., & Shaw, C. (1997). Spiritual well-being, religiosity, hope, depression, and other mood states in elderly people coping with cancer. *Oncology nursing forum*, 24(4), 663–671.

Fisher, J. (1998). *Spiritual health: Its nature and place in the school curriculum PhD thesis*. The University of Melbourne. Melbourne, Australia: Melbourne University Custom Book Centre.

Fisher, J. (2011). The four domains model: Connecting spirituality, health and well-being. *Religions*, 2, 17-28. https://doi.org/10.3390/rel2010017

Folkman, S., & Moskowitz, J.T. (2004). Coping: pitfalls and promise. *Annual Review of Psychology*, 67, 745-621. https://doi.org/10.1146/annurev.psych.55.090902.141456

Ford, T., Parker, C., Salim, J., Goodman, R., Logan, S., & Henley, W. (2018). The relationship between exclusion from school and mental health: A secondary analysis of the British Child and Adolescent Mental Health Surveys 2004 and 2007. *Psychological Medicine*, 48(4), 629-641. https://doi.org/10.1017/S003329171700215X

Frankl, V. E. (1962). *Man's search for meaning: An introduction to logotherapy.* Beacon Press.

Frenk, J. S. D. (1997). The Future of World Health: The New World Order and International Health. *British Medical Journal*, 314, 1404-1407. https://doi.org/10.1136/bmj.314.7091.1404

Freud, S. (1900). The interpretation of dreams. *Standard Edition*, 4(5), 1-627. https://psychclassics.yorku.ca/Freud/Dreams/dreams.pdf

Freud, S. (1928). *Totem and taboo: Resemblances between the psychic lives of savages and neurotics.* Dodd.

Freud, S. (1930). *Civilization and its discontents (Ed. and Trans.).* W. W. Norton.

Friedenberg, J. (2006). *Cognitive science, an introduction to the study of the mind.* Sage Publications.

Frydenberg, E. (1997). *Adolescent Coping: Theoretical and Research Perspectives.* Routledge.

Gallup, G. J. (1980). *Religion in America.* New Jersey: Princeton Religion Research Center.

Garcia-Moya, I., Rivera, F., & Moreno, C. (2013). School context and health in adolescence: The role of sense of coherence. *Scandinavian Journal of Psychology*, 54(3), 243–249. https://doi.org/10.1111/sjop.12041

Gartland, D. (2009). *Resilience in adolescents: The development and preliminary psychometric testing of a new measure (Unpublished doctoral thesis).* Swinburne: University of Technology, Melbourne, Australia.

Gecas, V. (1982). The self-concept. *Annual Review of Sociology*, 1, 1-33. https://doi.org/10.1146/ANNUREV.SO.08.080182.000245

Genia, V. (2001). Evaluation of spiritual well-being scale in a sample of college students. *International Journal for the Psychology of Religion*, 11(1), 25-33. https://doi.org/10.1207/S15327582IJPR1101_03

Gilot, L.B. (2000). Psychological and Spiritual Roots of Transpersonal Psychology in Europe. *International Journal of Transpersonal Studies*, 19(1), 133-140. https://doi.org/10.24972/ijts.2000.19.1.133

Gnanaprakash, C. (2013). Spirituality and resilience among postgraduate university students. *Journal of Health Management*, 15(3), 383-396. https://doi.org/10.1177/0972063413492046

Goldbeck, L., Schmitz, T.G., Besier, T., Herschbach, P., & Henrich, G. (2007). Life satisfaction decreases during adolescence. *Quality of Life Research*, 16(6), 969-979. https://doi.org/10.1007/s11136-007-9205-5

Goleman, D. (1996). *Emotional intelligence: why it can matter more than I.Q.* Bantam Books.

Good, M. (2008). Adolescence is a sensitive period for spiritual development. *Child Development Perspectives*, 2, 32-37. https://doi.org/10.1111/j.1750-8606.2008.00038.x

Goodloe, R., & Arreola, P. (1992). Spiritual health: out of the closet. *Health Education*, 23(4), 221-226. https://doi.org/10.1080/10556699.1992.10616295

Gopal, B. R., & Ritti, S. (2004). *Inscriptions of the Rulers of the Sangama Dynasty* (1336 A.D.- 1485 A.D). Indian Council of Historical Research and Northern Book Centre.

Gore, F. M., Bloem, P. J., Patton, G. C., Ferguson, J., Joseph, V., Coffey, C., Sawyer, S. M., & Mathers, C. D. (2011). Global burden of disease in young people aged 10-24 years: a systematic analysis. *Lancet (London, England)*, *377*(9783), 2093–2102. https://doi.org/10.1016/S0140-6736(11)60512-6

Gorsuch, R. L., & Miller, W. R. (1999). Assessing spirituality. In W. R. Miller (Ed.), *Integrating spirituality into treatment: Resources for practitioners* (pp. 47–64). American Psychological Association. https://doi.org/10.1037/10327-003

Gosain (n.d.). *A Healthy Mind in a Healthy Body: Ways to Prove it True.* Madeeasy.in. Retrieved August 25, 2020, from https://blog.madeeasy.in/healthy-mind-healthy-body-ways-prove-it-true.

Grof, S. (1988). *The Adventure of Self-Discovery. Dimensions of Consciousness and New Perspectives in Psychotherapy.* SUNY Press, Albany.

Grof, S. (1993). *The holotropic mind.* Harper San Francisco.

Guarino, A. J., Gamst, G. C., Meyers, L. S. (2006). Applied Multivariate Research: Design and Interpretation. SAGE Publications.

Guerra, L. A., Rajan, S., & Roberts, K. (2019). The Implementation of Mental Health Policies and Practices in Schools: An Examination of School and State Factors. *Journal of School Health*, 89(4), 328-338. https://doi.org/10.1111/josh.12738

Haber, M. G., Cohen, J. L., Lucas, T., & Baltes, B. B. (2007). The relationship between self-reported received and perceived social support: a meta-analytic review. *American journal of community psychology*, 39(1-2), 133–144. https://doi.org/10.1007/s10464-007-9100-9

Hamburg, B. A., & Varenhorst, B. B. (1972). Peer counseling in the secondary schools: a community mental health project for youth. *The American journal of orthopsychiatry*, 42(4), 566–581. https://doi.org/10.1111/j.1939-0025.1972.tb02523.x

Hankin, B. L. (2007). Sex differences in adolescent depression Stress exposure and reactivity models. *Child Development*, 78, 279-295.

Haranin, E.C., Huebner, E.S., & Suldo, S.M. (2007). Predictive and Incremental Validity of Global and Domain-Based Adolescent Life Satisfaction Reports. *Journal of Psychoeducational Assessment*, 25, 127 - 138. https://doi.org/10.1177/0734282906295620

Harnois, G., Gabriel, P., World Health Organization & International Labour Organisation. (2000). *Mental health and work: impact, issues and good practices.* World Health Organization. https://apps.who.int/iris/handle/10665/42346

Harris Friedma, H. & MacDonald, D. A. (2003). Editors' Introduction. *The International Journal of Transpersonal Studies.* 22(1).

Hateley, B. (1983). *Spiritual well-being through life-histories. A paper presented at the November Conference.* San Francisco, CA: Scientific Meeting of the Gerontological Society. http://dx.doi.org/10.1300/J491v01n02_06

Hawks, S. R., Hull, M. L., Thalman, R. L., & Richins, P. M. (1995). Review of spiritual health: definition, role, and intervention strategies in health promotion. *American journal of health promotion: AJHP*, 9(5), 371–378. https://doi.org/10.4278/0890-1171-9.5.371

Hay, D., Reich, K.H., & Utsch, M. (2006). Spiritual Development: Intersections and Divergence with Religious Development. *The Handbook of Spiritual Development in Childhood and Adolescence*, 46-59. https://doi.org/10.4135/9781412976657.N4

Hays, R. B., & Oxley, D. (1986). Social network development and functioning during a life transition. *Journal of Personality and*

Social Psychology, 50(2), 305–313. https://doi.org/10.1037/0022-3514.50.2.305

Heller, K. (1983). Social networks perceived social support and coping with stress in L. A. In R. D. Felner, *Preventive psychology: Theory, Research, and practice in community intervention.* Pergamon Press.

Hendren, R. W. (1994). *Mental health programmes in schools.* Geneva: World Health Organization.

Hess, E. D. & Ludwig, K. (2017). *Humility is the New Smart.* Berrett-Koehler Publishers.

Hettler, B. (1980). Wellness promotion on a university campus. *Family & community health,* 3(1), 77–95. https://doi.org/10.1097/00003727-198005000-00008

Hodges, S. (2002). Mental health, depression, and dimensions of spirituality and religion. *Journal of Adult Development,* 9(2), 109-115. http://dx.doi.org/10.1023/A:1015733329006

Holen, S., Waaktaar, T., & Sagatun, Å. (2018). A Chance Lost in the Prevention of School Dropout? Teacher-Student Relationships Mediate the Effect of Mental Health Problems on Noncompletion of Upper-Secondary School. *Scandinavian Journal of Educational Research,* 62(5), 737-753. https://doi.org/10.1080/00313831.2017.1306801

Hosman, C. & Jane-Llopis, E. (1999). Political challenges 2: Mental health. *In The Evidence of Health Promotion Effectiveness: Shaping Public Health in a New Europe,* (Chapter 3, 29-41). International Union for Health Promotion and Education, IUHPE, Paris: Jouve Composition & Impression.

Hsiao, Y. C., Chiang, H. Y., & Chien, L. Y. (2010). An exploration of the status of spiritual health among nursing students in Taiwan. *Nurse education today,* 30(5), 386–392. https://doi.org/10.1016/j.nedt.2009.05.001

Hurlock, E. (1972). *Child Development.* McGraw-Hill.

Hussong, A. (2000). Perceived peer context and adolescent adjustment. *Journal of Research on Adolescence,* 10, 391-415. https://doi.org/10.1207/SJRA1004_02

Iachini, A. L., Pitner, R. O., Morgan, F., & Rhodes, K. (2016). Exploring the principal perspective: implications for expanded school improvement and school mental health. *Children & Schools,* 38(1), 40-48. https://doi.org/10.1093/cs/cdv038

Ibrahim, N., Che Din, N., Ahmad, M., Amit, N., Ghazali, S.E., Wahab, S., Abdul Kadir, N.B., Halim, F.W., & A. Halim, M.R. (2019). The role of social support and spiritual wellbeing in predicting suicidal ideation among marginalized adolescents in Malaysia. *BMC Public Health,* 19, 553. https://doi.org/10.1186/s12889-019-6861-7

Israel, B. A., & Schurman, S. J. (1990). Social support, control, and the stress process. In K. Glanz, F. M. Lewis, & B. K. Rimer (Eds.), *Health behavior and health education: Theory, research, and practice* (pp. 187–215). Jossey-Bass/Wiley.

Ivtzan, I., Chan, C. P., Gardner, H. E., & Prashar, K. (2013). Linking religion and spirituality with psychological well-being: examining self-actualisation, meaning in life, and personal growth initiative. *Journal of religion and health,* 52(3), 915–929. https://doi.org/10.1007/s10943-011-9540-2

J., Adegoke, A., McCoy, J., & Brewer, T. (2011). Religious commitment, social support and life satisfaction among college students. *College Student Journal,* 45(2), 393.

Jacob, J. (2019, October). The Kerala Model School. *India Today.* Retrieved from https://www.indiatoday.in/india-today-insight/story/the-kerala-model-school-1606880-2019-10-07

Jafari, E., Dehshiri, G. R., Eskandari, H., Najafi, M., Heshmati, R., & Hoseinifar, J. (2010). Spiritual Well-Being and mental health in university students. *Procedia Social and Behavioral Sciences,* 5, 1477-1481. https://doi.org/10.1016/j.sbspro.2010.07.311

Jamali, S., Sabokdast, S., Sharif Nia, H., Goudarzian, A. H., Beik, S., & Allen, K. A. (2016). The Effect of Life Skills Training on Mental Health of Iranian Middle School Students: A Preliminary Study. *Iranian journal of psychiatry,* 11 (4), 269–272.

Jenkins, R. (2019). Global mental health and sustainable development 2018. *BJPsych International,* 16(2), 34-37. https://doi.org/10.1192/bji.2019.5

Jones, J. A. (2012). *The Vital Psoas Muscle: connecting physical, emotional and spiritual well-being.* North Atlantic Books.

Joseph, C. M. U. (2015). A study on the mental health of high school students. *Indian Journal of research,* 4(10), 63-64.

Joshi, S. (2017, October 8). We must educate young people about mental health like we do about sex, says Deepika Padukone. *The Times of India.* https://timesofindia.indiatimes.com/

home/sunday-times/all-that-matters/we-must-educate-young-people-about-mental-health-like-we-do-about-sex-says-deepika-padukone/articleshow/60988123.cms

Jung, C. G. (1969). The Archetypes and the Collective Unconscious. In C. G. Jung, Collected Works. Princeton University Press

Kahn, R. L. (1981). *Work and Health.* Wiley.

Kalashian, C. (2009). *Mental health services in secondary schools.* The Humanities and Social Sciences Collection. https://search.proquest.com/docview/305177388?accountid=50681

Kamya, H. A. (2000). Hardiness and spiritual well-being among social work students: Implications for social work education. *Journal of Social Work Education,* 36(2), 231-240. https://doi.org/10.1080/10437797.2000.10779004

Karen, R. (1998). *Becoming Attached: First Relationships and how They Shape Our Capacity to Love.* Oxford University Press.

Karstens, A. (2010). Towards an epistemological framework for a Life Orientation programme based on spirituality.

Keith, J. (1991). Age in social and cultural context: Anthropological perspectives. In I. R. (Eds.), *Handbook of ageing and the social sciences,* 3rd ed. (91-111). Academic Press.

Kelly B. D. (2016). Mental health, mental illness, and human rights in India and elsewhere: What are we aiming for?. *Indian journal of psychiatry, 58*(Suppl 2), S168–S174. https://doi.org/10.4103/0019-5545.196822

Kelly, B. (2011). Mental health legislation and human rights in England, Wales and the Republic of Ireland. *International Journal of Law and Psychiatry,* 34 (6), 439-54. https://doi.org/10.1016/j.ijlp.2011.10.009

Kelly, B.D. (2015). *Dignity, Mental Health and Human Rights: Coercion and the Law.* Abingdon. Routledge.

Kerala Mental Health Report: 11.36 per cent people in the state of unsound mind (2017, November 5). *The New Indian Express,* Kozhikode: The New Indian Express. https://www.newindianexpress.com/states/kerala/2017/nov/05/kerala-mental-health- report-1136-percent-people-in-the-state-of-unsound-mind-1692356.html

Kerala schools top CBSE Class XII. (2019). *The Times of India,* Kochi. Retrieved November Monday, 2019, from https://timesofindia.indiatimes.com/city/kochi/

98-2-kerala- schools-top-cbse-class-xii/articleshow/69155918.cms

Kessler, R. C., Berglund, P., Demler, O., Jin, R., Merikangas, K. R., & Walters, E. E. (2005). Lifetime prevalence and age-of-onset distributions of DSM-IV disorders in the National Comorbidity Survey Replication. *Archives of general psychiatry*, 62(6), 593– 602. https://doi.org/10.1001/archpsyc.62.6.593

Kimura, T., Sakuma, T., Isaka, H., Uchida, S., & Yamaoka, K. (2016). Depressive symptoms and spiritual well-being in Japanese university students. *International Journal of Culture and Mental Health*, 9(1), 14–30. https://doi.org/10.1080/17542863.2015.1074261

Kler, N. (2020, January 31). Mental health and budget 2020: Here's what is needed. *She the people.* https://www.shethepeople.tv/mental-health/mental- health- budget-2020-needed/

Kneipp, L. B., Kelly, K. E., & Cyphers, B. (2009). Feeling at peace with college: Religiosity, spiritual well-being, and college adjustment. *Individual Differences Research*, 7(3), 188-196.

Koller, J. R., & Bertel, J. M. (2006). Responding to Today's Mental Health Needs of Children, Familes and Schools: Revisiting the Preservice Training and Preparation of School-Based Personnel. *Education and Treatment of Children*, 29(2), 197–217. http://www.jstor.org/stable/42899882

Kort-Butler,L. A. (2017). Social Support Theory. *Wiley Online Library*, 1-4. htttps://doi.org/10.1002/9781118524275.ejdj0066

Kposowa A. J. (2001). Unemployment and suicide: a cohort analysis of social factors predicting suicide in the US National Longitudinal Mortality Study. *Psychological medicine*, 31(1), 127–138. https://doi.org/10.1017/s0033291799002925

Kramer, T. L., Blevins, D., Miller, T. L., Phillips, M. M., Davis, V., & Burris, B. (2007). Ministers' perceptions of depression: A model to understand and improve care. *Journal of Religion and Health*, 46, 123-139. https://doi.org/10.1007/s10943-006-9090-1

Krejcie, R.V., & Morgan, D.W. (1970). Determining sample size for research activities. *Educational and Psychological Measurement*, 30(3), 607-610. https://doi.org/10.1177/001316447003000308

Kutcher, S. & Wei, Y. (2012). Mental health and the school environment: Secondary schools, promotion and pathways to care. *Current Opinion in Psychiatry*, 25(4), 311. https://doi.org/10.1097/YCO.0b013e3283543976

Lakey, B. (2000). *Social support theory and selecting measures of social support.* Oxford.

Lakey, B., & Cohen, S. (2000). Social support theory and measurement. In S. Cohen, L. G. Underwood, & B. H. Gottlieb (Eds.), *Social support measurement and intervention: A guide for health and social scientists* (pp. 29–52). Oxford University Press. https://doi.org/10.1093/med:psych/9780195126709.003.0002

Lamers, S. M., Westerhof, G. J., Bohlmeijer, E. T., ten Klooster, P. M., & Keyes, C. L. (2011). Evaluating the psychometric properties of the Mental Health Continuum-Short Form (MHC-SF). *Journal of clinical psychology*, 67(1), 99–110. https://doi.org/10.1002/jclp.20741

Lazarus, R. S. (1984). *Lazarus, R. S. & Folkman, S.* Springer.

Lee, D. J. (2003). A study of quality of work-life, spiritual Well-being and life satisfaction. *Armonk, NY*, 209-230.

Lehner, G. (1962). *The Dynamics of Personal Adjustment.* Englewood Cliffs, N.J., Prentice-Hall.

Lendrum, A., Humphrey, N., & Wigelsworth, M. (2013). Social and emotional aspects of learning (SEAL) for secondary schools: implementation difficulties and their implications for school-based mental health promotion. *Child and adolescent mental health*, 18(3), 158–164. https://doi.org/10.1111/camh.12006

Lerner, R. M., & Steinberg, L. (2004). The scientific study of adolescent development: Past, present, and future. In R. M. Lerner & L. Steinberg (Eds.), *Handbook of adolescent psychology* (pp. 1–12). John Wiley & Sons, Inc.

Lester, L., Waters, S., & Cross, D. (2013). The Relationship Between School Connectedness and Mental Health During the Transition to Secondary School: A Path Analysis. *Australian Journal of Guidance and Counselling*, 23(2), 157-171. https://doi.org/10.1017/jgc.2013.20

Levav, I., Restrepo, H., & Guerra de Macedo, C. (1994). The restructuring of psychiatric care in Latin America: a new policy for mental health services. *Journal of public health policy*, 15(1), 71–85.

Lewis, S., Salins, N., Rao, M. R., & Kadam, A. (2014). Spiritual well-being and its influence on fatigue in patients undergoing active cancer directed treatment: a correlational study. *Journal of cancer research and therapeutics*, *10*(3), 676–680. https://doi.org/10.4103/0973-1482.138125

Li, Q., Guan, X., Wu, P., Wang, X., Zhou, L., Tong, Y., Ren, R., Leung, K. S. M., Lau, E. H. Y., Wong, J. Y., Xing, X., Xiang, N., Wu, Y., Li, C., Chen, Q., Li, D., Liu, T., Zhao, J., Liu, M., Tu, W., … Feng, Z. (2020). Early Transmission Dynamics in Wuhan, China, of Novel Coronavirus-Infected Pneumonia. *The New England journal of medicine*, *382*(13), 1199–1207. https://doi.org/10.1056/NEJMoa2001316

Livneh, H., Lott, S. M., & Antonak, R. F. (2004). Patterns of psychosocial adaptation to chronic illness and disability: A cluster analytic approach. *Psychology, Health & Medicine*, *9*(4), 411–430. https://doi.org/10.1080/1354850042000267030

Livni, E. (2018, May 30). *Individualized Transcendence, Columbia and Yale's scientists found the spiritual part of our brains—Religion not required*. Qz.com. https://qz.com/1292368/columbia-and-yale-scientists-just-found-the-spiritual-part-of-our-brains

Lurigio, A. J. (2011). People with serious mental illness in the criminal justice system: Causes, consequences, and correctives. *The Prison Journal*, *91*(3, Suppl), 66S–86S. https://doi.org/10.1177/0032885511415226

MacDonald, D. E. (2014). *Merge Group spiritual direction and faith maturity among emerging adults*, 1-159.

Macek, P. (2003). *Adolescence*. Praha: Portál.

Malecki, C. K. (2002). Measuring perceived social support: development of the child and adolescent social support scale (CASSS). *Psychology in the Schools*, *39*(1), 1-18. https://doi.org/10.1002/pits.10004.

Marin, P., & Brown, B. (2008). *The school environment and adolescent well-being: beyond academics*. Child Trends.

Mariu, K. R., Merry, S. N., Robinson, E. M., & Watson, P. D. (2012). Seeking professional help for mental health problems, among New Zealand secondary school students. *Clinical Child Psychology and Psychiatry*, *17*(2), 284-297. https://doi.org/10.1177/1359104511404176

Marmot, M, & Wilkinson, R. (2008). *Social determinants of health*. Translated by Ali Montazeri. Tehran: Iranian Institute for Health Sciences Research.

Marmot, M., & Wilkinson, R. (2008). *Social determinants of health.* Oxford Scholarship Online. https://doi.org/10.1093/acprof:oso/9780198565895.001.0001

Martsolf, D. S., & Mickley, J. R. (1998). The concept of spirituality in nursing theories: differing world-views and extent of focus. *Journal of advanced nursing, 27*(2), 294–303. https://doi.org/10.1046/j.1365-2648.1998.00519.x

Maslow, A. H. (1969). The farther reaches of human nature. *Journal of Transpersonal Psychology,* 1(1), 1-9.

Mathad, M.D., Rajesh, S.K., & Pradhan, B. (2019). Spiritual Well-Being and Its Relationship with Mindfulness, Self-Compassion and Satisfaction with Life in Baccalaureate Nursing Students: A Correlation Study. *Journal of Religion and Health, 58,* 554-565. https://doi.org/10.1007/s10943-017-0532-8

Maya, C. (2018, February 13). No.1, but State has a few hidden concerns. *The Hindu.* https://www.thehindu.com/news/national/kerala/no1-but-state-has-a-few-hidden-concerns/article22734487.ece

McCarroll, P. (2005). Assessing Plurality in Spirituality Definitions. In A. O. Meier & P. E. Van Katwyk (Ed.), *Spirituality and Health: Multidisciplinary Explorations* (pp. 43- 61). Wilfrid Laurier University Press.

McClain, C. S., Rosenfeld, B., & Breitbart, W. (2003). Effect of spiritual well-being on end-of-life despair in terminally-ill cancer patients. *Lancet (London, England), 361*(9369), 1603–1607. https://doi.org/10.1016/S0140-6736(03)13310-7

Mechanic, D. (2006). *Clinical Psychology: Science andPractice.* New Brunswick: Rutgen University. https://doi.org/10.1111/j.1468-2850.1997.tb00117.x

Merriam, S. B. (1988). *Case study research in education: A qualitative approach.* Jossey-Bass.

Mezulis, A. H., Funasaki, K. S., Charbonneau, A. M., & Hyde, J. S. (2010). Gender differences in the cognitive vulnerability-stress model of depression in the transition to adolescence. *Cognitive Therapy and Research, 34*(6), 501–513. https://doi.org/10.1007/s10608-009-9281-7

(2016, November 20). *Mental Depression High Among People of Kerala: Survey.* NDTV.com. https://www.ndtv.com/kerala-news/mental-depression-high-among-people-of-kerala-survey-1627899

Michael, J. Wallace. (1999). *Study Skills.* Cambridge University Press.
Moberg, D. O. (1971). *Spiritual well-being: Background and issues.* Washington, DC: White House Conference of Aging.
Moberg, D. O. (1979). The Development of Social Indicators for Quality of Life Research. *Sociological Analysis,* 40(1), 11–26. https://doi.org/10.2307/3710493
Moberg, D. O. (1990). *Spiritual well-being: Background and Issues.* Washington: White House Conference of Aging.
Moberg, D. O. (2002). Assessing and measuring spirituality: Confronting dilemmas of universal and particular evaluative criteria. Journal of Adult Development, 9(1), 47-60. https://doi.org/10.1023/A%3A1013877201375
Moberg, D. O. (2010). Spirituality research: Measuring the immeasurable? *Perspectives on Science and Christian Faith,* 62(2), 99-114.
Moberg, D. O., & Brusek, P. M. (1978). Spiritual well-being: A neglected subject in quality of life research. *Social Indicators Research,* 5, 303-323. https://doi.org/10.1007/BF00352936
Moksnes, U. K., Moljord, I. E. O., Espnes, G. A., & Byrne, D. G. (2010). The association between stress and emotional states in adolescents: The role of gender and self-esteem. *Personality and Individual Differences,* 49(5), 430–435. https://doi.org/10.1016/j.paid.2010.04.012
Monshouwer, K., Van Dorsselaer, S., Verdurmen, J., Bogt, T. T., De Graaf, R., Vollebergh, W., & Bogt, T. T. (2006). Cannabis use andmental health in secondary school children. Findings from a Dutch survey. *British Journal of Psychiatry,* 188, 148-153. https://doi.org/10.1192/bjp.188.2.148
Mũkoma, W., & Flisher, A. J. (2004). Evaluations of health-promoting schools: a review of nine studies. *Health promotion international,* 19(3), 357-368. https://doi.org/10.1093/heapro/dah309
Muldoon, M., & King, N. (1995). Spirituality, health care, and bioethics. *Journal of Religion & Health,* 34(4), 329–349. https://doi.org/10.1007/BF02248742
Muñoz-García, A., & Aviles-Herrera, M.J. (2014). Effects of academic dishonesty on dimensions of spiritual well-being and satisfaction: a comparative study of secondary school and university students. *Assessment & Evaluation in Higher Education,* 39, 349 - 363. https://doi.org/10.1080/02602938.2013.832729

Murphy, A. (2018, April 18). *What is the Meaning of Lokah Samastah Sukhino Bhavantu?* Gaia.com. https://www.gaia.com/article/what-is-the-meaning-of-lokah-samastah-sukhino-bhavantu

Musa, A. (2015). Spiritual beliefs and practices, religiosity, and spiritual well-being among Jordanian Arab Muslim university students in Jordan. *Journal of Spirituality in Mental Health,* 17, 34-49. https://doi.org/10.1080/19349637.2014.957609

Mutran, E. (1985). Intergenerational family support among blacks and whites: Response to culture or socioeconomic differences. *Journal of Gerontology, 40*(3), 382–389. https://doi.org/10.1093/geronj/40.3.382

Myer, L., Stein, D. J., Jackson, P. B., Herman, A. A., Seedat, S., & Williams, D. R. (2009). Impact of common mental disorders during childhood and adolescence on secondary school completion. *South African medical journal = Suid-Afrikaanse tydskrif vir geneeskunde, 99*(5 Pt 2), 354–356.

Nair, M. (2005). Family Life & Life Skills Education for Adolescents: Trivandrum Experience. *Journal of Indian Association for Child and Adolescent Mental Health,* 1(2), 278-284.

Nancy, R. P. (2011). *Spiritual Well-Being and Mental Health: A Study of Adolescents in colleges.* Tiruchirappalli: University of Bharathidasan.

Narayan, C. (2013). Indian legal system and mental health. *Indian J Psychiatry,* 55(2), 177- 181. https://doi.org/10.4103/0019-5545.105521

Nash, M. M. (2005). *Social work theories in action.* Jessica Kingsley.

National Interfaith Coalition on Aging. (1975). *Spiritual well-being: A definition.* Athens, GA, USA, NICA.

Neale, P., Thapa, S., & Boyce, C. (2006). *Preparing a case study: A guide for designing and conducting a case study for evaluation input.* Pathfinder International.

Ng, Josephine, W. Y & Tsang, Sandra K. M. (2008). School Bullying and the Mental Health of Junior Secondary School Students in Hong Kong. *Journal of School Violence,* 7(2), 3-20. https://doi.org/10.1300/J202v07n02_02

Nima, S. (2012). Influence of religion, religiosity and spirituality on the positive mental health of young people. *Mental Health, Religion & Culture,* 16, 435-443. https://doi.org/10.1080/13674676.2012.697879

NIMHANS (2016). *National Mental Health Survey of India*, 2015-16: Summary. Bangalore: National Institute of Mental Health and Neuro Sciences.

Ninaniya, P., Santosh, S., & Reena (2017). Attitude towards modernization of senior secondary school students. *Indian Journal of Health and Wellbeing*, 8(7), 716-719.

Nolan, P., & Crawford, P. (1997). Towards a rhetoric of spirituality in mental health care. *Journal of advanced nursing, 26*(2), 289–294. https://doi.org/10.1046/j.1365-2648.1997.1997026289.x

Odenbring, Y. (2017). Mental health, drug use and adolescence: Meeting the needs of vulnerable students in secondary school. *The Urban Review, 50*(3), 363-377. https://doi.org/10.1007/s11256-017-0437-6

Ojio, Y., Yonehara, H., Taneichi, S., Yamasaki, S., Ando, S., Togo, F., Nishida, A., & Sasaki, T. (2015). Effects of school-based mental health literacy education for secondary school students to be delivered by school teachers: A preliminary study. *Psychiatry and clinical neurosciences, 69*(9), 572–579. https://doi.org/10.1111/pcn.12320

Okasha A. (2003). The Presidential WPA Program on Child Mental Health. *World psychiatry: official journal of the World Psychiatric Association (WPA), 2*(3), 129–130.

Ola, B. A., & Morakinyo, O. (2008). Mental health and attitude towards education of secondary school students in Nigeria. *IFE Psychologia: An International Journal*, 16(2), 169-177. https://doi.org/10.4314/ifep.v16i2.23809

Oldnall A. (1996). A critical analysis of nursing: meeting the spiritual needs of patients. *Journal of advanced nursing, 23*(1), 138–144. https://doi.org/10.1111/j.1365-2648.1996.tb03145.x

Oman, D., Duggal, C., & Misra, G. (2018). Introduction to the Special Issue: Spirituality and Psychology, Emerging Perspectives. *Psychol Stud.* 63, 89–93. https://doi.org/10.1007/s12646-018-0458-6

Omar, I. A., & Mu'taz, F. A. (2018). Spiritual well-being perceived social support, and life satisfaction among university students, *International Journal of Adolescence and Youth*, 23(3), 291-298. https://doi.org/10.1080/02673843.2017.1352522

Osman, J. D., & Russell, R. D. (1979). The spiritual aspects of health. *Journal of School Health.* 49(6), 359. https://doi.org/10.1111/j.1746-1561.1979.tb07733.x

Pahlevanzadeh, F., Jarelahi O. (2011). Investigating the effect of social factors on the mental health of rural elders. *Journal of Rural development.* 3(1), 65–84.

Paloutzian, R. F. & Ellison, C. (1982). *The spiritual well-being scale.* Nyack.

Paloutzian, R. F. (1996). *Invitation to the psychology of religion.* Needtham Heights: M.A. and Allyn and Bacon.

Paloutzian, R. F., & Ellison, C.W. (1982). *Loneliness, spiritual well-being, and quality of life.* In L. A. Peplau & D. Perlman (Eds.), Loneliness: A sourcebook of current theory, research and therapy. Wiley.

Paloutzian, R. F., Bufford, R. K., & Wildman, A. J. (2012). Spiritual Well-Being Scale: Mental and physical health relationships. In M. Cobb, C. M. Puchalski, & B. Rumbold (Eds.), *Oxford textbook of spirituality in healthcare* (pp. 353–358). Oxford University Press. https://doi.org/10.1093/med/9780199571390.003.0048

Pandey, B. (1998). A psychological study on religion. *Indian Psycho Rev,* 33, 41–44.

Pandya S. P. (2017) Spirituality for Well-being of Bereaved Children in Residential Care: Insights for Spiritually Sensitive Child-Centred Social Work Across Country Contexts. *Child & Adolescent Social Work Journal.* 35(2), 181-195. https://doi.org/10.1007/s10560-017-0509-1

Pargament, K. I. (2009). The bitter and the sweet: An evaluation of the costs and benefits of religiousness. *Psychological Inquiry,* 13, 168-181. https://doi.org/10.1207/S153965PLI130302

Park, C. L., & Lee, S. Y. (2019). Unique effects of religiousness/spirituality and social support on mental and physical well-being in people living with congestive heart failure. *Journal of Behavioral Medicine,* 43(4), 630-637. https://doi.org/10.1007/s10865-019-00101-9.

Patel, V. (2001). Poverty, inequality, and mental health in developing countries. In Leon, D., & Walt, G. (Eds), *Poverty, inequality and health: an international perspective.* (pp. 247-261). Oxford University Press.

Patel, V. (2010). Global mental health: A new global health field comes of age. *Journal of the American Medical Association,* 303(19), 1976-1977. https://doi.org/10.1001/jama.2010.616

Patel, V., Flisher, A. J., Hetrick, S., & McGorry, P. (2007). The mental health of young people: a global public-health challenge.

Lancet, 369(9569), 1302–1313. https://doi.org/10.1016/S0140-6736(07)60368-7

Patton, G. C., Glover, S., Bond, L., Butler, H., Godfrey, C., Pietro, G. D., & Bowes, G. (2000). The Gatehouse Project: a systematic approach to mental health promotion in secondary schools. *Australian & New Zealand Journal of Psychiatry*, 34(4), 586-593. http://dx.doi.org/10.1046/j.1440-1614.2000.00718.x

Pearlin, L.I., Bierman A. Current issues andfuture directions in research into the stress process. In Aneshensel, C. S., Phelan, J. C., Bierman, A. (Eds), Handbook of the sociology of mental health. 2. New York: Springer; 2012. pp. 325–340. https://doi.org/10.1007/978-94-007-4276-5_16

Peck, M. S. (1998). *The road less travelled and beyond.* Touchstone.

Peltzer, K. (2008). Social support and suicide risk among secondary school students in Cape Town, South Africa. *Psychological Reports*, 103(3), 653-660. https://doi.org/10.2466/pr0.103.3.653-660

Peltzer, K., Kleintjes, S., Wyk, B. V., Thompson, E. A., & Mashego, T. (2008). Correlates of Suicide Risk Among Secondary School Students in Cape Town. *Social Behaviour & Personality: an international journal*, 36(4), 493-502. http://dx.doi.org/10.2224/sbp.2008.36.4.493

Phenwan, T., Peerawong, T., & Tulathamkij, K. (2019). The Meaning of Spirituality and Spiritual Well-Being among Thai Breast Cancer Patients: A Qualitative Study. *Indian Journal of Palliative Care*, 25, (1), 119-123. http://dx.doi.org/10.4103/IJPC.IJPC_101_18

Pillai, A., Andrews, T., & Patel, V. (2009). Violence, psychological distress and the risk of suicidal behaviour in young people in India. *International Journal of Epidemiology*, 8, 459-69. https://doi.org/10.1093/ije%2Fdyn166

Plante T. G. (2007). Integrating spirituality and psychotherapy: ethical issues and principles to consider. *Journal of clinical psychology*, 63(9), 891–902. https://doi.org/10.1002/jclp.20383

Population Council (2013). *Adolescents in India: A desk review of existing evidence and behaviours, programmes and policies.* New Delhi: Population Council & UNICEF.

Post, B. C., & Wade, N. G. (2009). Religion and spirituality in psychotherapy: a practice-friendly review of research. *Journal of clinical psychology*, 65(2), 131–146. https://doi.org/10.1002/jclp.20563

Praveenlal, K. (2000). *Family Suicide in Kerala: An explorative study into pattern, determinants and consequences.* Thiruvananthapuram. http://www.cds.ac.in/krpcds/report/praveenlal.pdf

Praveenlal. (2013, January 27-28). *Policy and programmes for mental health in Kerala.* Trivandrum, Kerala, India: BMC Proceedings. http://dx.doi.org/10.1186/1753-6561-7-S5-O12

Premkumar, S. (2020, July 20). Kerala Govt Focuses On Children's Mental Health After 66 Student Suicides During Lockdown. *Outlook.* https://www.outlookindia.com/website/story/india-news-kerala-govt-focuses-on-childrens-mental-health-after-student-suicide-shoots-up-during-lockdown/357055

Price, R. H. (1974). Aetiology, the social environment, and the prevention of psychological dysfunction. In I. P. (Eds.), *Health and the Social Environment* (pp. 287-300). Lexington, MA: Health.

Principe, W. (1983). Toward defining spirituality. *Studies in Religion,* 12, 127–41. https://doi.org/10.1177/000842988301200201

Procidano, M. E., & Heller, K. (1983). Measures of perceived social support from friends and from family: three validation studies. *American journal of community psychology,* 11(1), 1–24. https://doi.org/10.1007/BF00898416

Punia, P., & Berwal, S. (2013). Mental Health of Visually Impaired Children. *The Educand- Journal of Humanities and Social Sciences,* 3(1), 58-63.

Radhakrishnan, M. G. (2011, August 1). *Kerala's Mental Block, Mental illness, Alcoholism, Domestic Violence takes a toll on Kerala.* India Today. https://www.indiatoday.in/magazine/society-and-the-arts/story/20110801-kerala-mental-illness-alcoholism-domestic-violence-747003-2011-07-23

Rahman, A., Mubbashar, M., Harrington, R., & Gater, R. (2000). Developing child mental health services in developing countries. *Journal of child psychology and psychiatry, and allied disciplines,* 41(5), 539–546. https://doi.org/10.1111/1469-7610.00641

Rao, K. R. (1989). Religion and Secularism in, Shakir, Moin, (Ed.), *Religion State and Politics in India,* Ajanta Publications, Delhi,

Rao, S.K.R. (1985). Operational aspects of health concepts in the cultural context. In Bisht, D. B. (Ed.), *The Spiritual Dimension of Health.* New Delhi: Directorate General of Health Services.

Raufelder, D., Jagenow, D., Drury, K., & Hoferichter, F. (2013). Social relationships and motivation in secondary school: Four different motivation types. *Learning & Individual Differences*, 24, 89-95. https://doi.org/10.1016/j.lindif.2012.12.002

Raveesh, B. N., Gowda, G. S., & Gowda, M. (2019). How right is right-based mental health law?. *Indian journal of psychiatry*, *61*(Suppl 4), S640–S644. https://doi.org/10.4103/psychiatry.IndianJPsychiatry_115_19

Reker, G. T. (1994). Logotheory and Logotherapy: Challenges, opportunities, and some empirical findings. *International Forum for Logotherapy*, 17, 47-55.

Rich, A. (2012). Gender and spirituality: Are women more spiritual? *Liberty University Digital Commons*, 23-25.

Rilling, M. (2000). How the challenge of explaining learning influenced the origins and development of John B. Watson's behaviourism. *The American Journal of Psychology*, 113 (2),275-301. https://doi.org/10.2307/1423731

Robert, T. (2003). *The relationship between spiritual well-being and job satisfaction among adult workers*. Mississippi State University, Mississippi: unpublished doctoral dissertation.

Roehlkepartain, E. C., Benson, P. L., King, P. E., & Wagener, L. M. (2006). Spiritual Development in Childhood and Adolescence: Moving to the Scientific Mainstream. In E. C. Roehlkepartain, P. E. King, L. Wagener, & P. L. Benson (Eds.), *The handbook of spiritual development in childhood and adolescence* (pp. 1–15). Sage Publications, Inc. https://doi.org/10.4135/9781412976657.n1

Rogers. C.B. (1961). *On becoming a person*. Houghton Mifflin.

Rook K. S. (2015). Social Networks in Later Life: Weighing Positive and Negative Effects on Health and Well-Being. *Current directions in psychological science*, *24*(1), 45–51. https://doi.org/10.1177/0963721414551364

Rosa, M. C., & C, Preethi. (2012). Academic Stress and Emotional Maturity among Higher Secondary school students of Working and non-working mothers. *International Journal of Basic and Advanced Research*, 1(3), 40-43.

Rosenberg, M. (1981). The self-concept: Social product and social force. In M. Rosenberg & R. H. Turner (Eds.), *Social psychology: Sociological perspectives* (pp. 593-625). Basic Books.

Ross, L. J. (2018) Teaching Reproductive Justice: An Activist's Approach. In Perlow O., Wheeler D., Bethea S., Scott B. (Eds) *Black Women's Liberatory*. https://doi.org/10.1007/978-3-319-65789-9_9

Rovers, M.W., & Kocum, L. (2010). Development of a Holistic Model of Spirituality. *Journal of Spirituality in Mental Health, 12*, 2 - 24. https://doi.org/10.1080/19349630903495475

Rutter, M. (2006). *Genes and behaviour: Nature–nurture interplay explained.* Blackwell Publishing.

Ryff, C. D. (1989). In the eye of the beholder: views of psychological well-being among middle-aged and older adults. *Psychology and Ageing, 4*(2), 195–201. https://doi.org/10.1037//0882-7974.4.2.195

Sagone, E., & Indiana, M.L. (2017). The Relationship of Positive Affect with Resilience and Self-Efficacy in Life Skills in Italian Adolescents. *Psychology, 08*, 2226-2239. https://doi.org/10.4236/PSYCH.2017.813142

Saini, S., & Punia, V. (2013). Academic stress with self-efficacy and mindfulness among senior secondary school students. *Indian Journal of Health and Wellbeing, 1*, 194- 196.

Salovey, P., & Mayer, J. D. (1990). Emotional intelligence. *Imagination, Cognition and Personality, 9*(3), 185–211. https://doi.org/10.2190/DUGG-P24E-52WK-6CDG

Sandhu, J.P.S. (2011, February 6). *Updesh (teaching) to the Khalsa-SarblohGranth.* A blog about Vedic Astrology, Medical astrology, Jyotish, mantra procedures and remedies. https://bharatiyajyotishmantrasaadhana.blogspot.com/2011/02/

Sanford, N. (1972). Is the concept of prevention necessary or useful? In S. E. Golann & C. Eisdorfer (Eds.), *Handbook of community mental health* (pp. 461-471). Appleton-Century-Crofts.

Sarason, B. R., Sarason, I. G., & Gurung, R. A. R. (2001). Close personal relationships and health outcomes: A key to the role of social support. In B. R. Sarason & S. Duck (Eds.), *Personal relationships: Implications for clinical and community psychology* (pp. 15–41). John Wiley & Sons Ltd.

Sarason, I.G., Levine, H.M., Basham, R.B., & Sarason, B.R. (1983). Assessing Social Support: The Social Support Questionnaire. *Journal of Personality and Social Psychology, 44*, 127-139. https://doi.org/10.1037/0022-3514.44.1.127

Saraswati, Swami Dayananda (2018). The Vedic Version of God. *Vedanta*, 1.2-13. http://www.iosrjournals.org/iosr-jbm/papers/Vol19-issue9/Version-4/G1909043842.pdf

Sawatzky, R., Gadermann, A.M., & Pesut, B. (2009). An Investigation of the Relationships Between Spirituality, Health Status and

Quality of Life in Adolescents. *Applied Research in Quality of Life, 4,* 5-22. https://doi.org/10.1007/S11482-009-9065-Y

Saxena, S. (2015, November 12). 'CBSE launches web portal 'Saransh'. *The Times of India,* Dehradun, City, p. 8. https://timesofindia.indiatimes.com /city/dehradun/ CBSE-launches-web-portal-Saransh/articleshow/49760382.cms

Schwarzer, R., & Leppin, A. (1992). Possible impact of social ties and support on morbidity and mortality. In H. O. F. Veiel & U. Baumann (Eds.), *The meaning and measurement of social support* (pp. 65–83). Hemisphere Publishing Corp.

Schwarzer, R., Frensch, P. A. (Eds.) (2010). *Personality, human development and culture: international perspectives on psychological science.* Vol 2. Psychological press.

Seaward, B. L. (1991). Spiritual well-being: A health education model. *Journal of Health Education,* 22(3), 166-169. https://doi.org/10.1080/10556699.1991.10614606

Semo, R. (2011). Social Capital and Young People. Longitudinal Surveys of Australian Youth. Briefing Paper 26. *National Centre for Vocational Education Research.*

Semo, R. (2011). Social Capital and Young People. Longitudinal Surveys of Australian Youth. Briefing Paper 26. *National Centre for Vocational Education Research.*

Seth, A. (2016). Study of mental health and burnout with teacher effectiveness among secondary school teachers. *Indian Journal of Health and Well-Being,* 7(7), 769-773.

Shabani, J., Hassan, S.A., Ahmad, A.B., & Baba, M. (2010). Age as Moderated Influence on the Link of Spiritual and Emotional Intelligence with Mental Health in High School Students. *Journal of American Science.,* 6(11), 394-400.

Shaffer, L. F. (Ed.). (1948). *Personal Adjustment.* Hoboken, NJ: John Wiley & Sons, Inc.

Shah, A.V. (1982). Integration of mental health. *Indian Journal of Psychiatry.* 24(1), 3-7.

Shakeri N. I. (2012). Effect of Social Assists and Hopefulness in Elderly Health Status with Chronic Pain. *Salmand: Iranian Journal of Ageing,* 7 (1) 7-15. http://salmandj.uswr.ac.ir/article-1-491-en.html

Sharma, S., & Varma, L. P. (1984). History of mental hospitals in Indian sub-continent. *Indian journal of psychiatry,* 26(4), 295–300.

Shastri P. C. (2009). Promotion and prevention in child mental health. *Indian journal of psychiatry*, 51(2), 88–95. https://doi.org/10.4103/0019-5545.49447

Sheffield, D. D. (1994). Stress, social support, and psychological and physical well-being in secondary school teachers. *Work & Stress*, 8(3), 235-243. http://dx.doi.org/10.1080/02678379408259995

Shek, D. (2014). Spirituality, overview. In A. Michalos (ed.), *Encyclopedia of Quality of Life and Well-Being Research*(pp. 6289–6295). Springer.

Siewert, P. T. (1999). Mental illness in a multicultural context. In C. A. Phelan (Eds.), *Handbook of the Sociology of Mental Health* (pp. 19-36). Springer.

Singh, A.K., & Gupta, A.S. (1983). Manual for Mental Health Battery. *Lucknow Ankur Psychological Agency*, 1-11

Singh, R. (2013). *Emotional maturity among senior secondary school students in relation to their self-esteem, home environment and mental health* (Unpublished thesis). Maharshi Dayanand University, Rohtak, Haryana, India

Sithey, G., Li, M., Wen, L. M., Kelly, P. J., & Clarke, K. (2018). Socioeconomic, religious, spiritual and health factors associated with symptoms of common mental disorders: a cross-sectional secondary analysis of data from Bhutan's Gross National Happiness Study, 2015. *BMJ open*, 8(2), e018202. https://doi.org/10.1136/bmjopen-2017-018202

Sivaraman, A. (2017). Women in the Kerala Model of Development, *Jindal Journal of Public Policy*, 3, 1, 97-104.

Skok, A. H. (2006). Perceived stress, perceived social support, and well-being among mothers of school-aged children with cerebral palsy. *Journal of Intellectual and Developmental Disability*, 31, 53-57. https://doi.org/10.1080/13668250600561929

Smith, C. (2005). *Soul Searching: The Religious and Spiritual lives of American Teenagers*. Oxford University Press.

Sonawat, R. (2001). Understanding families in India: a reflection of societal changes. *Psicologia: Teoria e Pesquisa*, 17, 2, 177-186. https://dx.doi.org/10.1590/S0102-37722001000200010

Spitznagel, R.J. (1992). Fitting the spiritual within the context of adjustment services: An historical perspective. Special issue: Silver anniversary edition of the. In R. J. services., *Vocational Evaluation and Work Adjustment Bulletin* (pp. 100-101).

Srivastava, K., Chatterjee, K., & Bhat, P.S. (2016). Mental health awareness: The Indian scenario. *Industrial Psychiatry Journal, 25(2)*, 131 - 134. https://doi.org/10.4103/ipj.ipj_45_17

Srivastava, V. (2002). Some thoughts on the anthropology of mental health and mental illness with particular reference to India. *The Anthropologist, 4*, 149 - 161. https://doi.org/10.1080/09720073.2002.11890741

St Clair-Thompson, H., Bugler, M., Robinson, J., Clough, P., McGeown, S. P., & Perry, J. (2015). Mental toughness in education: Exploring relationships with attainment, attendance, behaviour and peer relationships. *Educational Psychology, 35*(7), 886–907. https://doi.org/10.1080/01443410.2014.895294

Stake, R. E. (1988). Case study methods in education research: Seeking sweeter waters. In Jaeger, R. M., (Ed.), *Complementary Methods for Education Research* (pp. 253-278). Washington, D.C., AERA.

Stangor, C. (2012). States of Consciousness. In C. Stangor (Ed.), Introduction to Psychology (1st ed.): flat world Knowledge.

Steese, S., Dollette, M., Phillips, W., Hossfeld, E., Matthews, G., & Taormina, G. (2006). Understanding Girls' Circle as an intervention on perceived social support, body image, self-efficacy, locus of control, and self-esteem. *Adolescence, 41*(161), 55–74.

Stevenson, R. (2004). Constructing knowledge of educational practices from case studies. *Environmental Education Research, 10*(1), 39-51. https://doi.org/10.1080/1350462032000173698

Stoll, L., Michaelson, J., & Seaford, C. (2012). Well-Being Evidence for Policy: A review. *New Economics Foundation.*

Stolz, H., Olsen, J., Henke, T., & Barber, B. (2013). Adolescent Religiosity and Psychosocial Functioning: Investigating the Roles of Religious Tradition, National-Ethnic Group, and Gender. *Child Development Research,* 1-13. https://doi.org/10.1155/2013%2F814059

Sturman, A. (1997). Case study methods. In I. J. (ed.)., *Educational Research, Methodology and Measurement: an International Handbook* (2nd ed). (pp. 61-66). Pergamon. https://doi.org/10.1016/B978-008043349-3%2F50010-4

Sullivan, G., Burnam, A., & Koegel, P. (2000). Pathways to homelessness among the mentally ill. *Social psychiatry and psychiatric epidemiology, 35*(10), 444–450. https://doi.org/10.1007/s001270050262

Tacey, D. (2004). *The Spirituality Revolution: The emergence of contemporary.* Brunner-Routledge.

Takizawa, R., Maughan, B., & Arseneault, L. (2014). Adult health outcomes of childhood bullying victimization: evidence from a five-decade longitudinal British birth cohort. *The American journal of psychiatry, 171*(7), 777–784. https://doi.org/10.1176/appi.ajp.2014.13101401

Tao, S., Dong, Q., Pratt, M. W., Hunsberger, B., & Pancer, S. M. (2000). Social support: Relations to coping and adjustment during the transition to university in the People's Republic of China. *Journal of Adolescent Research, 15*(1), 123–144. https://doi.org/10.1177/0743558400151007

Teich, J. L., Robinson, G., & Weist, M. D. (2007). What kind of mental health services. *Advances in School Mental Health*, 1, 13-22.

The Times of India. (2018). One out of five teens in Kerala suffer from psychological distress. *The Times of India.* https://timesofindia.indiatimes.com/city/kochi/one-out-of-five-teens-in-kerala-suffer-from-psychological-distress-study/articleshow/66146766.cms

Thoits, P. A. (1986). Social support as coping assistance. *Journal of Consulting and Clinical Psychology, 54*(4), 416–423. https://doi.org/10.1037/0022-006X.54.4.416

Thomson, N. L. (1988). *Social Support, Stress and the Secondary public school administrator.* University of Kansas: University of Kansas, ProQuest Dissertations Publishing.

Thornicroft, G. (2012). Evidence-based mental health care and implementation science in low- and middle-income countries. *Epidemiology and Psychiatric Sciences.*, 21(3), 241-244. https://doi.org/10.1017/S2045796012000261

Tierney, T. & Dowd, R. (2000). The use of social skills groups to support girls with emotional difficulties in secondary schools. *Support for Learning*, 15(2), 82-85. https://doi.org/10.1111/1467-9604.00151

Tung, R., & Koch, J. (1980). School Administrators: Sources of Stress and Ways of Coping with it. In C. Cooper and J. Marshall (Eds.), *White Collar and Professional Stress.* John Wiley and Sons.

Tvorogova, N. (2011). Spiritual Well-Being. *Psychology in Russia:* State of the Art, 193-203. https://doi.org/10.11621/pir.2011.0011

Tyagi, A., & Cohen, M. (2014). Yoga and hypertension: a systematic review. *Alternative therapies in health and medicine, 20*(2), 32–59.

Uchino, B. (2006). Social support and health: a review of physiological processes potentially underlying links to disease outcomes. *Journal of Behavioral Medicine, 29*(4), 377–387. https://doi.org/10.1007/s10865-006-9056-5

UNI (2018, October 9). Mental health problems on the rise among Indian adolescents: study. *United News of Inida.* Kochi, Kerala, India.

UNICEF (2012). *Progress for children-A report card on adolescents.* United Nations Children's Fund.

UNICEF (2013). *Every Child's Birth Right: Inequities and trends in birth registration, Data and Analytics Section, Division of Policy and Strategy.* UNICEF.

United Nations (1948). *Universal Declaration of Human Rights.* Geneva, United Nations.

United Nations (1991). *Principles for the Protection of Persons with Mental Illness and the Improvement of Mental Health Care.* United Nations.

United Nations High Commissioner for Human Rights (2017). Mental health and human rights: *Report of the United Nations High Commissioner for Human Rights.* UN High Commissioner for Human Rights.

Unterrainer, H. F., Lewis, A. J. & Fink, A. (2014). Religious/Spiritual Well-Being, Personality and Mental Health: A Review of Results and Conceptual Issues. *Journal of Religion and Health.* 53(2), 82-392. https://doi.org/10.1007/s10943-012-9642-5

Vágnerová, M. (2000). *Vývojová psychologie.*Praha : Portál.

Vaineta, J. (2016). Spiritual health as an integral component of human well-being. *Applied Research In Health And Social Sciences: Interface And Interaction,* 13(1), 3-13. http://dx.doi.org/10.1515/arhss-2016-0002

Valde, E. A. (1993). *The role of student counselling in a senior secondary school in orientation towards working life and vocational choice.* ProQuest Dissertations & Theses Global: The Humanities and Social Sciences Collection (304097337).

Van Droogenbroeck, F., Spruyt, B., & Keppens, G. (2018). Gender differences in mental health problems among adolescents and the role of social support: results from the Belgian health interview surveys 2008 and 2013. *BMC psychiatry*, 18(1), 1-9. https://doi.org/10.1186/s12888-018-1591-4

Van Gastel, W. A., Tempelaar, W., Bun, C., Schubart, C. D., Kahn, R. S., Plevier, C., & Boks, M. P. (2013). Cannabis use as an indicator of risk for mental health problems in adolescents: a population-based study at secondary schools. *Psychological Medicine.*, 43(9), 1849-1856. https://doi.org/10.1017/S0033291712002723

Vandenbroeck, P., Dechenne, R., Becher, K., Eyssen, M., & Van den Heede, K. (2013). Soliciting stakeholders' views on the organization of child and adolescent mental health services: a system in trouble. *Child and Adolescent Psychiatry and Mental Health*, 7, 42 - 42. https://doi.org/10.1186/1753-2000-7-42

Vaus, D., & McAllister, I. (1982). Gender differences in religion: A test of the structural location theory. *American Sociological Review*, 52(4), 472-81. https://doi.org/10.2307/2095292

Verma, L.P. (1965). Psychiatry in Ayurveda. *Indian Journal of Psychiatry*. 7, 292.

Vijaykumar, L. (2007). Suicide and its prevention: The urgent need in India. *Indian Journal of Psychiatry*, 49(2), 81-84. https://doi.org/10.4103/0019-5545.33252

Vilchinsky, N., & Kravetz, S. (2005). How Are Religious Belief and Behavior Good for You? An Investigation of Mediators Relating Religion to Mental Health in a Sample of Israeli Jewish Students. *Journal for the Scientific Study of Religion*, 44(4), 459-471. https://doi.org/10.1111/J.1468-5906.2005.00297.Xhttp://www.jstor.org/stable/3590557

Vinney, C. (2020, April 22). *Psychodynamic Theory: Approaches and Proponents.* https://www.thoughtco.com/psychodynamic-theory-4588302

Vos, T. A. (2013). Global, regional, and national incidence, prevalence, and years lived with disability for 301 acute and chronic diseases and injuries in 188 countries: a systematic analysis for the Global Burden of Disease Study. *The Lancet*, 386(9995), 743-800. https://doi.org/10.1016/S0140-6736(15)60692-4

Wagani, R., & Colucci, E. (2018). Spirituality and Well-being in the Context of a Study on Suicide Prevention in North India. *Religions*, 9(183), 1-18. https://doi.org/10.3390/REL9060183

Wainberg, M. L., Scorza, P., Shultz, J. M., Helpman, L., Mootz, J. J., Johnson, K. A., Neria, Y., Bradford, J. E., Oquendo, M. A., & Arbuckle, M. R. (2017). Challenges and Opportunities in Global Mental Health: a Research-to-Practice Perspective. *Current psychiatry reports, 19*(5), 28. https://doi.org/10.1007/s11920-017-0780-z

Walsh, R. (1993). *Paths beyond ego.* Tarcher.

Wei, Y., & Kutcher, S. (2012). Innovations in practice: 'Go-to' Educator Training on the mental health competencies of educators in the secondary school setting: a program evaluation. *Child & Adolescent Mental Health,* 19(3), 219-222. https://doi.org/10.1111/camh.12056

WHO & Partners (2017). *Global Accelerated Action for the Health of Adolescents* (AA- HA). Geneva: World Health Organization.

WHO (1946). *Constitution of the World Health Organization.* Geneva: World Health Organization.

WHO (1951). *Annual Report of the Director-General to the World Health Organization and the United Nations.*Geneva: World Health Organization.

WHO (1961). *The teaching of psychiatry and mental health.*Geneva: World Health Organization.

WHO (1978). *Declaration of Alma Ata. Geneva.* World Health Organization.

WHO (1985). Handbook of Resolutions and Decisions. *The Determinants of Health.* (pp. 5- 6). Geneva: World Health Organization. http://www.who.int/hia/ evidence/doh/en.

WHO (1998). *Report on WHO Consultation JUNE 22-24. 1998.* World Health Organization, Division of Mental Health and Prevention of substance abuse.

WHO (2001). *World Health Report.* World Health Organization: Geneva. Retrieved November 25, 2019, http://www.who.int/whr/en

WHO (2003). *The Mental Health Context.* (Mental Health Policy and Service Guidance Package). Geneva, World Health Organization.

WHO (2004). *Promoting Mental Health:* concepts, emerging evidence, practice (Summary Report) Geneva. Geneva, World Health Organization.

WHO (2005). *Child and Adolescent Mental Health Policies and Plans.* Geneva: World Health Organization.

WHO (2005). *Mental health: facing the challenges, building solutions.* Report from the WHO European Ministerial Conference. Copenhagen, WHO. http://www.euro.who.int/__data/assets/pdf_file/0008/96452/E87301.pdf

WHO (2005). *Resource Book on Mental health, Human Rights and Legislation.* Geneva, World Health Organization.

WHO (2017). *Global Accelerated Action for the Health of Adolescents (AA-HA).* Geneva: World Health Organization. http://docs.scalingupnutrition.org/wp-content/uploads/2017/06/9789241512343-annexes-eng.pdf

WHO (n.d.). *International statistical classification of diseases and related health problems (ICD-10) in occupational health.* https://www.who.int/publications/i/item/International-statistical-classification-of-diseases-and-related-health-problems-icd-10-in-occupational-health

WHO International Consortium in Psychiatric Epidemiology (2000). Cross-national comparisons of the prevalences and correlates of mental disorders / WHO International Consortium in Psychiatric Epidemiology. *Bulletin of the World Health Organization: the International Journal of Public Health 2000*; 78(4): 413-426. https://apps.who.int/iris/handle/10665/57240

Wilber, K. (1999). An approach to integral psychology. *Journal of Transpersonal Psychology*, 31(2), 109-136.

Wilber, K. (2000). *Sex, ecology, spirituality: The spirit of evolution* (rev. ed.). Shambhala.

Wilkinson, J., Francis, L., J., & McKenna, U. (2018). Personal prayer, worship attendance and spiritual well-being: a study among fourth, fifth and sixth class students attending Church of Ireland schools in the Republic of Ireland. *Journal of Religious Education*, 66, 203-212. https://doi.org/10.1007/s40839-018-0068-6

Wills, T. A., & Ainette, M. C. (2012). Social networks and social support. In A. Baum, T. A. Revenson, & J. Singer (Eds.), *Handbook of health psychology* (pp. 465–492). Psychology Press.

Wilson, C. (2011). *The expatriate spouse: A study of their adjustment to expatriate life.* (Doctoral dissertation, University of Massey, Albany, New Zealand, 2011). https://mro.massey.ac.nz/bitstream/handle/10179/2852/02_whole.pdf

Wilson, C.J., Deane, F.P., Ciarrochi, J., & Rickwood, D. (2002). *Mental health help-seeking in young people. (Report for National Health and*

Medical Research Council of Australia, Grant YS060). Wollongong, NSW: the University of Wollongong, Illawarra Institute for Mental Health.

Wolters, N., Knoors, H., Cillessen, A. H., & Verhoeven, L (2014). Social Adjustment of Deaf Early Adolescents at the Start of Secondary School: The Divergent Role of Withdrawn Behavior in Peer Status. *Exceptional Children. Summer of 2014.* 80(4), 438-453. https://doi.org/10.1177/0014402914527242

Woolfson, R., Woolfson, L., Mooney, L., & Bryce, D. (2009). Young people's views of mental health education in secondary schools: a Scottish study. *Child: care, health and development*, 35(6), 790–798. https://doi.org/10.1111/j.1365-2214.2008.00901.x

Xiu -lun, T., Yong, Z., & J. -J.-l. (2003). Mental health of high school and secondary technical school students before graduation. *Chinese Journal of Clinical Psychology*, 11(4), 313. https://search.proquest.com/docview

Yin, R. K. (2009). *Case Study Research: Design and Methods (4th ed.).* Sage Publications.

Yogesh, M. K., Mohan, K., Roy, G., & Basu, S. (2004). Spiritual well-being: An empirical study with yogic perspectives. *Trans: Internet Journal for Cultural Sciences*, 15. http://www.inst.at/trans/15nr/03_8/yohan15.html.

Yogeshkumar, V. P. (2015). Occupational Stress and Mental Health of Primary School Teachers. *International Journal of Public Mental Health and Neurosciences*, 2(3), 7-9.

Yolak, B. B., Kiziltepe, Z., & Seggie, F. N. (2019). The Contribution of Remedial Courses on the Academic and Social Lives of Secondary School Students. *Journal of Education*, 199(1), 24-34. https://doi.org/10.1177/0022057419836434

Yuang, X. (2000). Correlation between self-esteem and mental health of secondary normal school students. *Chinese Journal of Clinical Psychology*, 8(2), 102-103.

Yuen (2017). Spiritual health, school engagement and civic engagement of secondary students in Hong Kong. *Journal of Youth Studies*, 20(1), 144-155.

Zare, A., Bahia, N.J., Eidy, F., Adib, N., Sedighe, F., (2019). The relationship between spiritual well-being, mental health, and quality of life in cancer patients receiving chemotherapy. *Journal of Family Medicine and Primary Care*, 8, 1701-1705. https://doi.org/10.4103/jfmpc.jfmpc_131_19.

www.ingramcontent.com/pod-product-compliance
Lightning Source LLC
LaVergne TN
LVHW091637070526
838199LV00044B/1108